Mandolin Songbook for Beginners

100 Timeless Folk and Children Songs with Tabs and Chords

ONLINE MP3

Collected and arranged by
Peter Upclaire

Peter Upclaire
Mandolin Songbook for Beginners
100 Timeless Folk and Children Songs with Tabs and Chords

First edition: August 2021

Available from Amazon.com and other book stores.

Copyright © 2021 Peter Upclaire
All rights are reserved. No part of this book may be in any way reproduced, stored, or copied without the prior written consent of the copyright owner.

More information can be found online at www.lovelymelodies.com.

Online MP3

Contents

A Sailor Went to Sea	7	Lavender's Blue	47
Amazing Grace	8	Lazy Sheep, Pray Tell Me Why	48
Aura Lea	10	Little Jack Horner	49
Baa, Baa, Black Sheep	12	Little Bo-Peep	50
Bingo	13	Li'l Liza Jane	51
Boys and Girls Come Out To Play	14	Little Miss Muffet	52
Brother John	15	Little Polly Flinders	53
Curly Locks	16	Looby Loo	54
Dance a Baby Diddy	17	London Bridge Is Falling Down	56
Did You Ever See a Lassie?	18	Lucy Locket	56
Five Little Monkeys	19	Mary Had a Little Lamb	57
Down in the Valley	20	Mistress Bond	58
Doctor Foster	21	Mary, Mary, Quite Contrary	58
Five Little Ducks	22	My Bonnie Lies over the Ocean	60
For He's a Jolly Good Fellow	23	Oh Dear What Can The Matter Be	62
Five Little Speckled Frogs	24	Oh Where Has My Little Dog Gone	63
Georgie Porgie	25	Oh My Darling, Clementine	64
Good King Arthur	26	Oh, Susanna	66
Goosey Goosey Gander	27	Old King Cole	68
Greensleeves	28	Old MacDonald Had a Farm	70
Head, Shoulders, Knees and Toes	29	Old Woman Who Lived in a Shoe	72
Happy Birthday To You	30	On Top of Old Smoky	73
Hark, Hark! The Dogs Do Bark	30	Over in the Meadow	74
Hickory Dickory Dock	31	One, Two, Three, Four, Five	76
Here We Go Round The Mulberry Bush	32	Pat-a-cake	77
Hot Cross Buns	33	Pop! Goes the Weasel	78
Home on the Range	34	Polly, Put the Kettle On	78
Humpty Dumpty	36	Rock-a-bye Baby	79
Hush Little Baby	37	Rain, Rain Go Away	80
I Had a Little Nut Tree	38	Ring a Ring o' Roses	80
I Saw Three Ships	39	Red River Valley	81
I Love Little Kitty	40	Row, Row, Row Your Boat	82
It's Raining, It's Pouring	40	Rub-a-dub-dub	82
Jack Sprat	41	See Saw Margery Daw	83
Jingle Bells	42	She'll Be Coming 'Round the Mountain	84
Jack and Jill	44	Ride a Cock Horse to Banbury Cross	86
John Jacob Jingleheimer Schmidt	45	Silent Night	87
Kumbaya	46	Sing a Song of Sixpence	88

Skip to My Lou	89	The Riddle Song	100
Skidamarink	90	There Came To My Window	101
Sur le Pont d'Avignon	91	This Old Man	102
Sleep, Baby, Sleep	92	Tom, Tom, the Piper's Son	104
The A.B.C.	93	Three Craws	106
Swing Low Sweet Chariot	94	Three Little Kittens	107
Ten Little Teddy Bears	95	Twinkle, Twinkle, Little Star	108
The Bear Went Over the Mountain	96	We wish you a merry Christmas	109
The Farmer in the Dell	97	Wee Willie Winki	110
The Muffin Man	98	When the Boat Comes In	112
The King Of France	98	When the Saints Go Marching In	113
The North Wind Does Blow	99	Yankee Doodle	114

Introduction

Young people often do not know the price of browsing the Internet. And my daughter also believes in the saying that you can get everything on the Internet for free. When she wanted to learn to play a few songs on guitar, she spent almost 1 hour searching for a single, not-too-quality song. When I told her that she would spend 100 hours of her life searching for 100 songs or, in other words, that she could earn $ 1,000 in 100 hours or play 100 hours more guitar, she began to think. But when I wanted to buy her a quality book of guitar songs, I couldn't find it. So I published my first paper and e-book in the field of music. Others followed, and this book on playing the mandolin is one of many.

The "Mandolin Songbook for Beginners" contains 100 of the most popular folk and children's songs, which have delighted music lovers for several generations. As the title suggests, the book is intended primarily for beginners, but with the remark that the book is not intended for complete beginners. It is intended for those of you who, to some extent, already master the basics of music. I expect you to know what a tablature is, know three or more chords, and that you know how to rhythmically strum the strings.

Unlike other books, each song is presented with a melody in standard notation and tablature, with chord diagrams and lyrics. Thus, it can be used by almost complete beginners, as well as already musically educated musicians.

You can download free online audio tracks for all 100 songs at www.lovelymelodies.com. MP3s collected there are intended primarily for learning about traditional melodies. Since traditional melodies and lyrics change throughout history, we rarely find two identical melodies and lyrics of the same song in a certain period. Therefore, the songs in this book sometimes differ from the songs found on Youtube channels, and whose performances and arrangements are often copyrighted.

Due to the reduced cost of recording many songs from these books, the songs are recorded using computer programs and MIDI files arranged and used to print the book. Therefore, the performance of the song is somewhat mechanical, with no personal interpretations of the melody. And in some cases, the songs also lack the real sound of the instrument. Nevertheless, I found it better to add such music recordings to the book. A book with music recordings has a much greater value than a book without a piece of music. There are quite a few reasons for this. Listening to a song specifies the version of the melody. The song can be used to play while listening, and mechanical playing can also be used instead of the metronome. This will allow you to improve your playing technique. So your first task is to capture the given rhythm as accurately as possible.

The chords accompanying the melody are played at the beginning of each musical measure or when changing chords. Once you've mastered changing chords, you can find the right strumming pattern, as you've probably learned from books for complete beginners. In the beginning, it's best to play the chords next to each syllable of the song. And only a little later, try to find a suitable pattern that matches the whole melody of the song.

The book is also adapted for playing in a duet. The first instrument can play a melody and the second chords. Of course, you can also spice things up by singing.

But that's not all. All the songs from the books in this series are also adapted for other instruments. The song that someone plays on the mandolin is the same as in other books arranged for guitalele, ukulele, guitar, banjo, etc. Readers of books from this series who play different instruments can therefore play together at any time without any problems.

I arranged the songs so that playing requires as little effort as possible on the musician's part. I used the chords with open strings that produce the so-called ringing tones. These once extremely popular chords are intended for beginners and lovers of old sounds. For other contemporary-oriented musicians, I also added slightly more complex chords. I avoided the popular bare chords. These chords are difficult to play well, and the tones are often quite muted and shorter in duration.

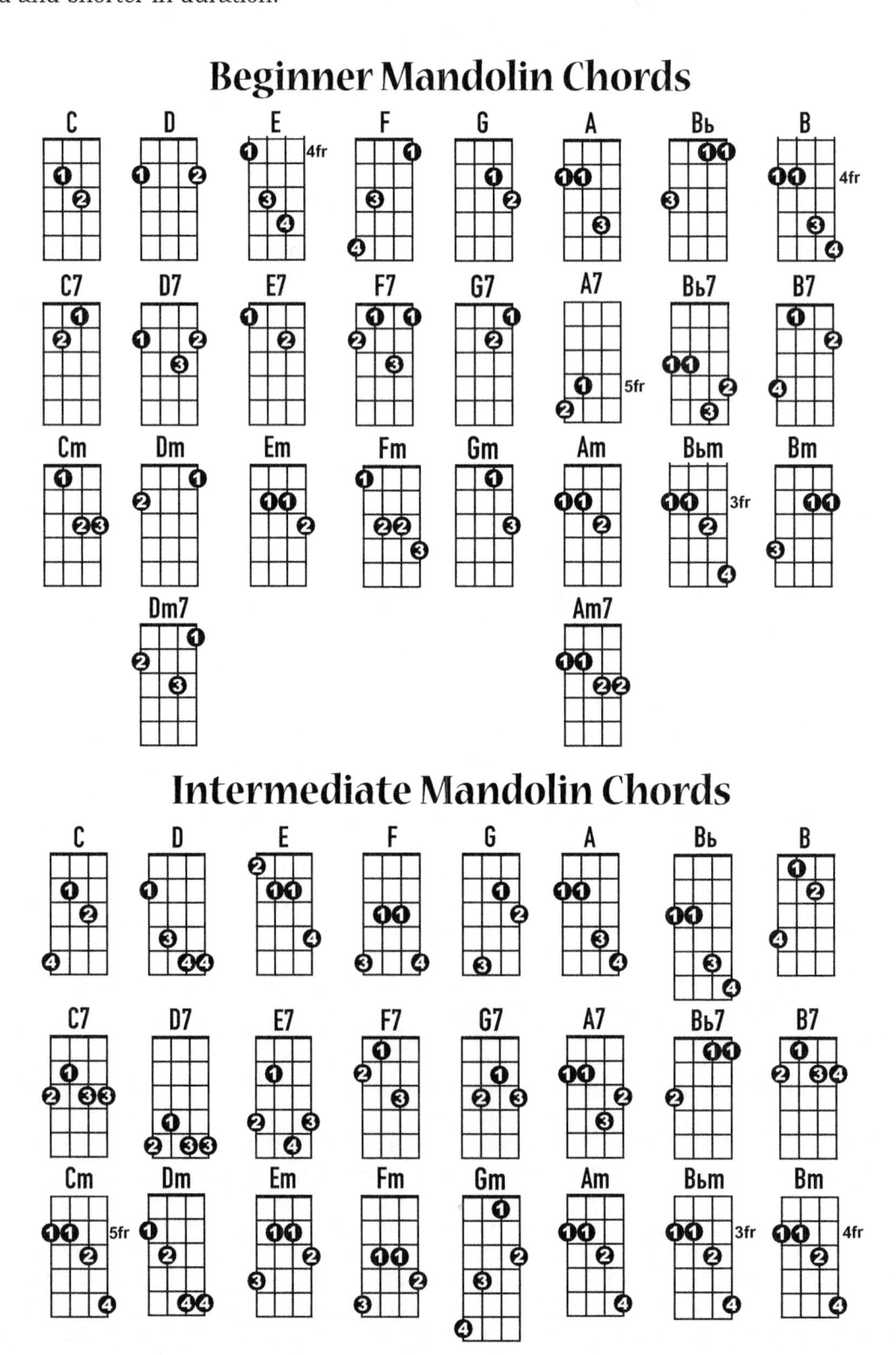

Beginner Mandolin Chords

Intermediate Mandolin Chords

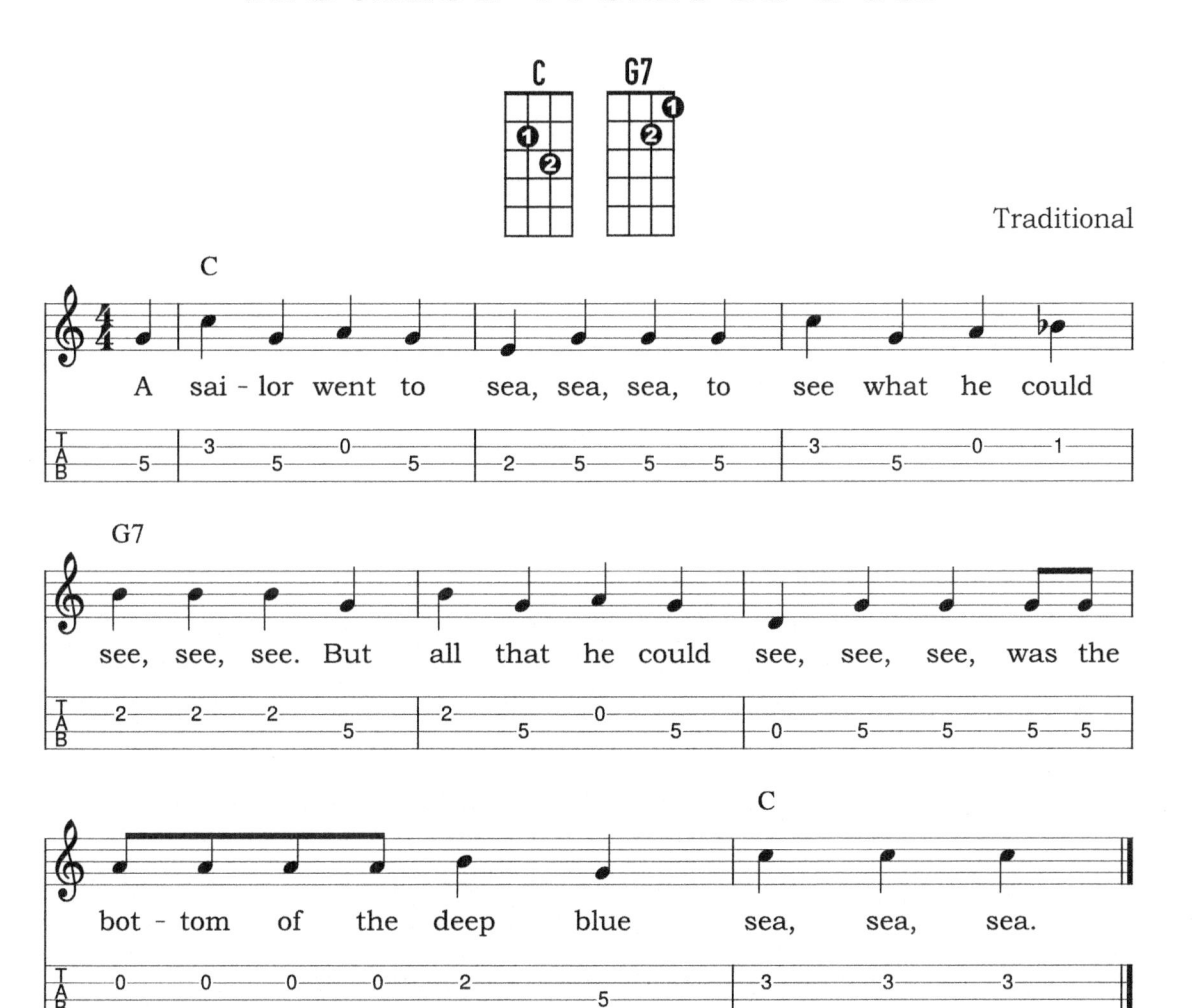

A Sailor Went to Sea

Traditional

A sai-lor went to sea, sea, sea, to see what he could see, see, see. But all that he could see, see, see, was the bot-tom of the deep blue sea, sea, sea.

A sailor went to sea, sea, sea,
To see what he could see, see, see.
But all that he could see, see, see
Was the bottom of the deep blue sea, sea, sea.

A sailor went to chop, chop, chop,
To see what he could chop, chop, chop.
But all that he could chop, chop, chop
Was the bottom of the deep blue chop, chop, chop.

A sailor went to knee, knee, knee,
To see what he could knee, knee, knee,
But all that he could knee, knee, knee,
Was the bottom of the deep blue knee, knee, knee.

A sailor went to sea, chop, knee,
To see what he could sea, chop, knee,
But all that he could sea, chop, knee,
Was the bottom of the deep blue sea, chop, knee.

Amazing Grace

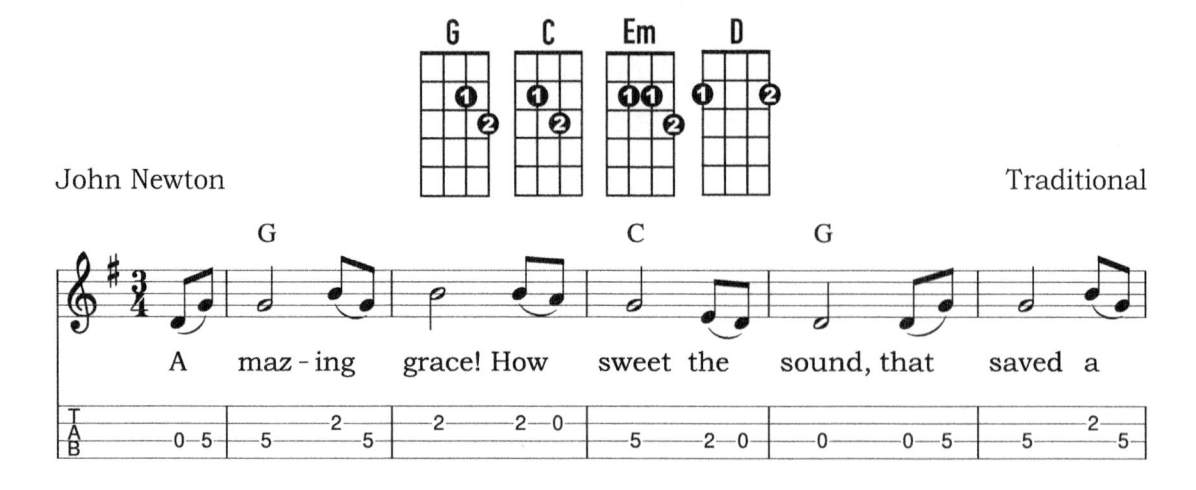

John Newton
Traditional

Amazing grace! How sweet the sound, that saved a wretch like me. I once was lost, but now I'm found. Was blind, but now I see.

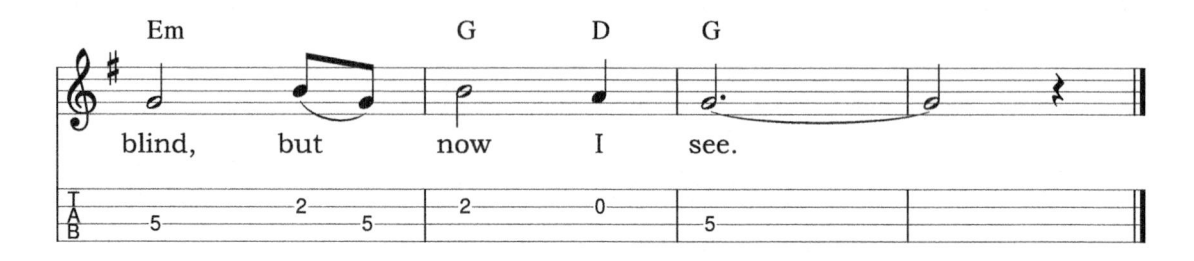

Amazing grace! How sweet the sound
That saved a wretch like me!
I once was lost, but now am found;
Was blind, but now I see.

Twas grace that taught my heart to fear,
And grace my fears relieved;
How precious did that grace appear
The hour I first believed.

Through many dangers, toils, and snares,
I have already come;
Tis grace hath brought me safe thus far,
And grace will lead me home.

The Lord has promised good to me,
His Word my hope secures;
He will my Shield and Portion be,
As long as life endures.

Yea, when this flesh and heart shall fail,
And mortal life shall cease,
I shall possess, within the veil,
A life of joy and peace.

The earth shall soon dissolve like snow,
The sun forbear to shine;
But God, who called me here below,
Will be forever mine.

When we've been there ten thousand years,
Bright shining as the sun,
We've no less days to sing God's praise
Than when we'd first begun.

Aura Lea

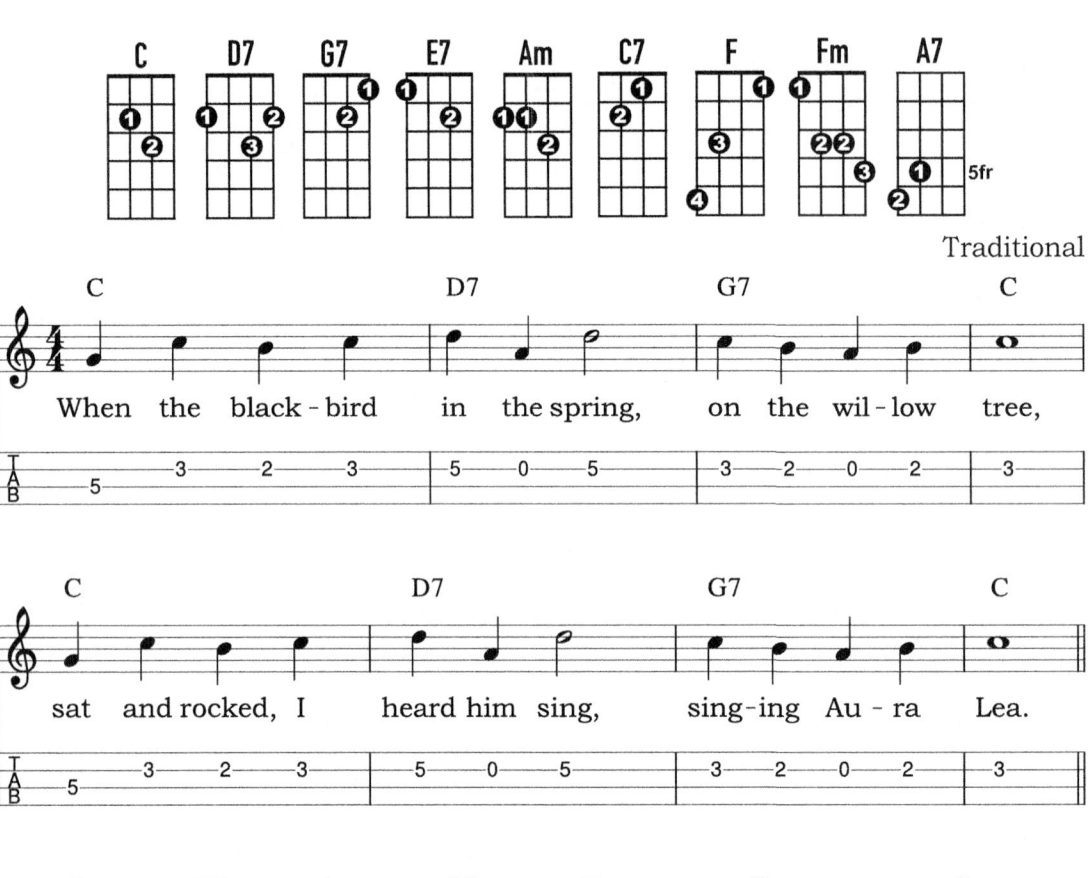

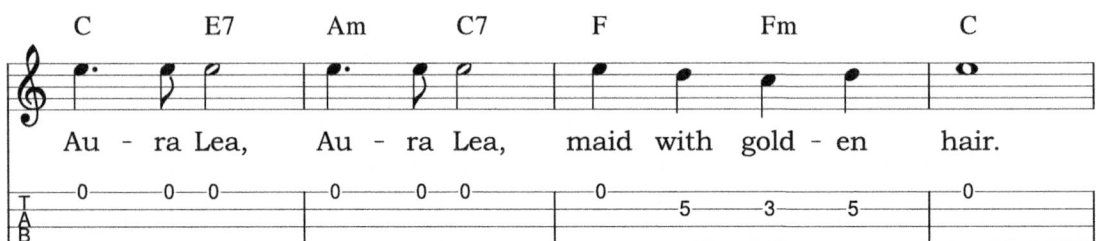

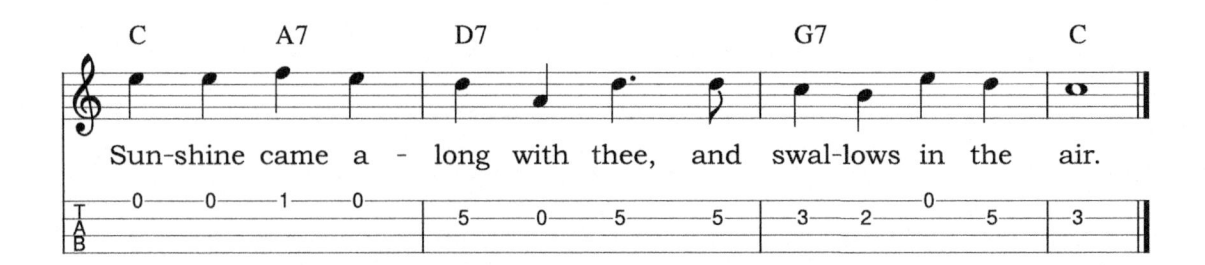

Traditional

When the black-bird in the spring, on the wil-low tree,

sat and rocked, I heard him sing, sing-ing Au-ra Lea.

Au-ra Lea, Au-ra Lea, maid with gold-en hair.

Sun-shine came a-long with thee, and swal-lows in the air.

When the blackbird in the Spring,
On the willow tree,
Sat and rocked, I heard him sing,
Singing Aura Lea.
Aura Lea, Aura Lea,
Maid with golden hair;
Sunshine came along with thee,
And swallows in the air.

Aura Lea, Aura Lea,
Maid with golden hair;
Sunshine came along with thee,
And swallows in the air.

In thy blush the rose was born,
Music, when you spake,
Through thine azure eye the morn,
Sparkling seemed to break.
Aura Lea, Aura Lea,
Birds of crimson wing,
Never song have sung to me,
As in that sweet spring.

Aura Lea, Aura Lea,
Maid with golden hair;
Sunshine came along with thee,
And swallows in the air.

Aura Lea! the bird may flee,
The willow's golden hair
Swing through winter fitfully,
On the stormy air.
Yet if thy blue eyes I see,
Gloom will soon depart;
For to me, sweet Aura Lea
Is sunshine through the heart.

Aura Lea, Aura Lea,
Maid with golden hair;
Sunshine came along with thee,
And swallows in the air.

When the mistletoe was green,
Midst the winter's snows,
Sunshine in thy face was seen,
Kissing lips of rose.
Aura Lea, Aura Lea,
Take my golden ring;
Love and light return with thee,
And swallows with the spring.

Aura Lea, Aura Lea,
Maid with golden hair;
Sunshine came along with thee,
And swallows in the air.

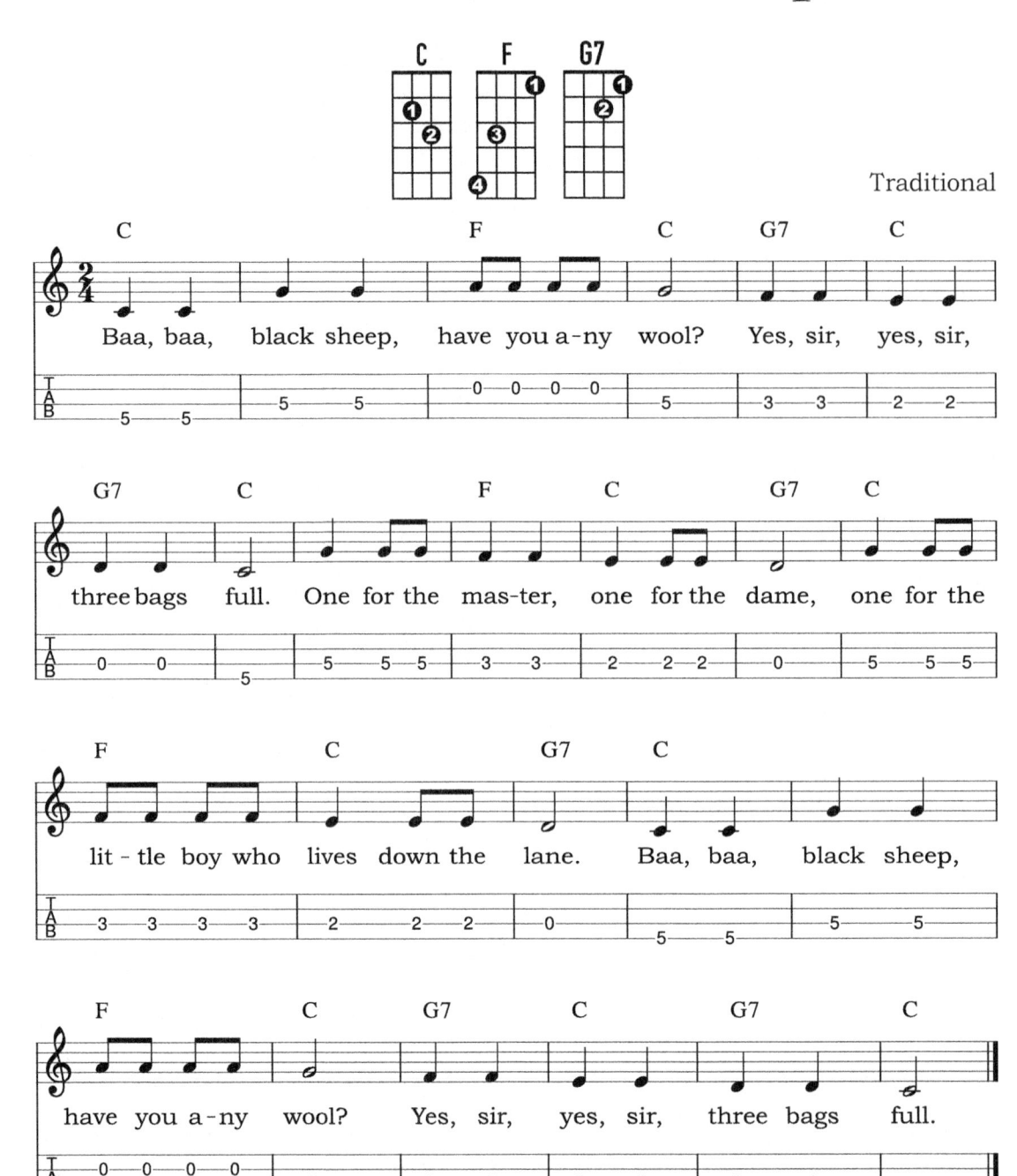

Baa, Baa, Black Sheep

Traditional

Baa, baa, black sheep, have you a-ny wool? Yes, sir, yes, sir, three bags full. One for the mas-ter, one for the dame, one for the lit-tle boy who lives down the lane. Baa, baa, black sheep, have you a-ny wool? Yes, sir, yes, sir, three bags full.

Bingo

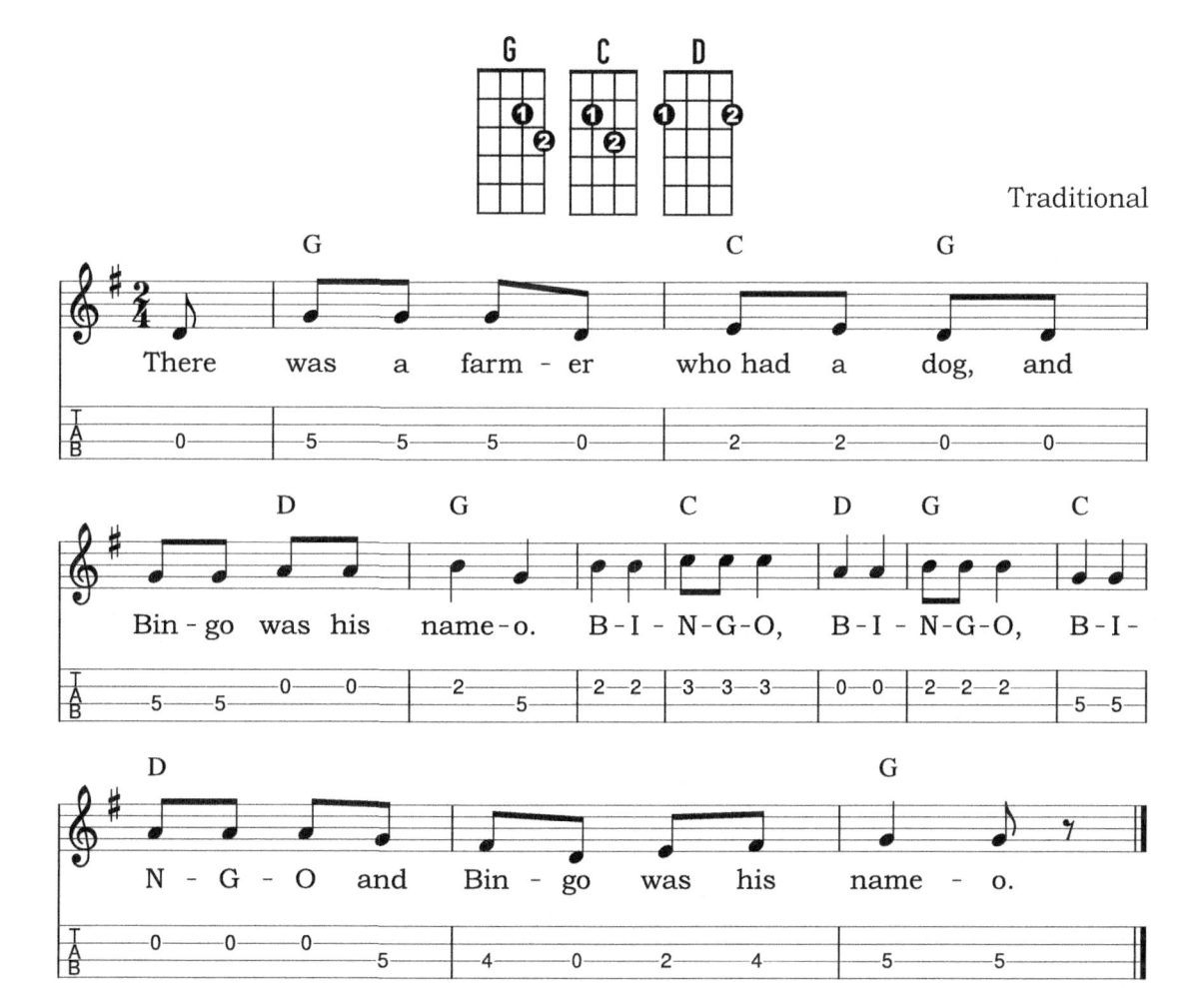

Traditional

There was a farmer who had a dog, and Bingo was his name-o. B-I-N-G-O, B-I-N-G-O, B-I-N-G-O and Bingo was his name-o.

There was a farmer who had a dog,
and Bingo was his name-o.
B-I-N-G-O
B-I-N-G-O
B-I-N-G-O
And Bingo was his name-o.

There was a farmer who had a dog,
and Bingo was his name-o.
(clap)-I-N-G-O
(clap)-I-N-G-O
(clap)-I-N-G-O
And Bingo was his name-o.

There was a farmer who had a dog,
and Bingo was his name-o.
(clap)-(clap)-N-G-O
(clap)-(clap)-N-G-O
(clap)-(clap)-N-G-O
And Bingo was his name-o.

There was a farmer who had a dog,
and Bingo was his name-o.
(clap)-(clap)-(clap)-G-O
(clap)-(clap)-(clap)-G-O
(clap)-(clap)-(clap)-G-O
And Bingo was his name-o.

There was a farmer who had a dog,
and Bingo was his name-o.
(clap)-(clap)-(clap)-(clap)-O
(clap)-(clap)-(clap)-(clap)-O
(clap)-(clap)-(clap)-(clap)-O
And Bingo was his name-o.

There was a farmer who had a dog,
and Bingo was his name-o.
(clap)-(clap)-(clap)-(clap)-(clap)
(clap)-(clap)-(clap)-(clap)-(clap)
(clap)-(clap)-(clap)-(clap)-(clap)
And Bingo was his name-o.

Boys and Girls Come Out To Play

Traditional

Girls and boys, come out to play, the moon doth shine as bright as day. Leave your sup-per, and leave your sleep, come with your play-fel-lows in the street. Come with a whoop, and come with a call. Come with a good will or not at all. Up the lad-der and down the wall, a half-pen-ny roll will serve us all.

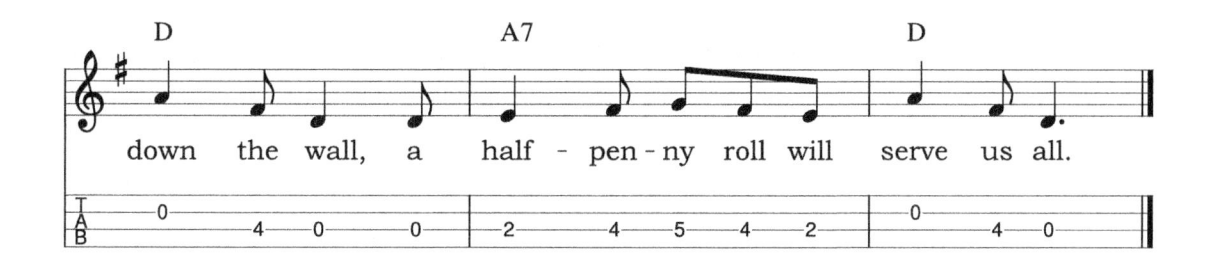

Brother John

Traditional

Are you sleep-ing? Are you sleep-ing?

Bro-ther John, bro-ther John?

Mor-ning bells are ring-ing! Mor-ning bells are ring-ing!

Ding, dang, dong. Ding, dang, dong.

Curly Locks

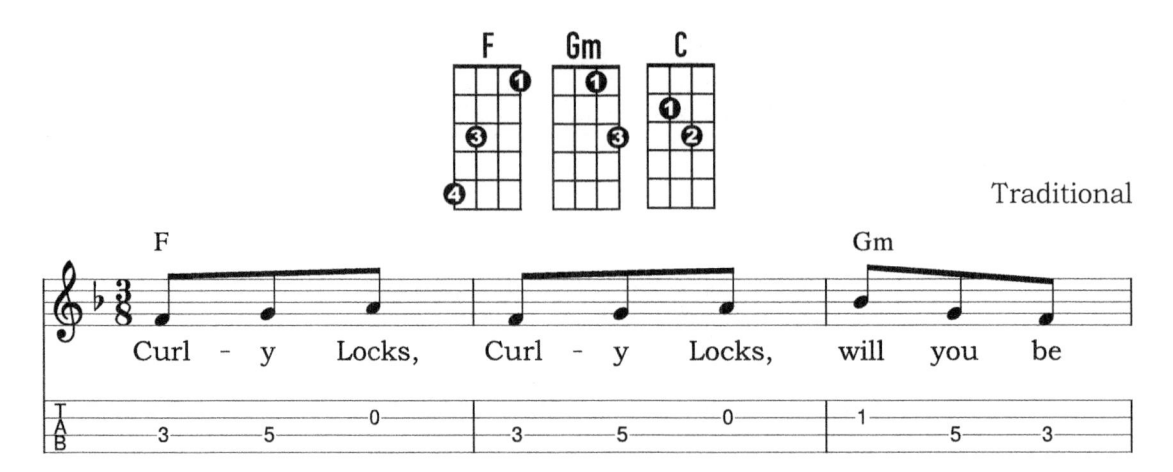

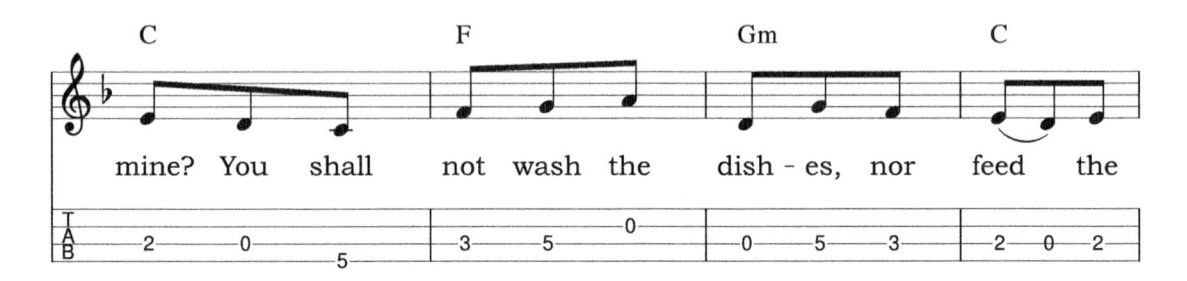

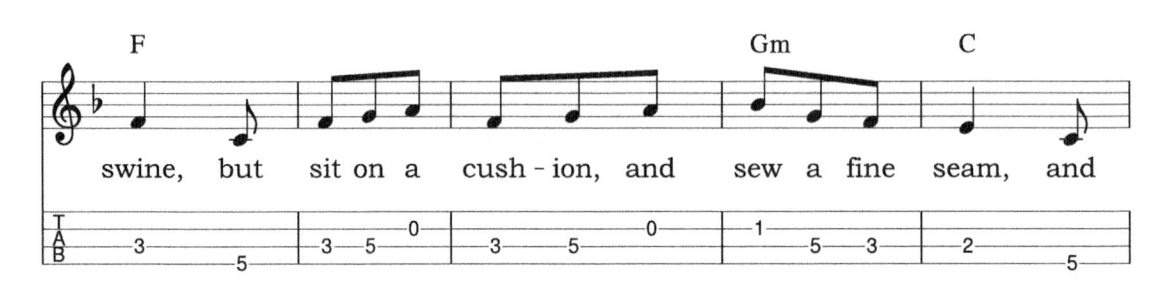

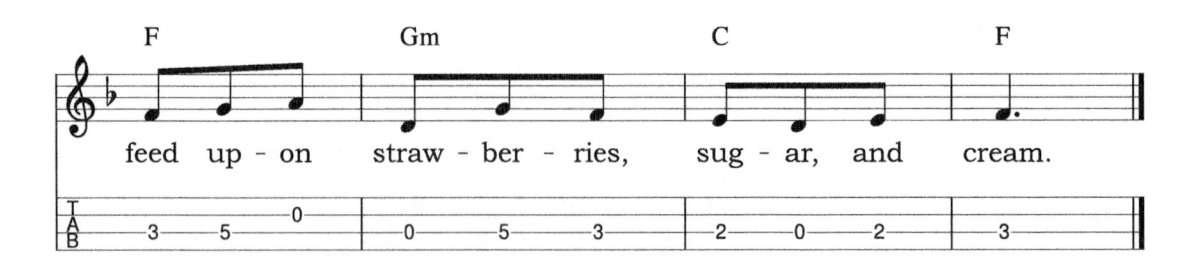

Traditional

Curl - y Locks, Curl - y Locks, will you be mine? You shall not wash the dish - es, nor feed the swine, but sit on a cush - ion, and sew a fine seam, and feed up - on straw - ber - ries, sug - ar, and cream.

Dance a Baby Diddy

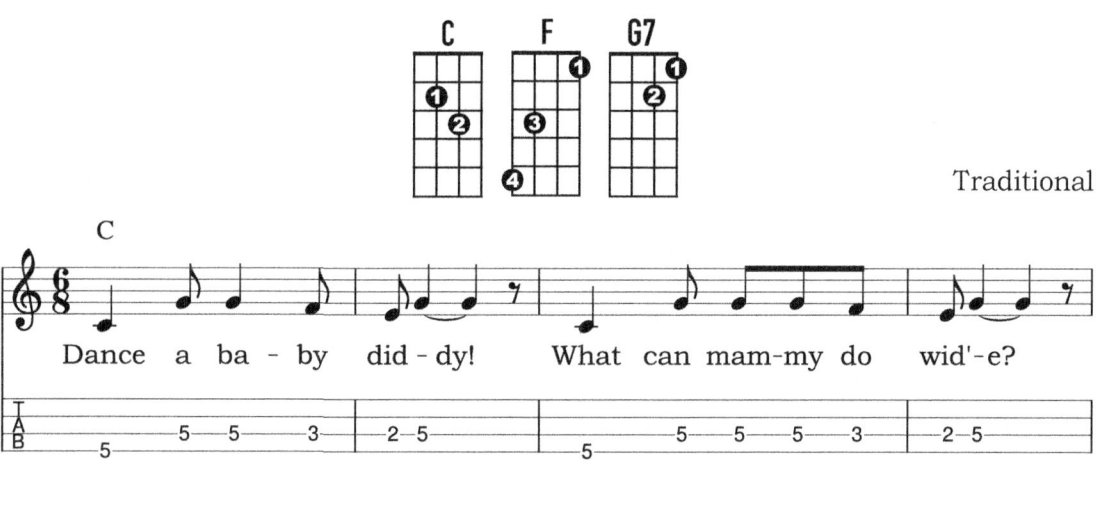

Traditional

Dance a baby, diddy;
What can a mammy do wid 'e?
Sit in a lap, give it some pap,
And dance a baby, diddy.

Smile, my baby, bonny;
What will time bring on 'e?
Sorrow and care, frowns and grey hair,
So smile my baby, bonny.

Laugh, my baby, beauty;
What will time do to 'e?
Furrow your cheek, wrinkle your neck,
So laugh, my baby, beauty.

Dance, my baby, deary;
Mother will never be weary,
Frolic and play now while you may,
So dance, my baby, deary.

Did You Ever See a Lassie?

Traditional

Did you ever see a lassie, a lassie, a lassie? Did you ever see a lassie, go this way and that? Go this way and that way, go this way and that way. Did you ever see a lassie, go this way and that?

Did you ever see a lassie,
A lassie, a lassie?
Did you ever see a lassie,
Go this way and that?
Go this way and that way,
Go this way and that way.
Did you ever see a lassie,
Go this way and that?

Did you ever see a laddie,
A laddie, a laddie?
Did you ever see a laddie,
Go this way and that?
Go this way and that way,
Go this way and that way.
Did you ever see a laddie,
Go this way and that?

Five Little Monkeys

Traditional

Five little monkeys jumping on the bed,
One fell off and bumped her head,
Mama called the doctor and the doctor said,
"No more monkeys jumping on the bed!"

Four little monkeys jumping on the bed,
One fell off and bumped his head,
Mama called the doctor and the doctor said,
"No more monkeys jumping on the bed!"

Three little monkeys jumping on the bed,
One fell off and bumped her head,
Mama called the doctor and the doctor said,
"No more monkeys jumping on the bed!"

Two little monkeys jumping on the bed,
One fell off and bumped his head,
Mama called the doctor and the doctor said,
"No more monkeys jumping on the bed!"

One little monkey jumping on the bed,
He fell off and bumped his head,
Mama called the doctor and the doctor said,
"Put those monkeys to bed!"

Down in the Valley

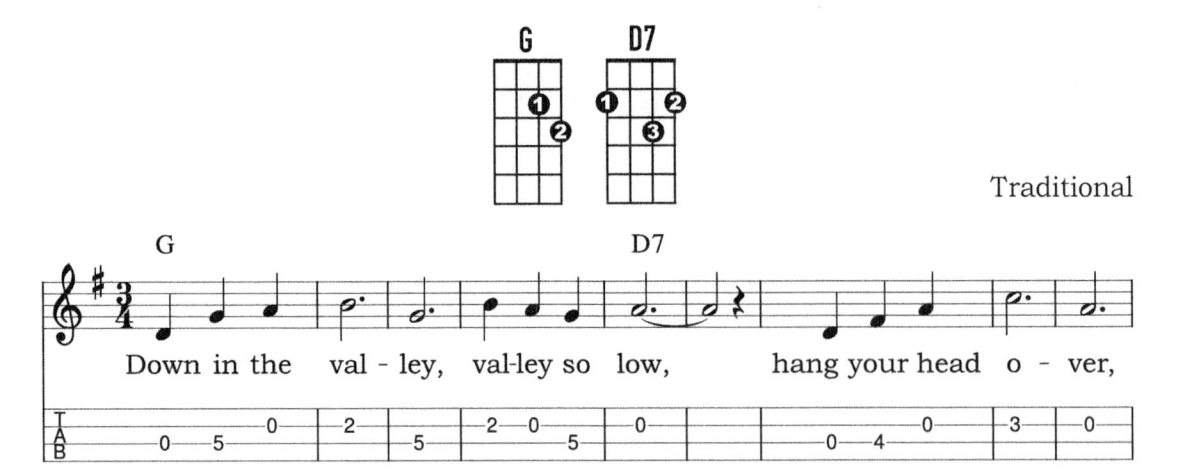

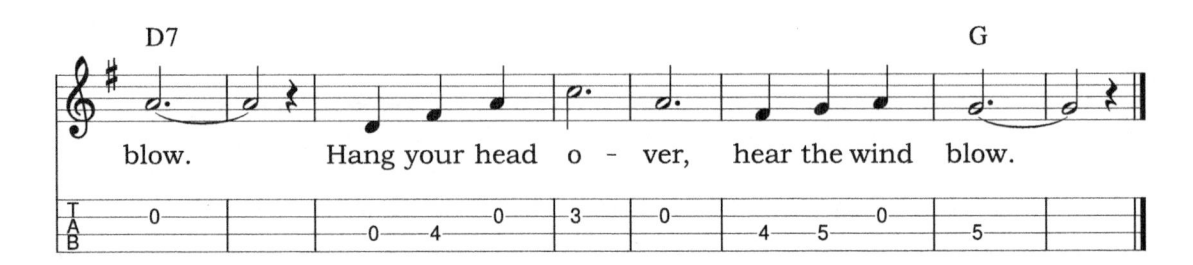

Traditional

Down in the val - ley, val-ley so low, hang your head o - ver, hear the wind blow. Hear the wind blow, love, hear the wind blow. Hang your head o - ver, hear the wind blow.

Down in the valley, valley so low.
Hang your head over hear the wind blow.
Hear the wind blow, dear, hear the wind blow.
Hang your head over hear the wind blow.

Roses love sunshine; violets love dew.
Angels in heaven know I love you.
Know I love you dear, know I love you.
Angels in heaven know I love you.

If you don't love me, love, whom you please.
Throw your arms 'round me, give my heart ease.
Give my heart ease, love, give my heart ease.
Throw your arms round me, give my heart ease.

Build me a castle forty feet high
So I can see him as he rides by.
As he rides by, love, as he rides by.
So I can see him as he rides by.

Write me a letter, send it by mail.
Send it in care of Birmingham jail.
Birmingham jail, love, Birmingham jail.
Send it in care of Birmingham jail.

Down in the valley, valley so low.
Hang your head over, hear the wind blow.
Hear the wind blow, love, hear the wind blow.
Hang your head over, hear the wind blow.

Doctor Foster

Traditional

Doc - tor Fos - ter went to Glos - ter in a show-er of rain. He stepped in a pud - dle right up to his mid - dle, and nev - er went there a - gain.

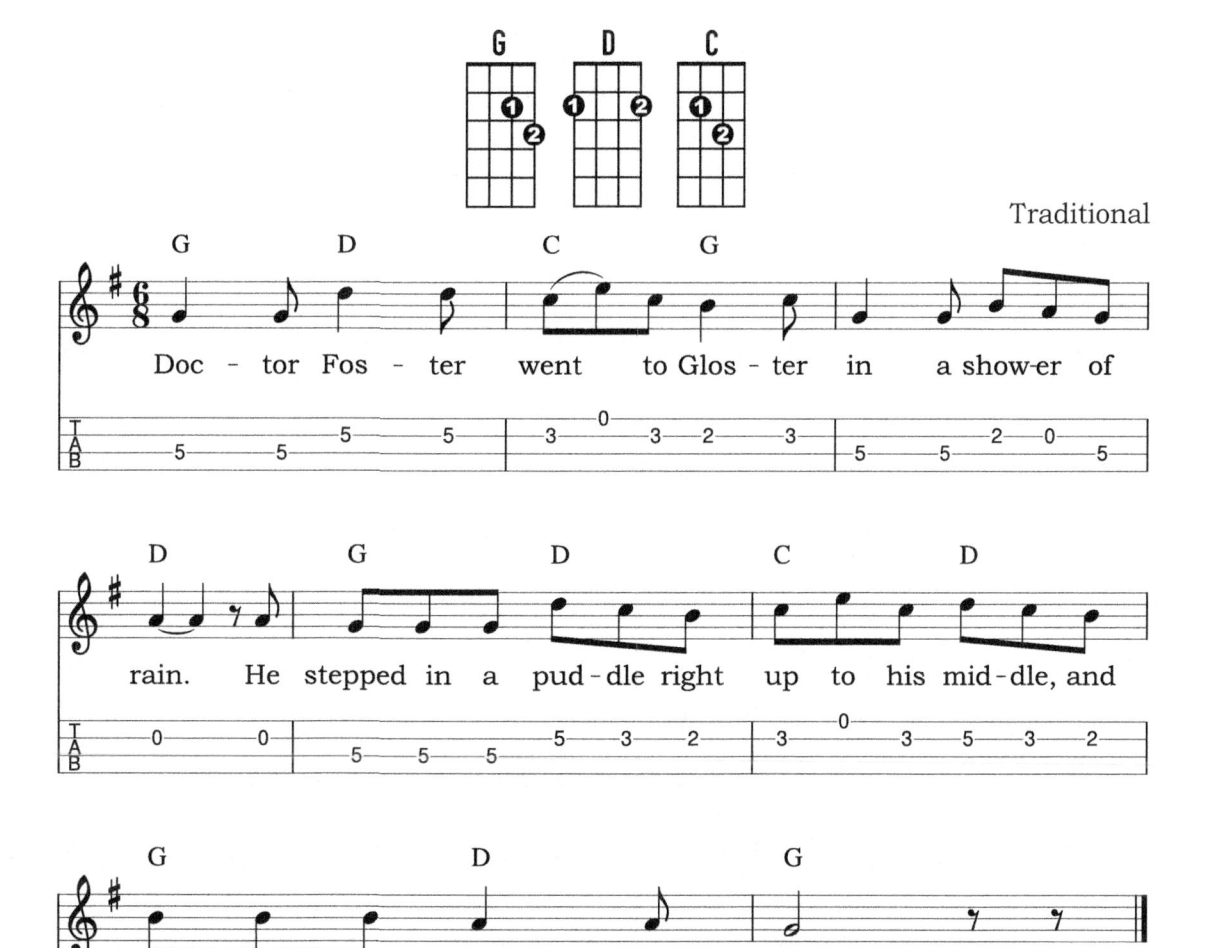

Five Little Ducks

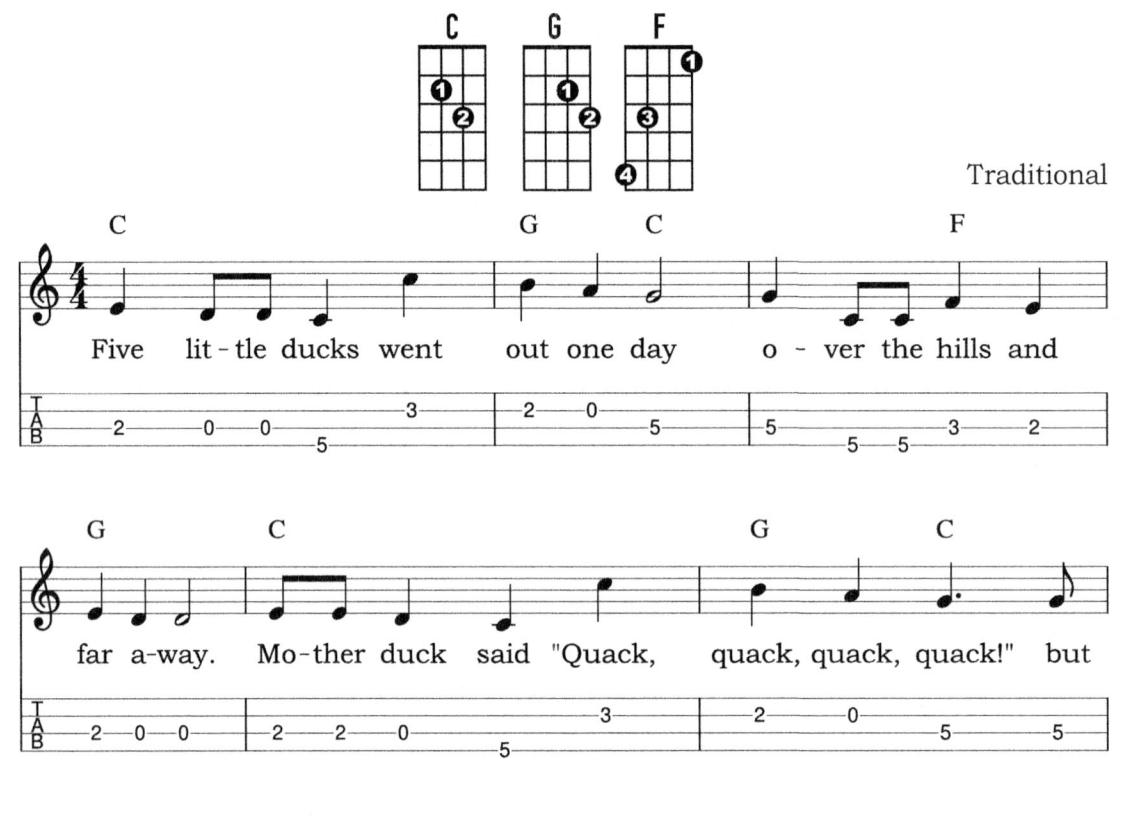

Traditional

Five little ducks went out one day,
Over the hills and far away.
Mother duck said, "quack quack quack quack,"
But only four little ducks came back.

Four little ducks went out one day,
Over the hills and far away.
Mother duck said, "quack quack quack quack,"
But only three little ducks came back.

Three little ducks went out one day,
Over the hills and far away.
Mother duck said, "quack quack quack quack,"
But only two little ducks came back.

Two little ducks went out one day,
Over the hills and far away.
Mother duck said, "quack quack quack quack,"
But only one little duck came back.

One little duck went out one day,
Over the hills and far away.
Mother duck said, "quack quack quack quack,"
But none of the five little ducks came back.

So sad Mother duck went out one day,
Over the hills and far away.
Mother duck said, "quack quack quack quack,"
And all of the five little ducks came back.

For He's a Jolly Good Fellow

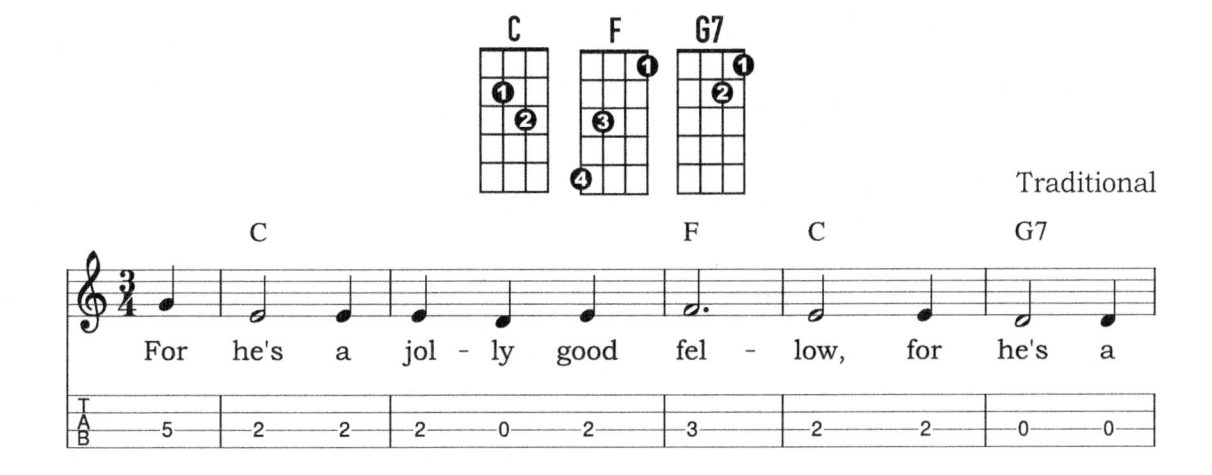

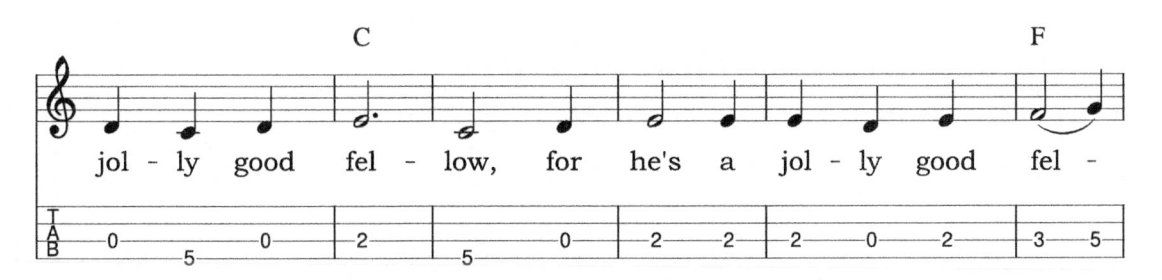

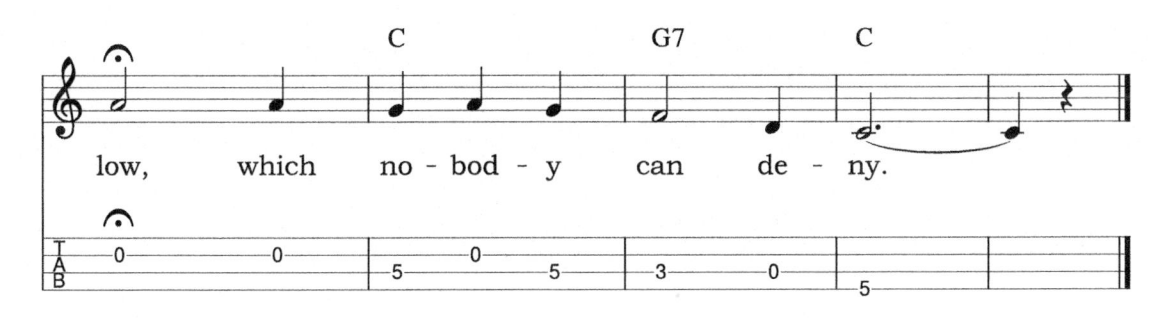

Traditional

Five Little Speckled Frogs

Traditional

Five little speckled frogs
Sat on a speckled log
Eating some most delicious bugs.
Yum-yum!
One jumped into the pool,
Where it was nice and cool
Then there were four speckled frogs.
Glub! Glub!

Four little speckled frogs
Sat on a speckled log
Eating some most delicious bugs.
Yum-yum!
One jumped into the pool,
Where it was nice and cool
Then there were three speckled frogs.
Glub! Glub!

Three little speckled frogs
Sat on a speckled log
Eating some most delicious bugs.
Yum-yum!
One jumped into the pool,
Where it was nice and cool
Then there were two speckled frogs.
Glub! Glub!

Two little speckled frogs
Sat on a speckled log
Eating some most delicious bugs.
Yum-yum!
One jumped into the pool,
Where it was nice and cool
Then there was one speckled frog.
Glub! Glub!

One little speckled frog
Sat on a speckled log
Eating some most delicious bugs.
Yum-yum!
One jumped into the pool,
Where it was nice and cool
Then there were no more speckled frogs.
Glub! Glub!

Georgie Porgie

Traditional

Geor-gie Por-gie pud-ding and pie, kissed the girls and made them cry, when the girls came out to play, Geor-gie Por-gie ran a-way.

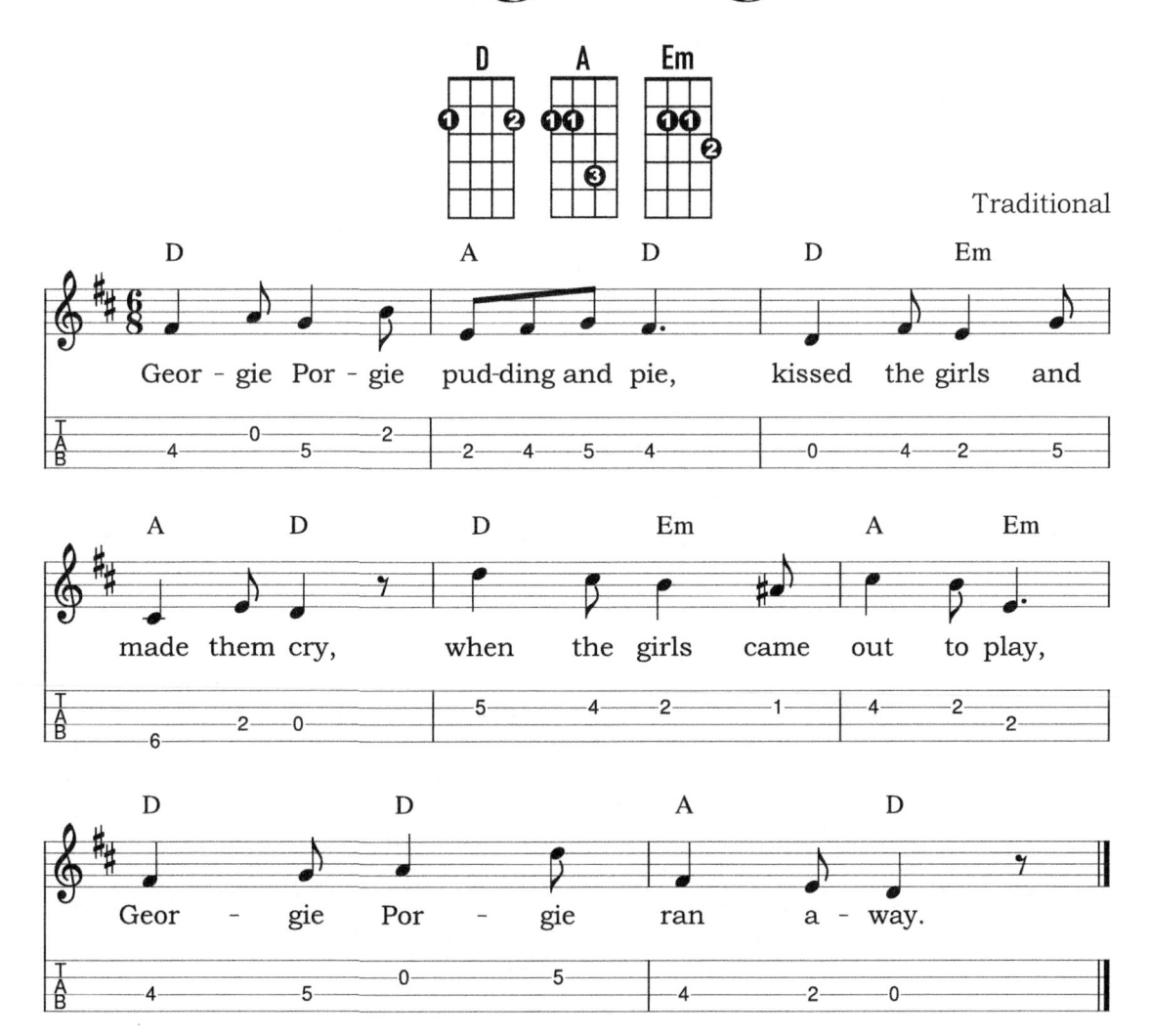

Good King Arthur

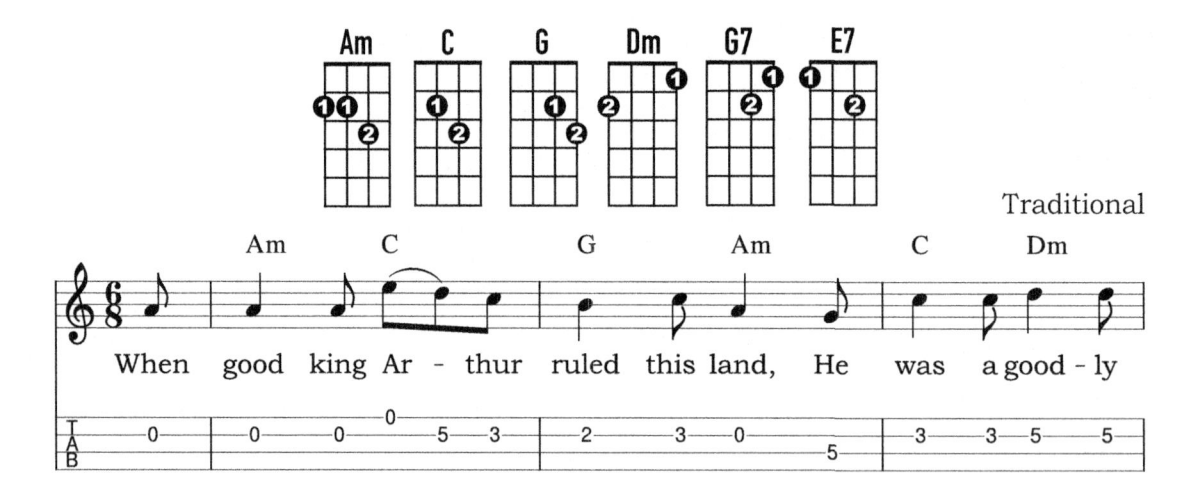

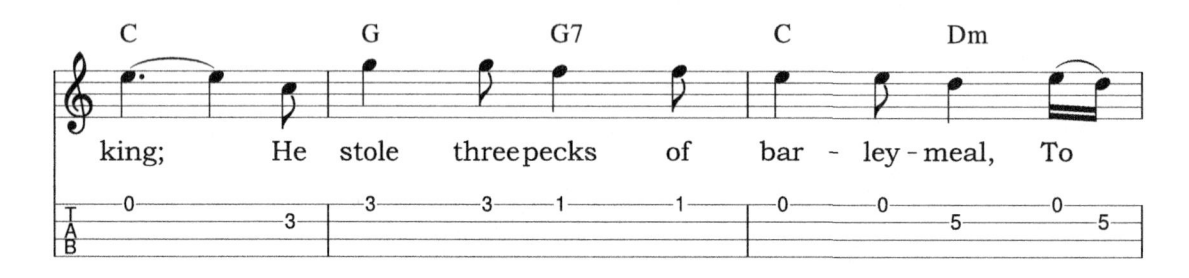

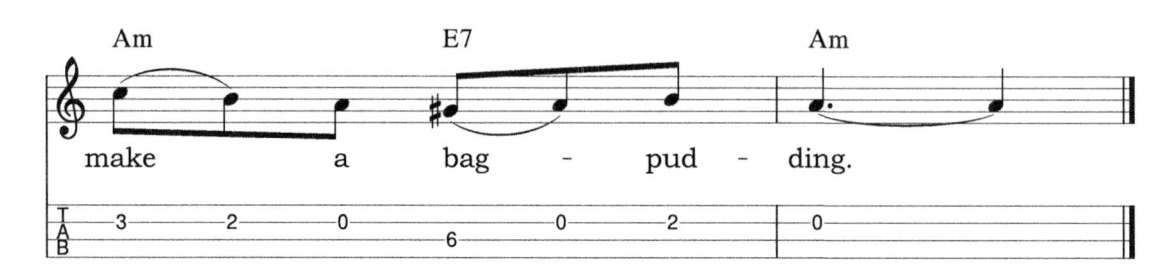

Traditional

When good king Arthur ruled this land,
He was a goodly king;
He stole three pecks of barley-meal,
To make a bag-pudding.

A bag-pudding the king did make,
And stuffed it well with plums:
And in it put great lumps of fat,
As big as my two thumbs.

The king and queen did eat thereof,
And noblemen beside;
And what they could not eat that night,
The queen next morning fried.

Goosey Goosey Gander

Traditional

Goos-ey, goos-ey, gan - der, where shall I wan-der? -

Up - stairs and down - stairs and in my la-dy's cham - ber.

There I met an old man who would-n't say his pray-ers, so I

took him by his left leg and threw him down the stairs.

Greensleeves

Traditional

Head, Shoulders, Knees and Toes

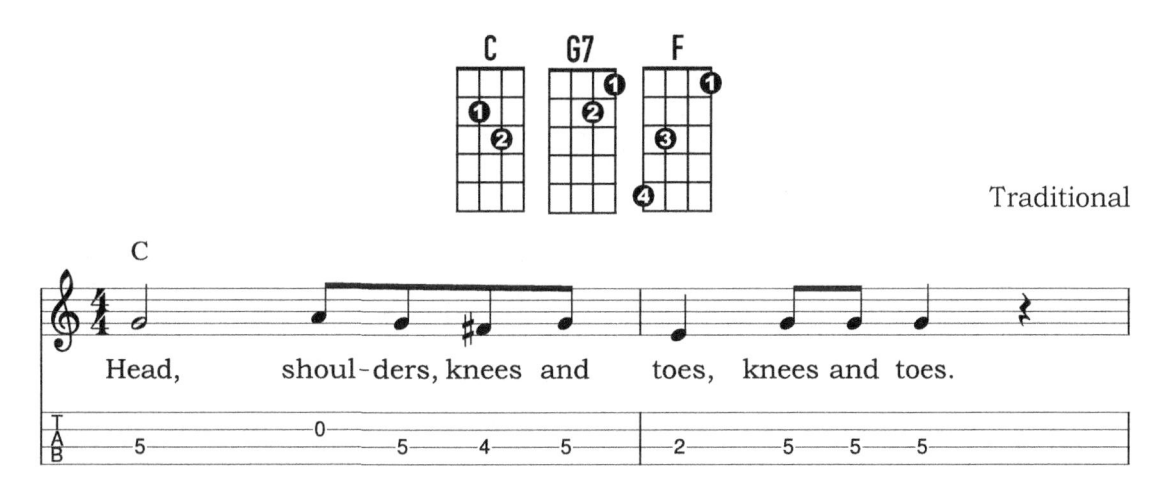

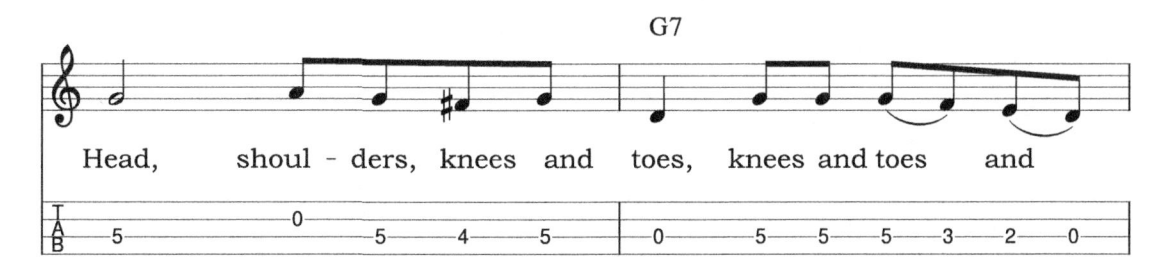

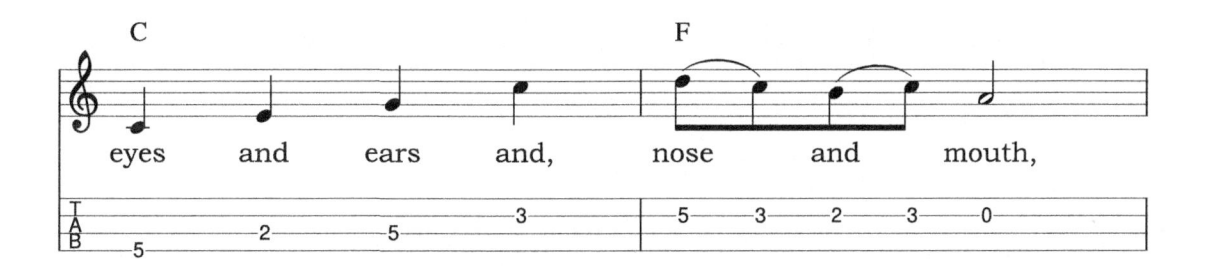

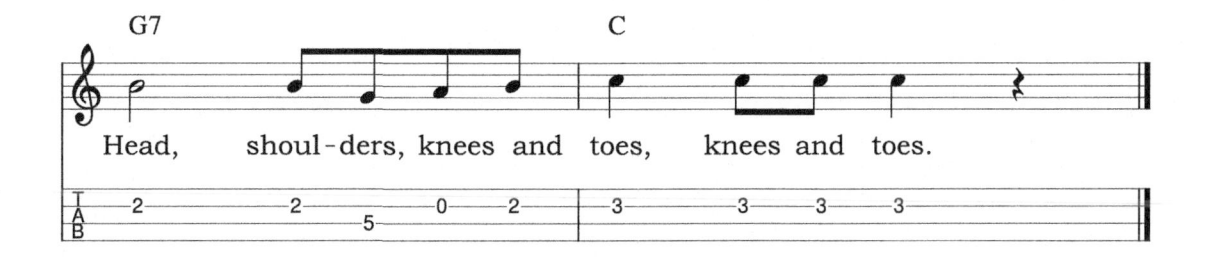

Traditional

Happy Birthday To You

Traditional

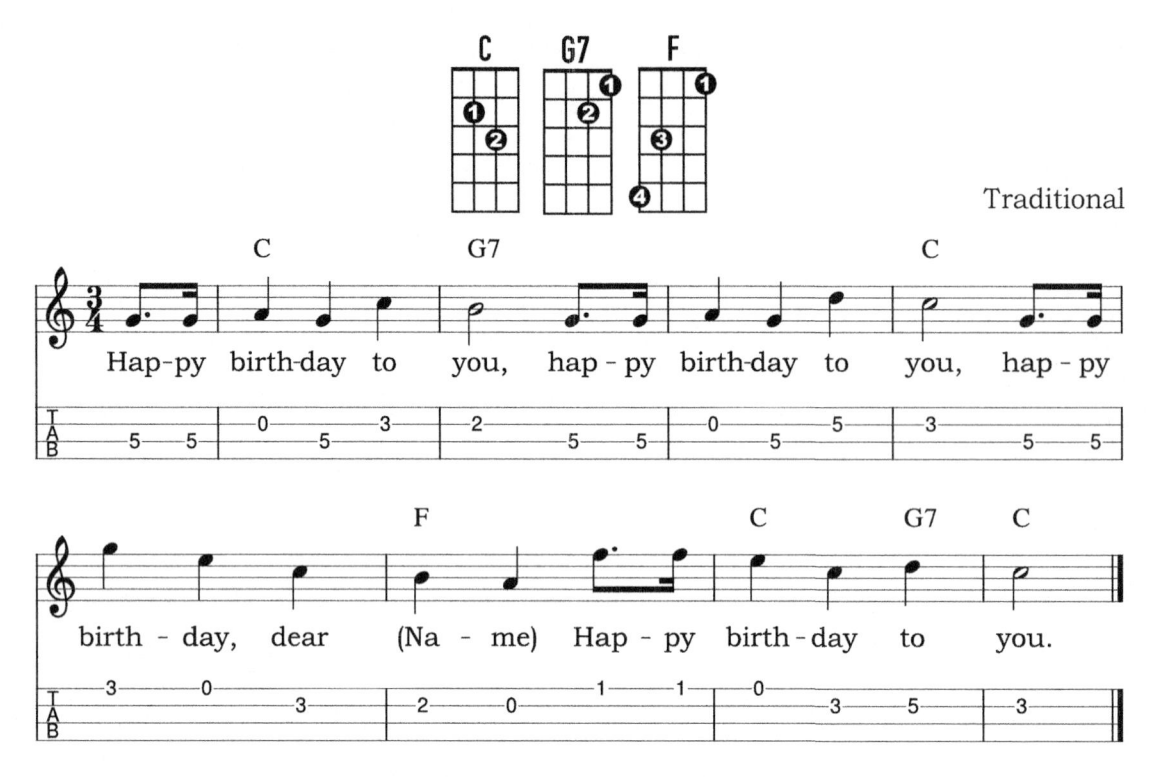

Hap-py birth-day to you, hap-py birth-day to you, hap-py birth-day, dear (Na - me) Hap-py birth-day to you.

Hark, Hark! The Dogs Do Bark

Traditional

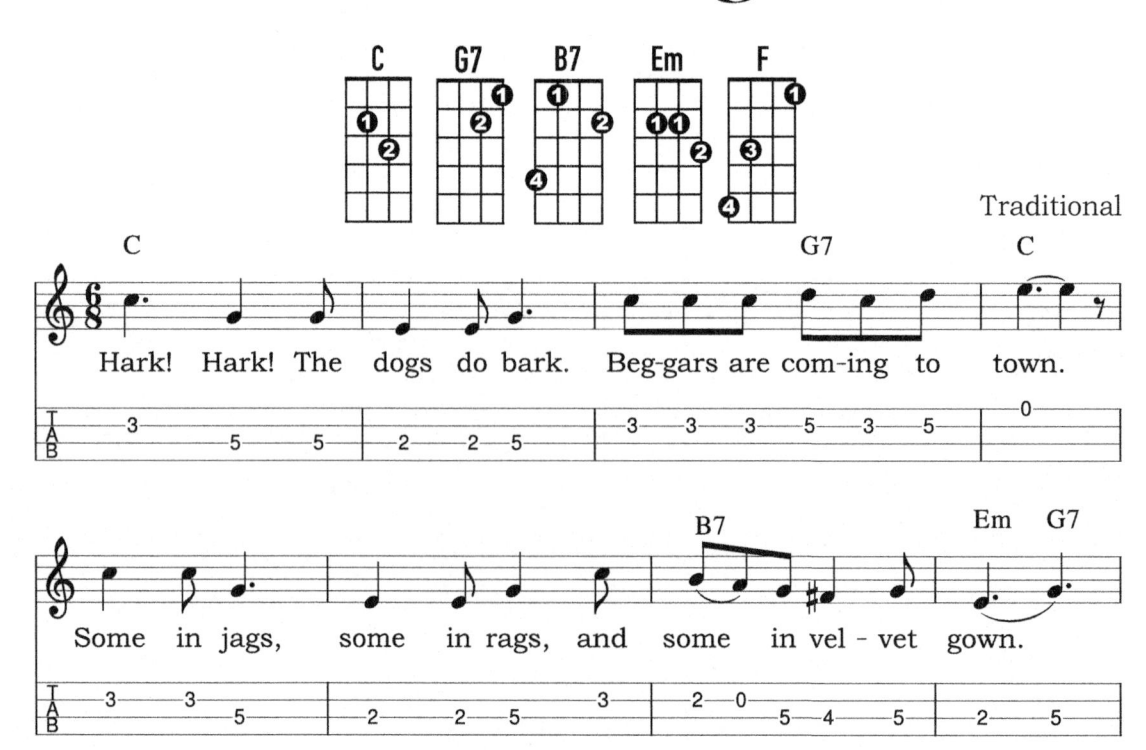

Hark! Hark! The dogs do bark. Beg-gars are com-ing to town.
Some in jags, some in rags, and some in vel - vet gown.

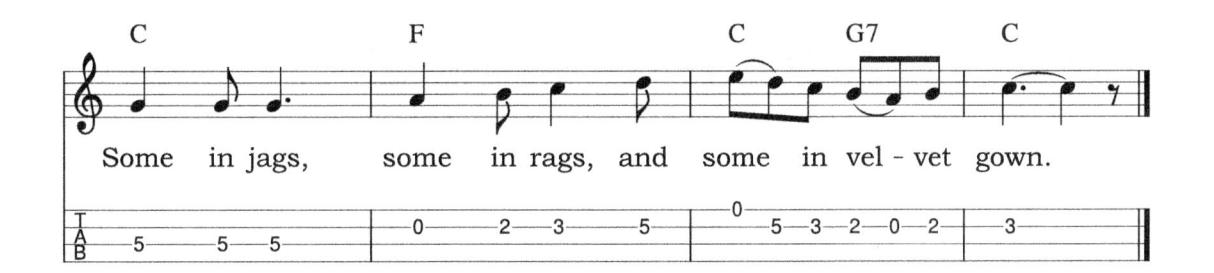

Some in jags, some in rags, and some in vel-vet gown.

Hickory Dickory Dock

Traditional

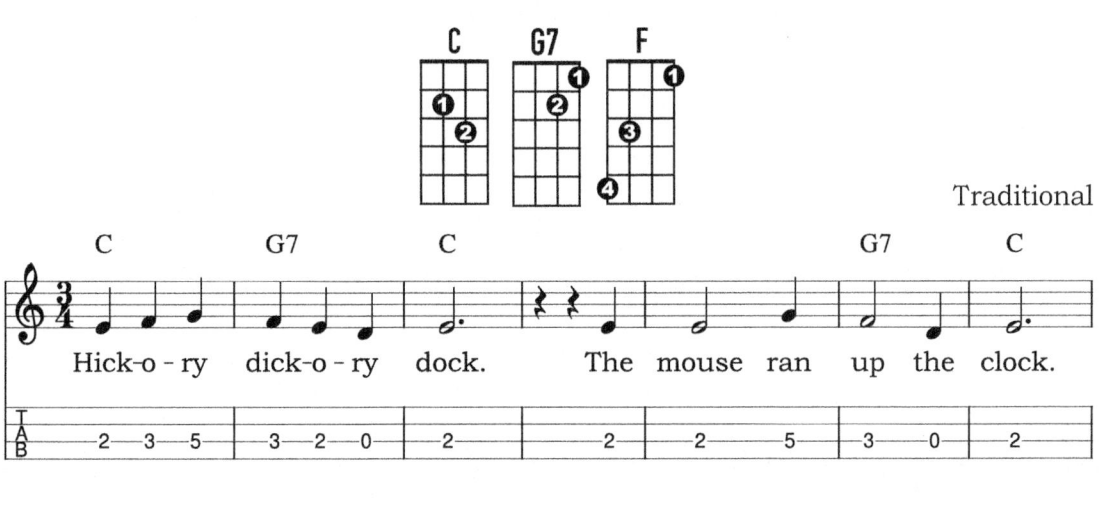

Hick-o-ry dick-o-ry dock. The mouse ran up the clock.

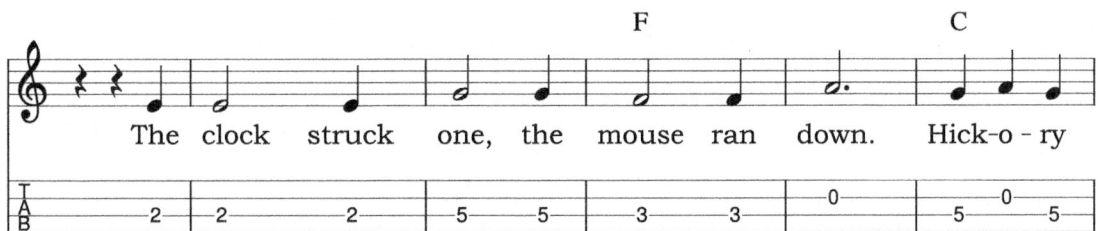

The clock struck one, the mouse ran down. Hick-o-ry

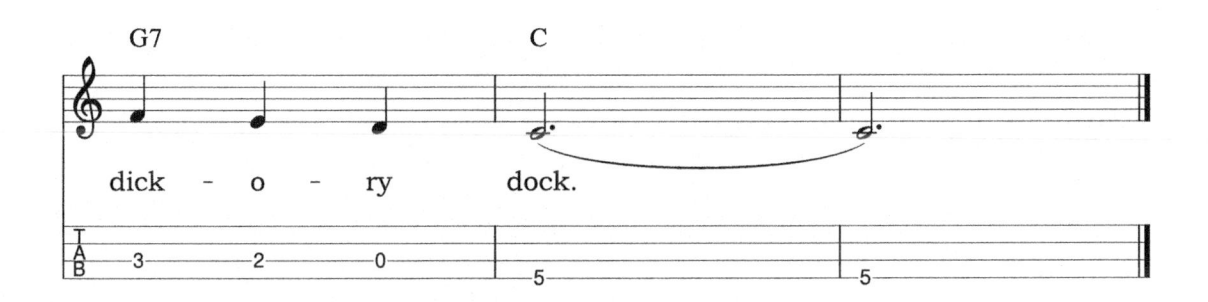

dick - o - ry dock.

Here We Go Round The Mulberry Bush

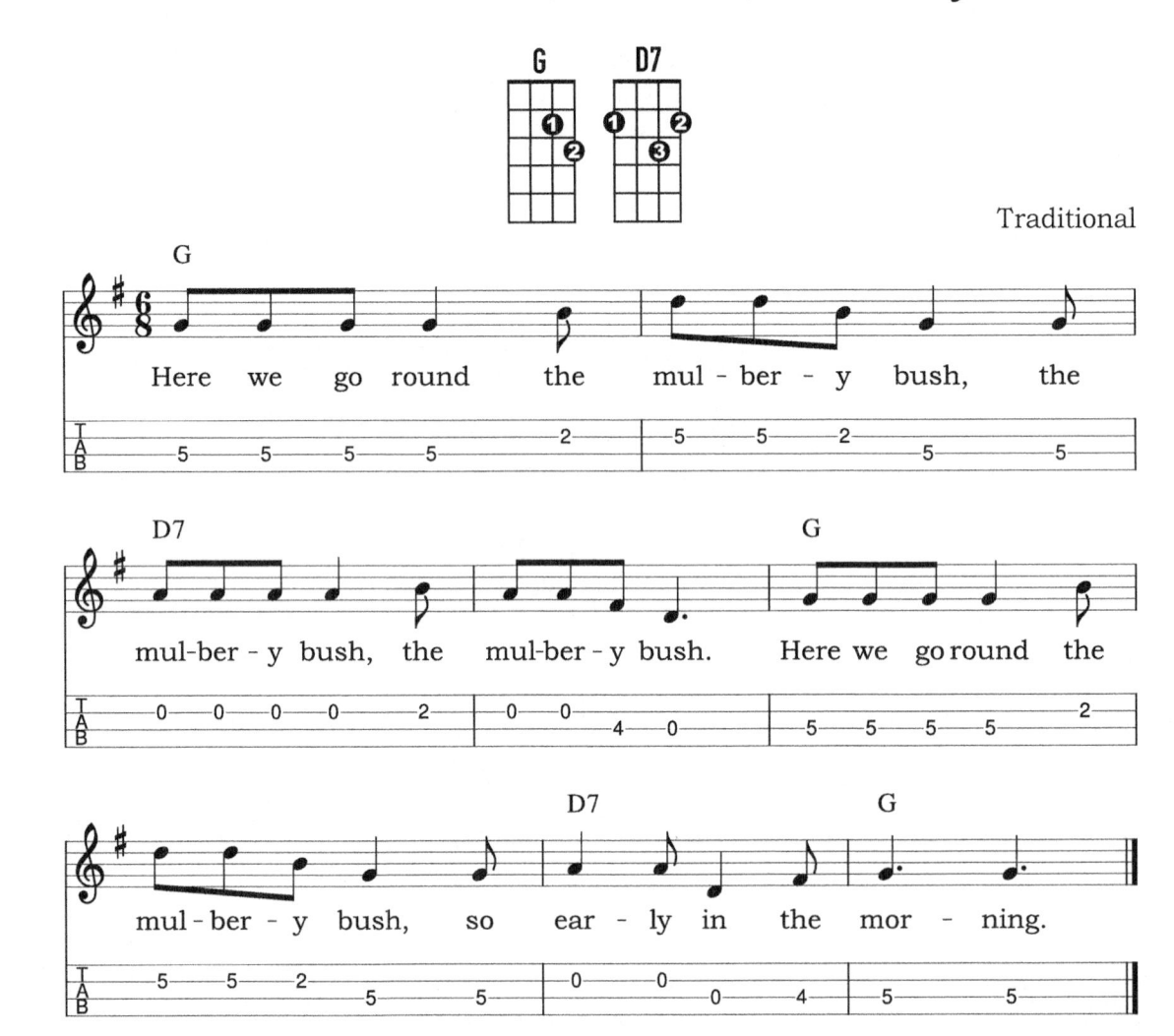

Traditional

Here we go round the mulberry bush, the mul-ber-y bush, the mul-ber-y bush, the mul-ber-y bush. Here we go round the mul-ber-y bush, so ear-ly in the mor-ning.

Here we go round the mulberry bush,
The mulberry bush,
The mulberry bush.
Here we go round the mulberry bush
So early in the morning.

This is the way we wash our face,
Wash our face,
Wash our face.
This is the way we wash our face
So early in the morning.

This is the way we comb our hair,
Comb our hair,
Comb our hair.
This is the way we comb our hair
So early in the morning.

This is the way we brush our teeth,
Brush our teeth,
Brush our teeth.
This is the way we brush our teeth
So early in the morning.

This is the way we put on our clothes,
Put on our clothes,
Put on our clothes.
This is the way we put on our clothes
So early in the morning.

Here we go round the mulberry bush,
The mulberry bush,
The mulberry bush.
Here we go round the mulberry bush
So early in the morning.

Hot Cross Buns

Traditional

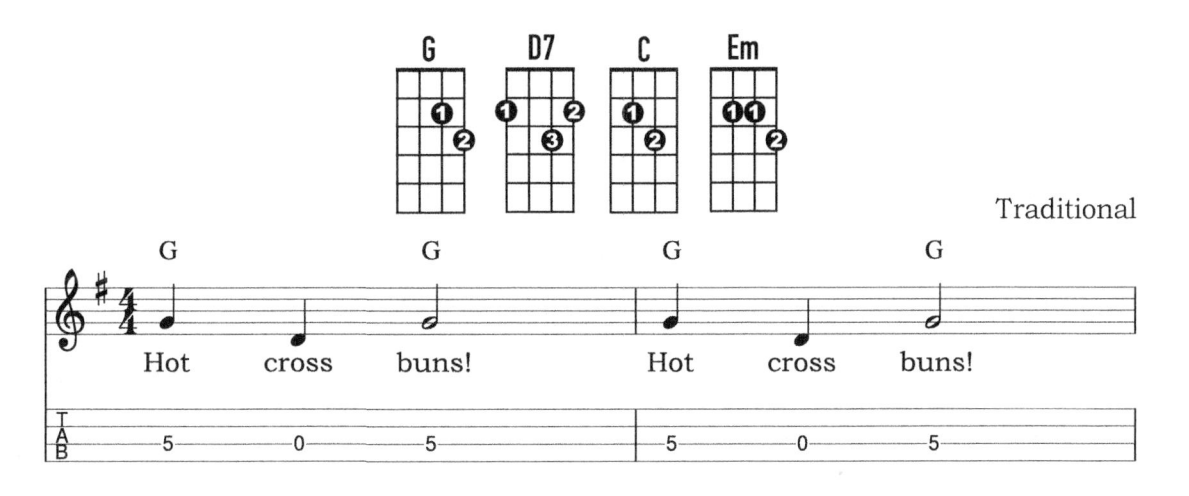

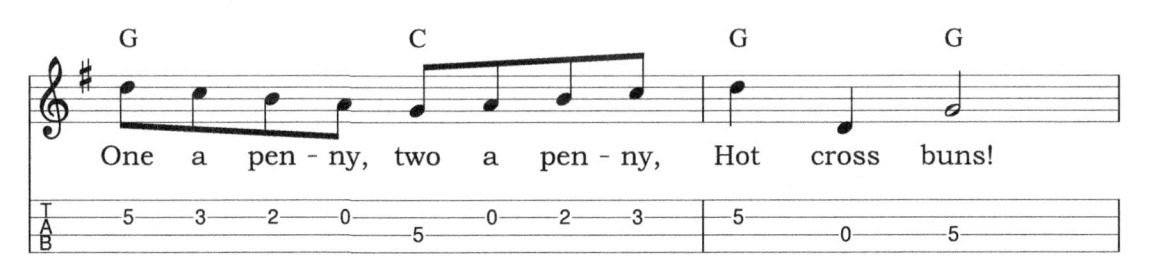

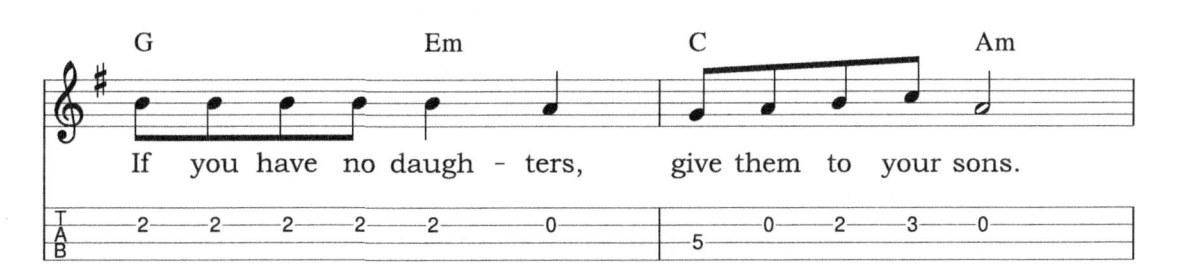

Hot cross buns! Hot cross buns!
One a pen-ny, two a pen-ny, Hot cross buns!
If you have no daugh-ters, give them to your sons.
One a pen-ny, two a pen-ny, Hot cross buns!

Home on the Range

Brewster M. Higley　　　　　　　　　　　　　　　　　　　Daniel E. Kelley

Oh give me a home where the buf-fa-lo roam, where the deer and the an-te-lope play, where sel-dom is heard a dis-cour-ag-ing word, and the skies are not cloud-y all day. Home, home on the range, where the deer and the an-te-lope play, where sel-dom is heard a dis-cour-ag-ing word, and the

34

Oh, give me a home where the buffalo roam,
Where the deer and the antelope play,
Where seldom is heard a discouraging word
And the skies are not cloudy all day.

Home, home on the range,
Where the deer and the antelope play;
Where seldom is heard a discouraging word
And the skies are not cloudy all day.

Where the air is so pure, the zephyrs so free,
The breezes so balmy and light,
That I would not exchange my home on the range
For all of the cities so bright.

The red man was pressed from this part of the West,
He's likely no more to return
To the banks of Red River where seldom if ever
Their flickering camp-fires burn.

How often at night when the heavens are bright
With the light from the glittering stars,
Have I stood here amazed and asked as I gazed
If their glory exceeds that of ours.

Oh, I love these wild flowers in this dear land of ours,
The curlew I love to hear scream,
And I love the white rocks and the antelope flocks
That graze on the mountain-tops green.

Oh, give me a land where the bright diamond sand
Flows leisurely down the stream;
Where the graceful white swan goes gliding along
Like a maid in a heavenly dream.

Then I would not exchange my home on the range,
Where the deer and the antelope play;
Where seldom is heard a discouraging word
And the skies are not cloudy all day.

Home, home on the range,
Where the deer and the antelope play;
Where seldom is heard a discouraging word
And the skies are not cloudy all day.

Humpty Dumpty

Traditional

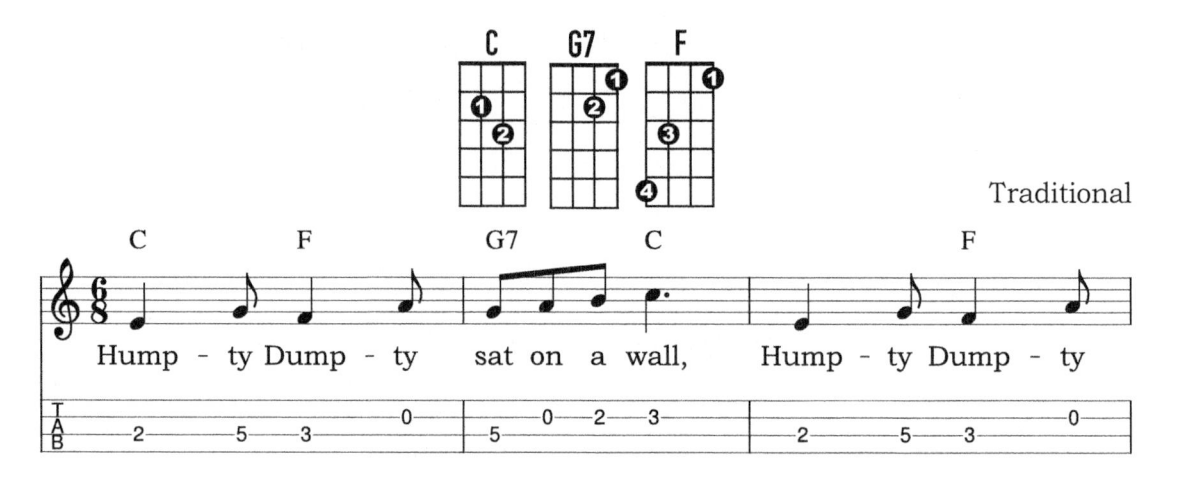

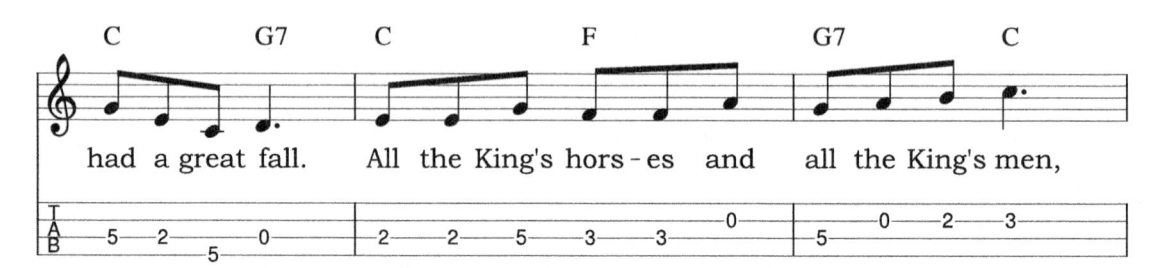

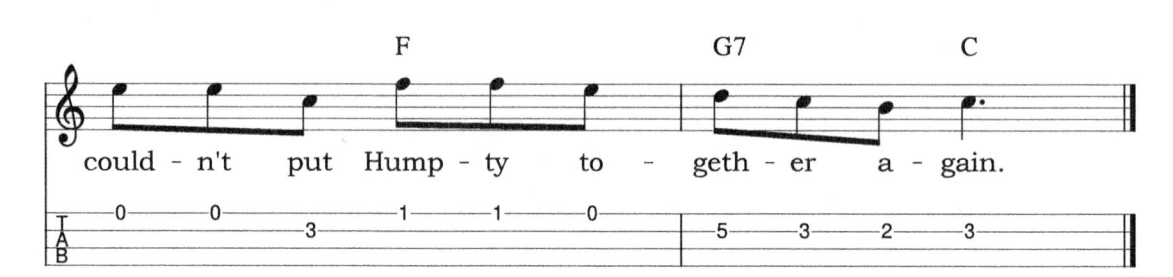

Hump - ty Dump - ty sat on a wall, Hump - ty Dump - ty had a great fall. All the King's hors - es and all the King's men, could - n't put Hump - ty to - geth - er a - gain.

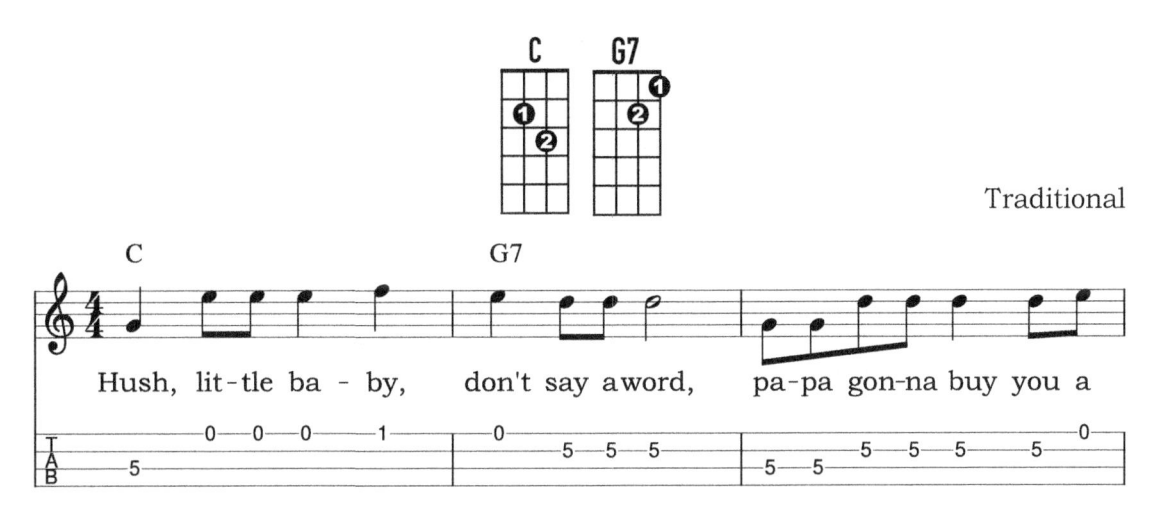

Hush Little Baby

Traditional

Hush, lit-tle ba-by, don't say a word, pa-pa gon-na buy you a mock-ing bird. If that mock-ing bird don't sing, pa-pa's gon-na buy you a dia-mond ring.

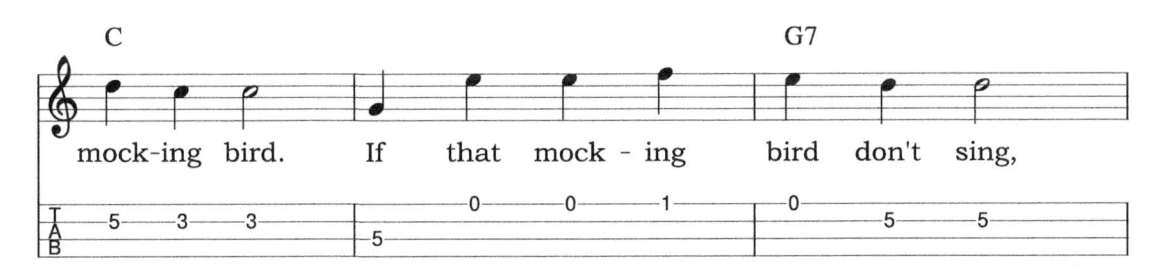

Hush little baby, don't say a word,
Papa's gonna buy you a mockingbird.
If that mockingbird don't sing,
Papa's gonna buy you a diamond ring.

If that diamond ring turns to brass,
Papa's gonna buy you a looking glass.
If that looking glass gets broke,
Papa's gonna buy you a billy goat.

If that billy goat won't pull,
Papa's gonna buy you a cart and bull.
If that cart and bull turn over,
Papa's gonna buy you a dog named Rover.

If that dog named Rover won't bark,
Papa's gonna buy you a horse and cart.
If that horse and cart fall down,
You'll still be the sweetest little baby in town!

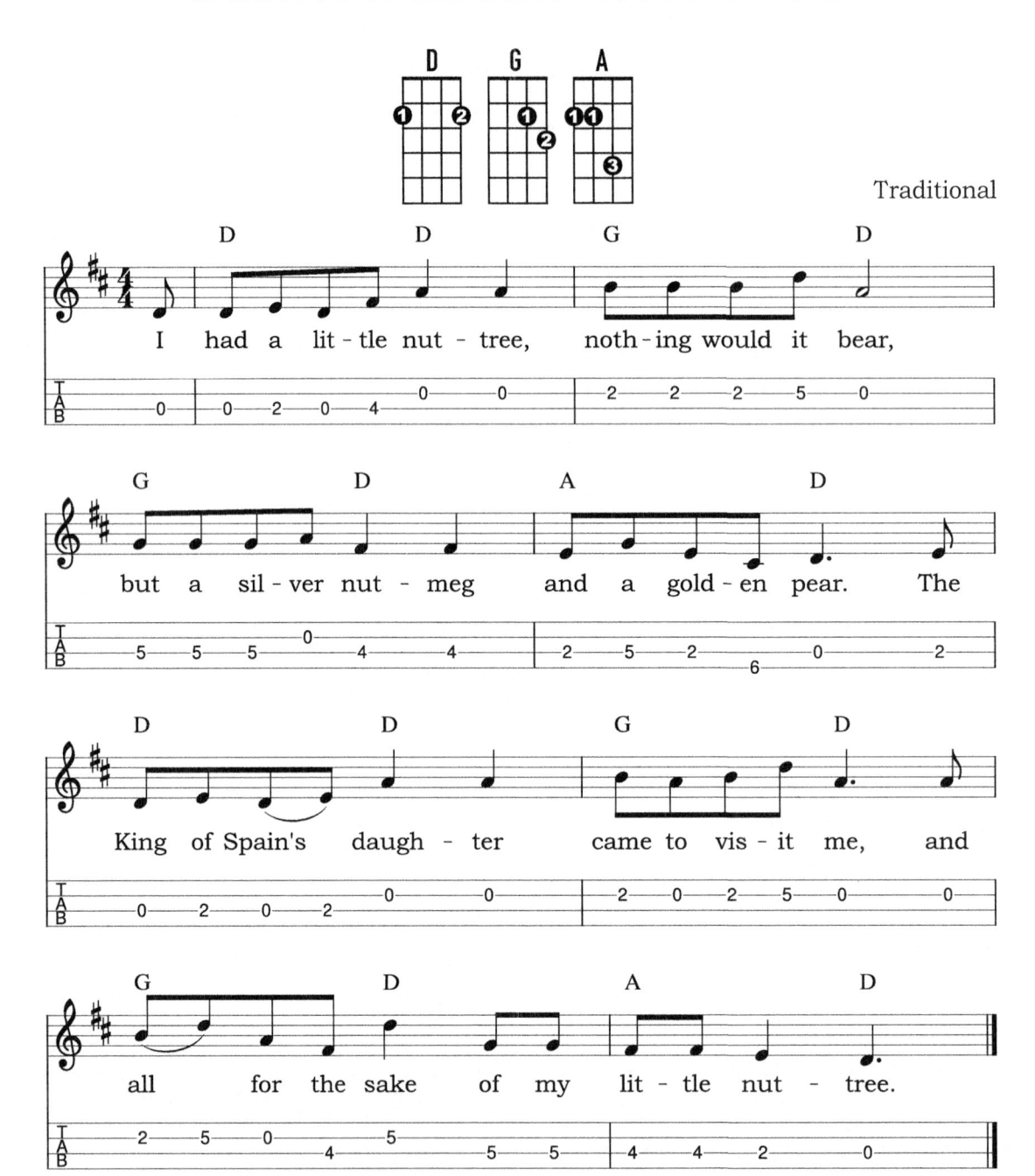

I Had a Little Nut Tree

Traditional

I had a little nut-tree, nothing would it bear,
but a silver nutmeg and a golden pear. The
King of Spain's daughter came to visit me, and
all for the sake of my little nut-tree.

I had a little nut tree,
Nothing would it bear,
But a silver nutmeg
And a golden pear.
The King of Spain's daughter
Came to visit me,
And all for the sake
Of my little nut tree.

Her dress was made of crimson,
Jet black was her hair,
She asked me for my nutmeg
And my golden pear.
I said, "So fair a princess
Never did I see,
I'll give you all the fruit
From my little nut tree."

I Saw Three Ships

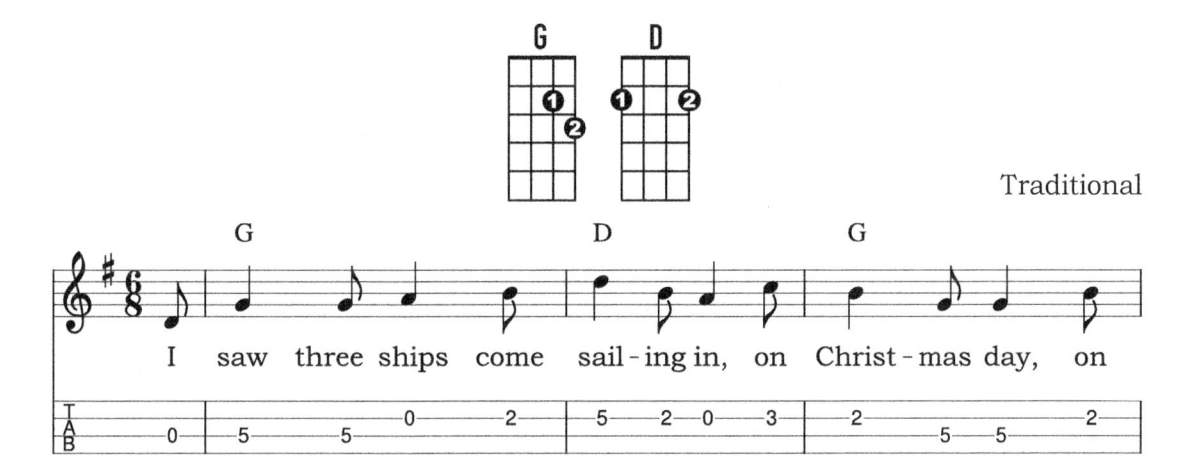

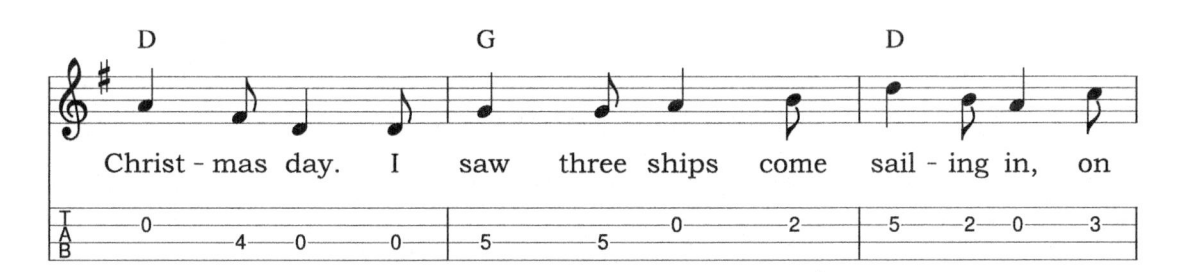

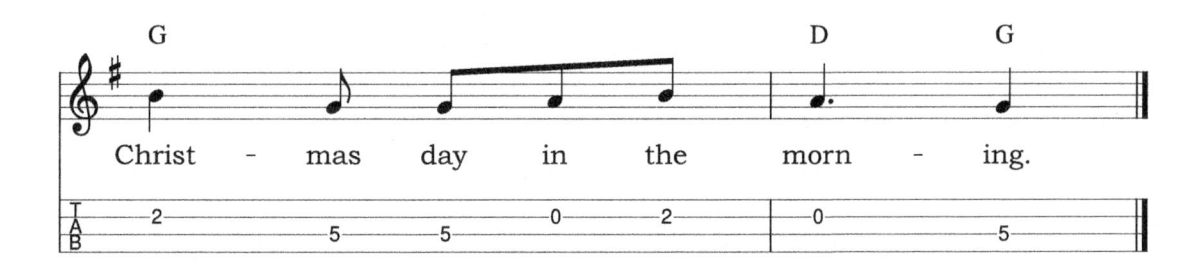

Traditional

I saw three ships come sailing in, on Christ-mas day, on Christ-mas day. I saw three ships come sail-ing in, on Christ-mas day in the morn-ing.

I saw three ships come sailing in
On Christmas Day, on Christmas Day.
I saw three ships come sailing in
On Christmas Day in the morning.

And what was in those ships all three
On Christmas Day, on Christmas Day?
And what was in those ships all three
On Christmas Day in the morning?

Our Savior Christ and His lady
On Christmas Day, on Christmas Day.
Our Savior Christ and His lady
On Christmas Day in the morning.

Pray, wither sailed those ships all three
On Christmas Day, on Christmas Day.
Pray, wither sailed those ships all three
On Christmas Day in the morning.

O, they sailed into Bethlehem
On Christmas Day, on Christmas Day.
O, they sailed into Bethlehem
On Christmas Day in the morning.

And all the bells on Earth shall ring
On Christmas Day, on Christmas Day.
And all the bells on Earth shall ring
On Christmas Day in the morning.

I Love Little Kitty

Traditional

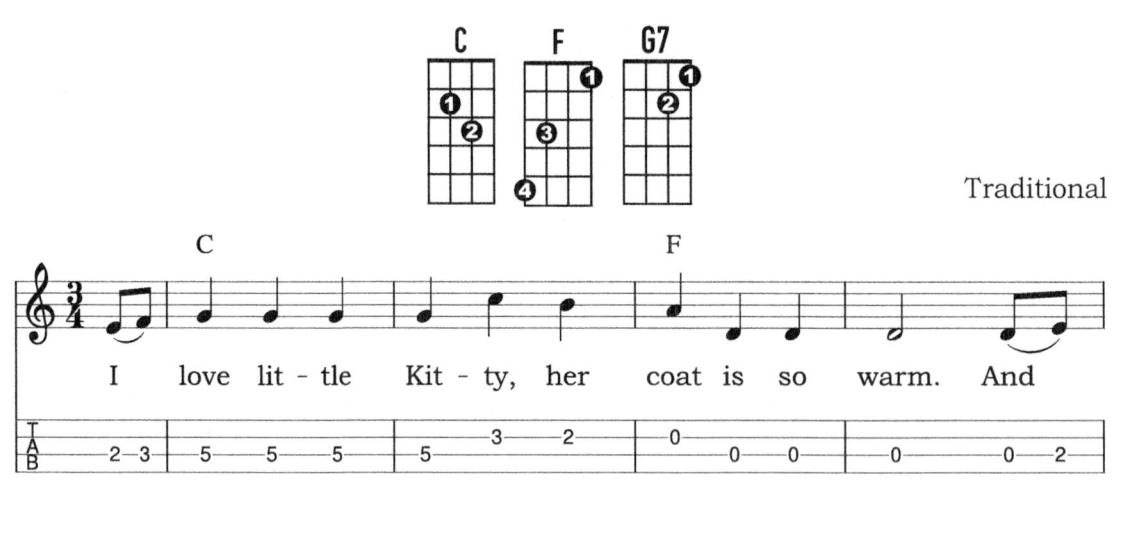

I love little Kitty, her coat is so warm. And if I don't hurt her, she'll do me no harm.

I love little kitty,
Her coat is so warm,
And if I don't hurt her,
She'll do me no harm.

So I'll not pull her tail,
Nor drive her away,
But kitty and I,
Very gently will play.

It's Raining, It's Pouring

Traditional

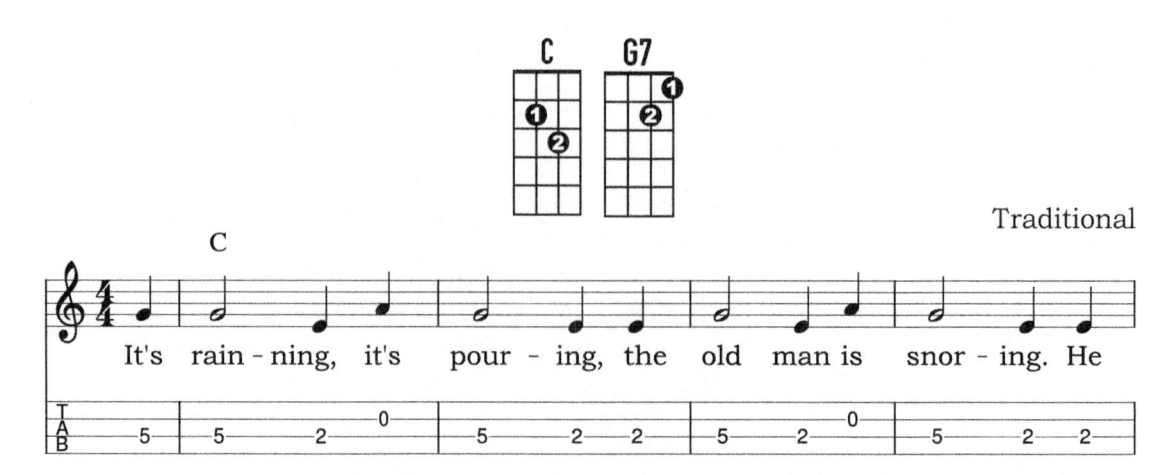

It's rain-ning, it's pour-ing, the old man is snor-ing. He

40

G7

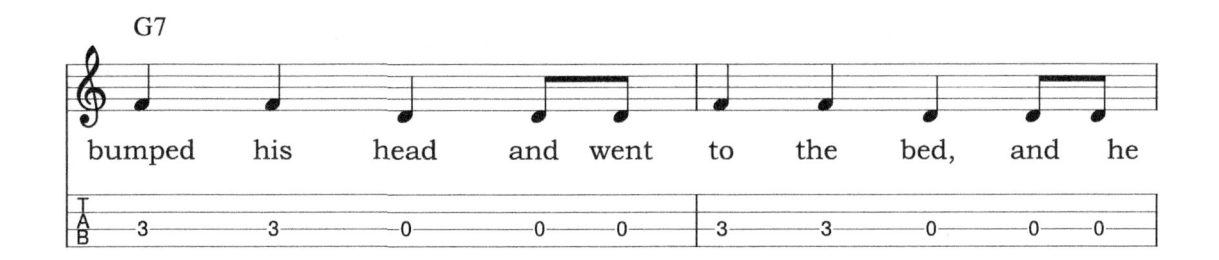

bumped his head and went to the bed, and he

could-n't get up in the **C** morn - ing.

Jack Sprat

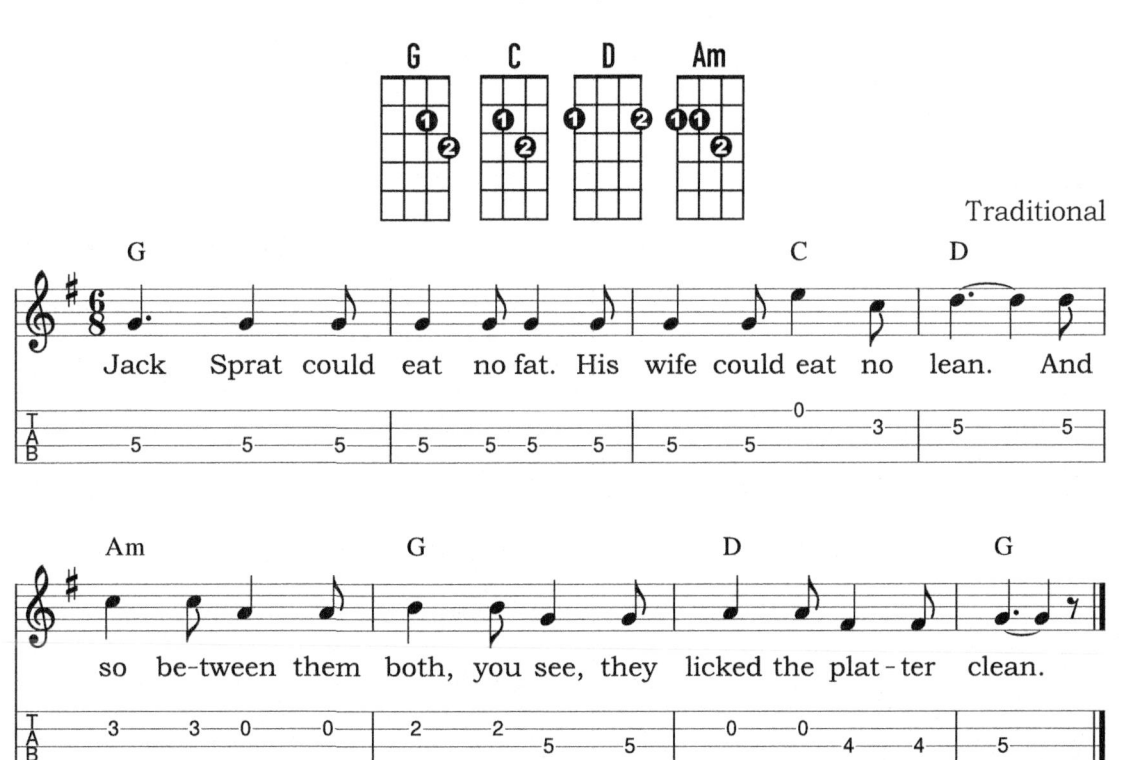

Traditional

G Jack Sprat could eat no fat. His wife could eat no **C** **D** lean. And

Am so be-tween them **G** both, you see, they **D** licked the plat-ter **G** clean.

Jingle Bells

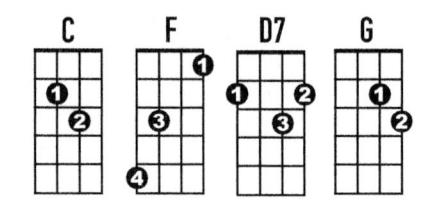

James Lord Pierpon

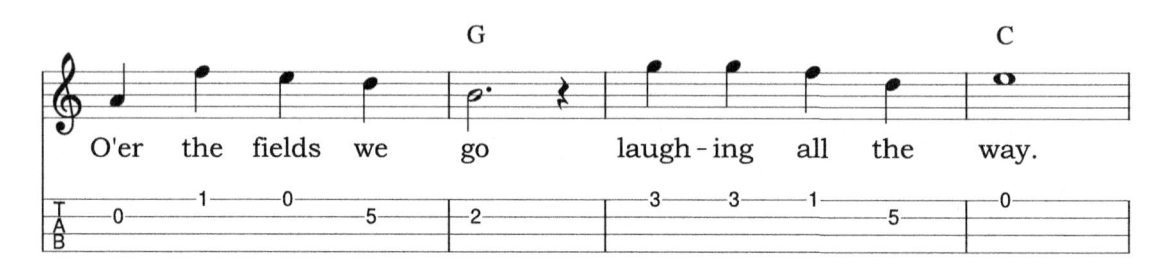

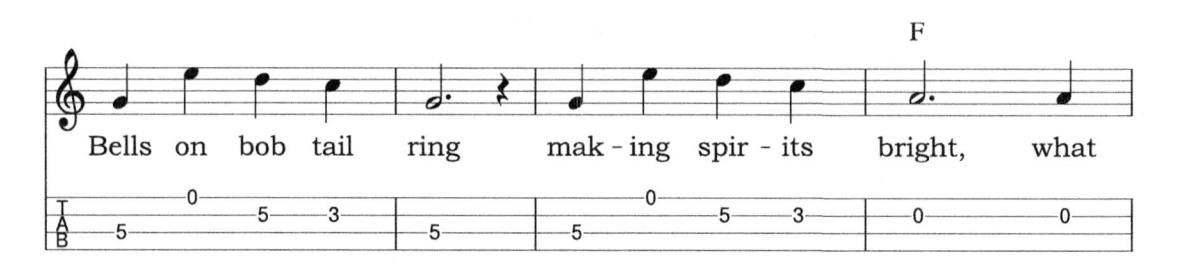

Dash - ing through the snow in a one-horse o - pen sleigh.
O'er the fields we go laugh - ing all the way.
Bells on bob tail ring mak - ing spir - its bright, what
fun it is to ride and sing a sleigh - ing song to - night!
Jing - le bells, jing - le bells, jing - le all the way!

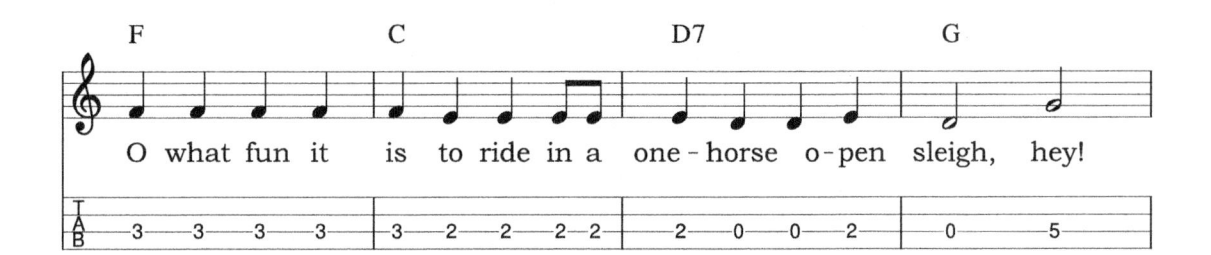

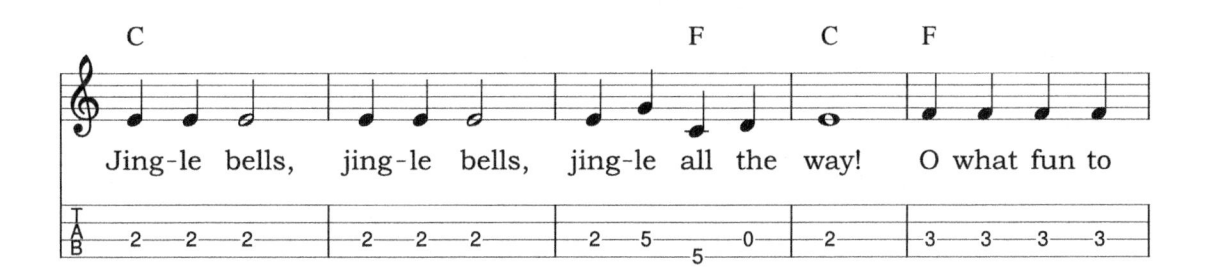

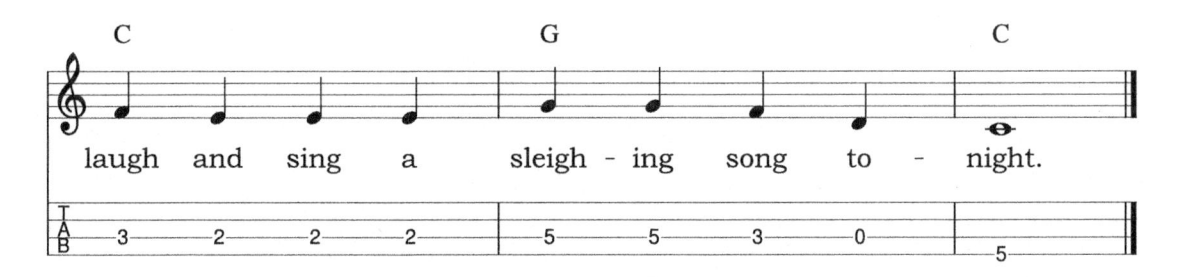

Dashing through the snow
In a one-horse open sleigh
O'er the fields we go
Laughing all the way
Bells on bob tail ring
Making spirits bright
What fun it is to ride and sing
A sleighing song tonight!

Jingle bells, jingle bells,
Jingle all the way.
Oh! what fun it is to ride
In a one-horse open sleigh.
Jingle bells, jingle bells,
Jingle all the way;
Oh! what fun it is to ride
In a one-horse open sleigh.

A day or two ago,
The story I must tell
I went out on the snow,
And on my back I fell;
A gent was riding by
In a one-horse open sleigh,
He laughed as there I sprawling lie,
But quickly drove away.

Jingle bells, jingle bells,
Jingle all the way.
Oh! what fun it is to ride
In a one-horse open sleigh.
Jingle bells, jingle bells,
Jingle all the way;
Oh! what fun it is to ride
In a one-horse open sleigh.

Now the ground is white
Go it while you're young,
Take the girls tonight
and sing this sleighing song;
Just get a bobtailed bay
Two forty as his speed[b]
Hitch him to an open sleigh
And crack! you'll take the lead.

Jingle bells, jingle bells,
Jingle all the way.
Oh! what fun it is to ride
In a one-horse open sleigh.
Jingle bells, jingle bells,
Jingle all the way;
Oh! what fun it is to ride
In a one-horse open sleigh.

Jack and Jill

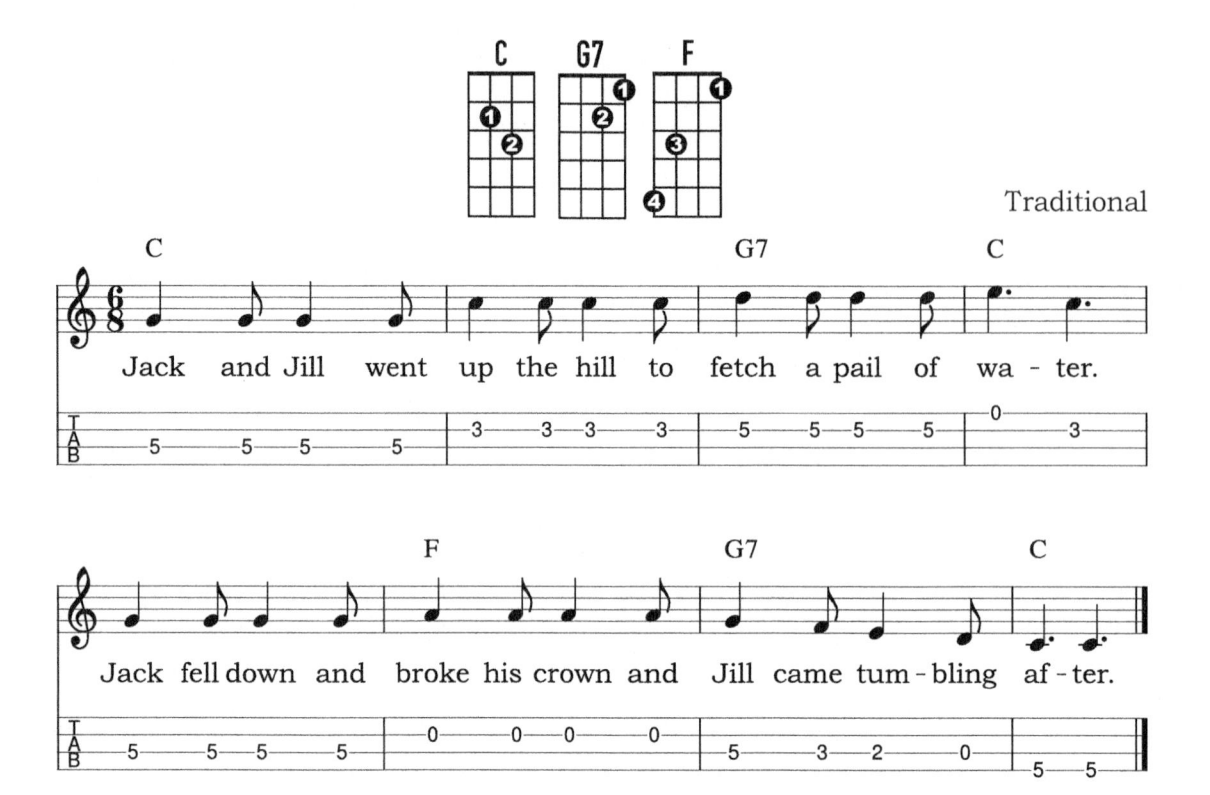

Traditional

Jack and Jill went up the hill to fetch a pail of wa - ter.
Jack fell down and broke his crown and Jill came tum - bling af - ter.

Jack and Jill
Went up the hill
To fetch a pail of water
Jack fell down and broke his crown
And Jill came tumbling after.

Up Jack got
And home did trot,
As fast as he could caper;
Went to bed
To mend his head
With vinegar and brown paper.

Jill came in
And she did grin
To see his paper plaster;
Mother, vex'd,
Did whip her next
For causing Jack's disaster.

John Jacob Jingleheimer Schmidt

Traditional

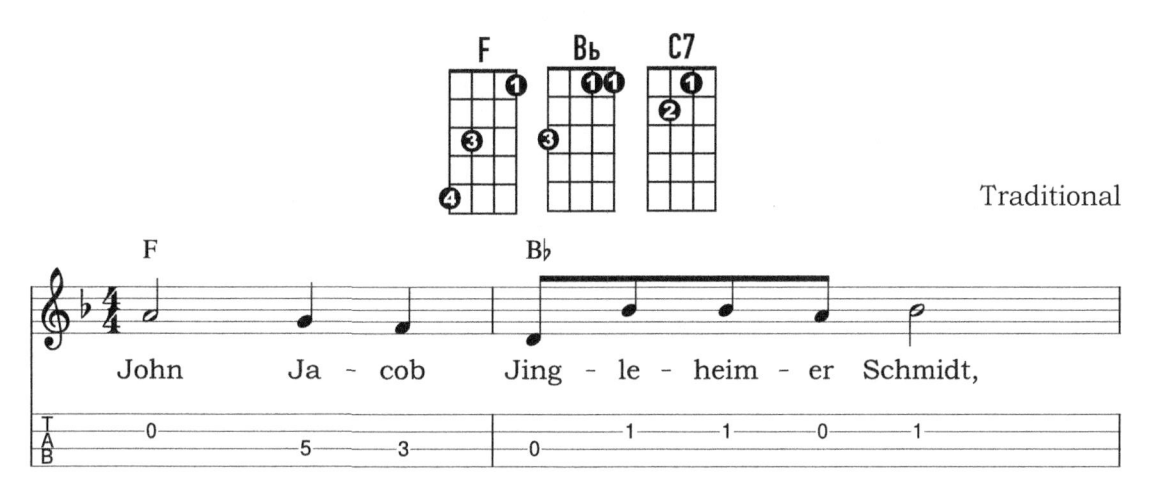

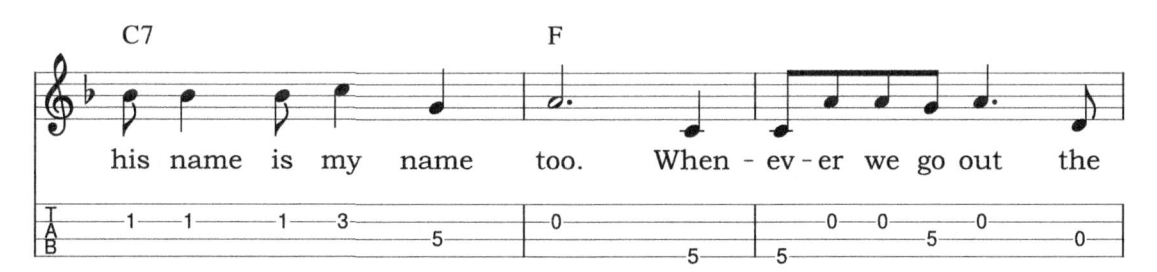

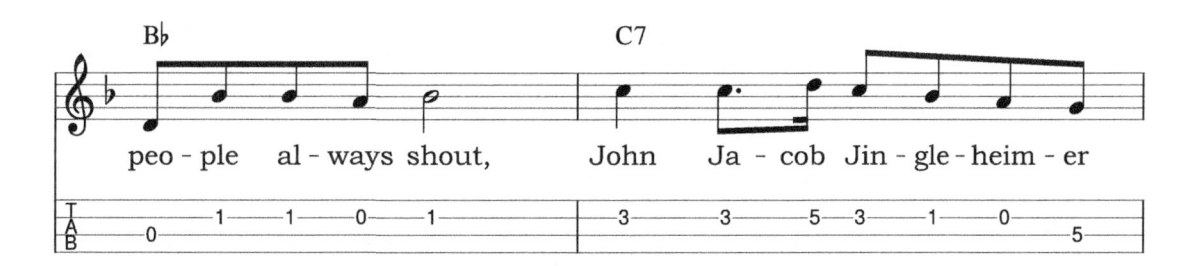

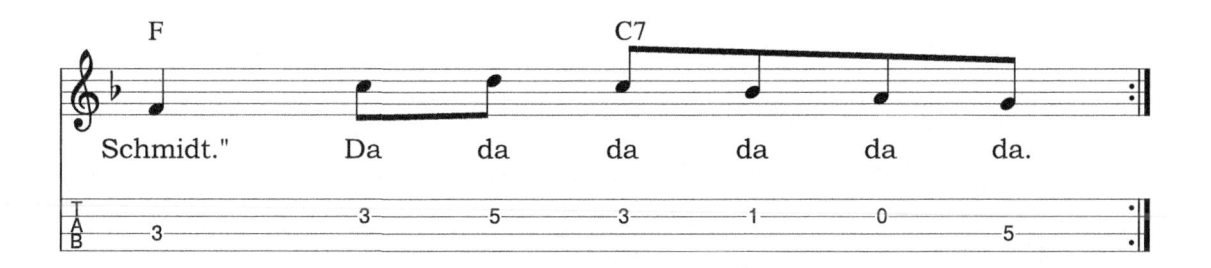

John Jacob Jingleheimer Schmidt, his name is my name too. Whenever we go out the people always shout, "John Jacob Jingleheimer Schmidt." Da da da da da da.

Kumbaya

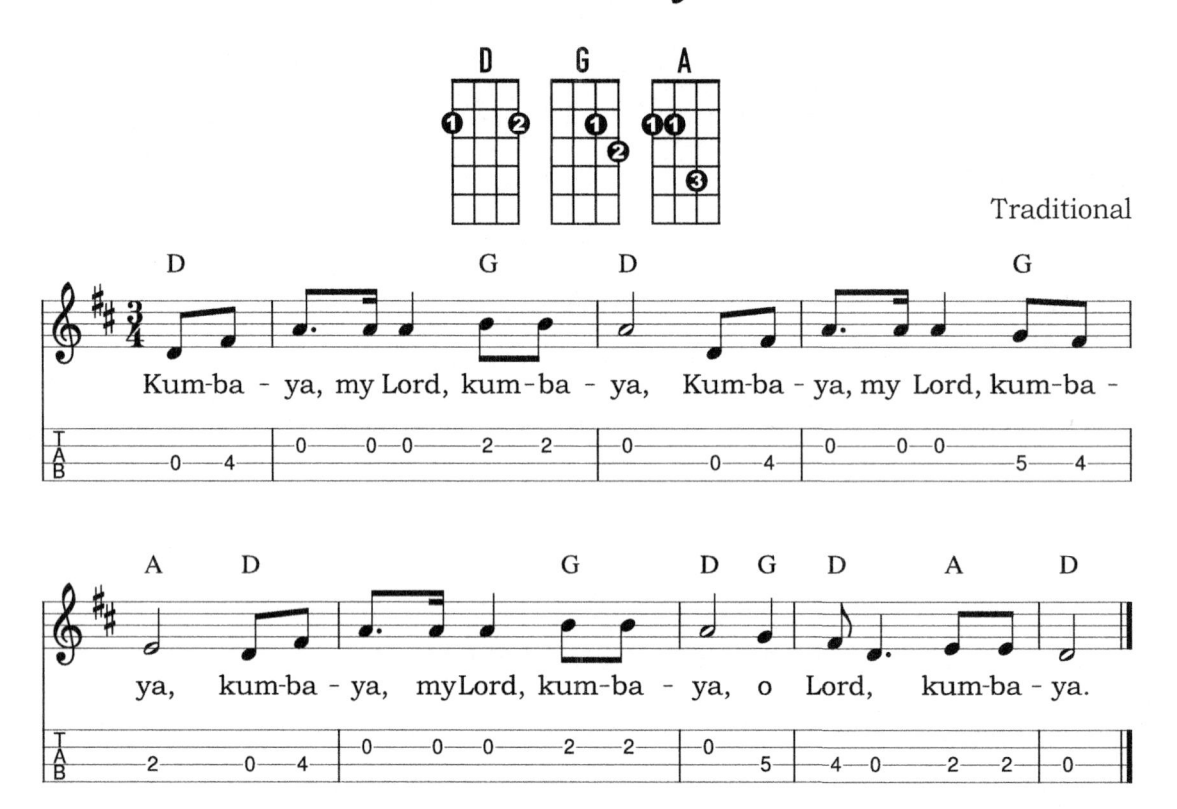

Traditional

Kum-ba - ya, my Lord, kum-ba - ya, Kum-ba - ya, my Lord, kum-ba - ya, kum-ba - ya, my Lord, kum-ba - ya, o Lord, kum-ba - ya.

Someone's laughing, Lord, kum bay ya;
Someone's laughing, Lord, kum bay ya;
Someone's laughing, Lord, kum bay ya,
O Lord, kum bay ya.

Someone's crying, Lord, kum bay ya;
Someone's crying, Lord, kum bay ya;
Someone's crying, Lord, kum bay ya,
O Lord, kum bay ya.

Someone's praying, Lord, kum bay ya;
Someone's praying, Lord, kum bay ya;
Someone's praying, Lord, kum bay ya,
O Lord, kum bay ya.

Someone's singing, Lord, kum bay ya;
Someone's singing, Lord, kum bay ya;
Someone's singing, Lord, kum bay ya,
O Lord, kum bay ya.

Lavender's Blue

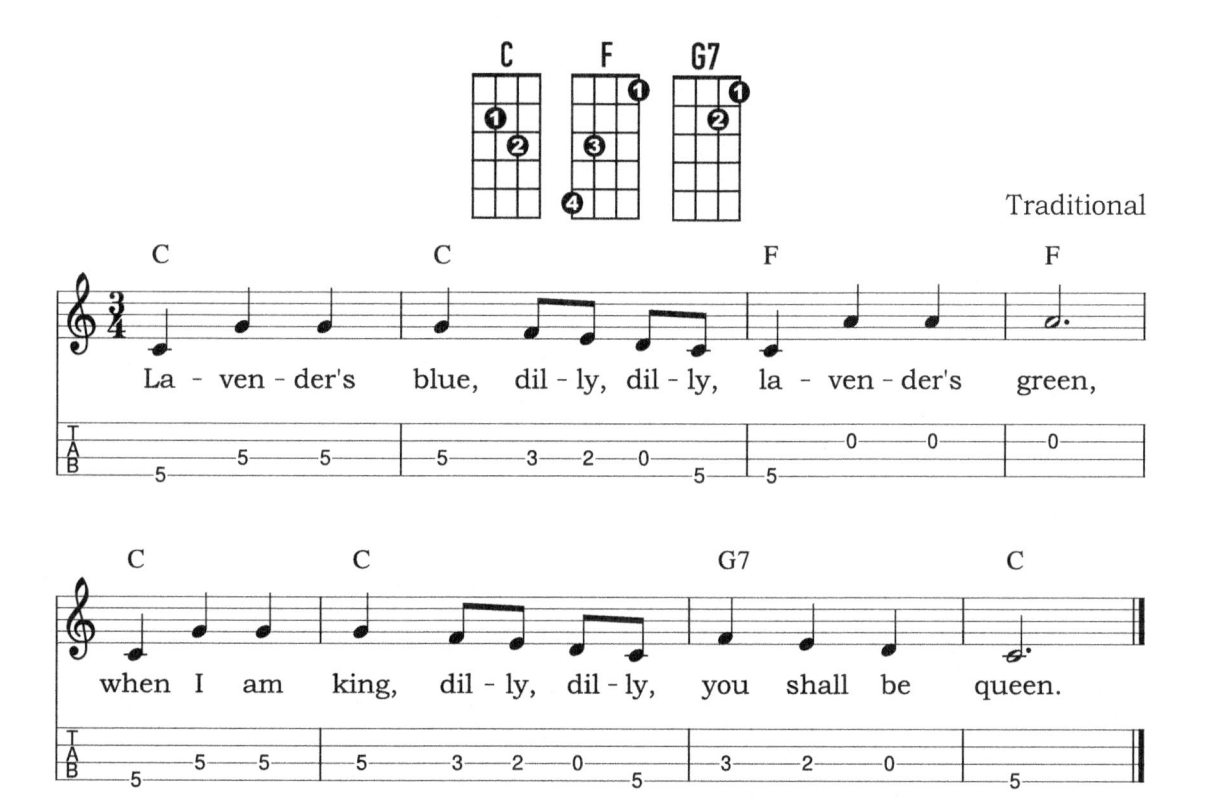

Traditional

Lavender's blue, dil-ly, dil-ly, la-ven-der's green,
when I am king, dil-ly, dil-ly, you shall be queen.

Lavender's blue, dilly dilly, lavender's green,
When I am king, dilly dilly, you shall be queen:

Who told you so, dilly dilly, who told you so?
'Twas mine own heart, dilly dilly, that told me so.

Call up your men, dilly dilly, set them to work,
Some with a rake, dilly dilly, some with a fork;

Some to make hay, dilly dilly, some to thresh corn,
Whilst you and I, dilly dilly, keep ourselves warm.

If you should die, dilly dilly, as it may hap,
You shall be buried, dilly dilly, under the tap;

Who told you so, dilly dilly, pray tell me why?
That you might drink, dilly dilly, when you are dry.

Lazy Sheep, Pray Tell Me Why

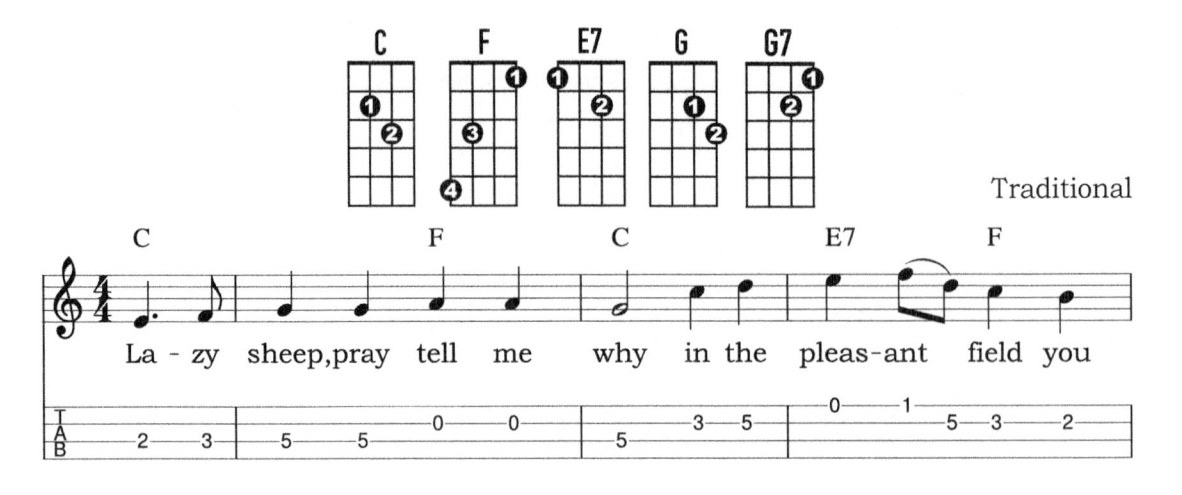

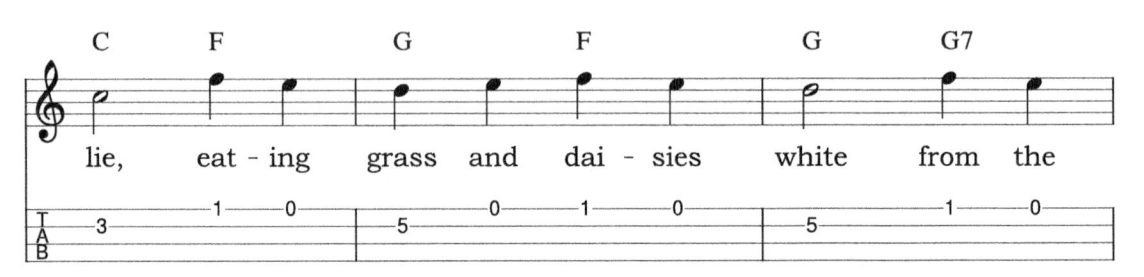

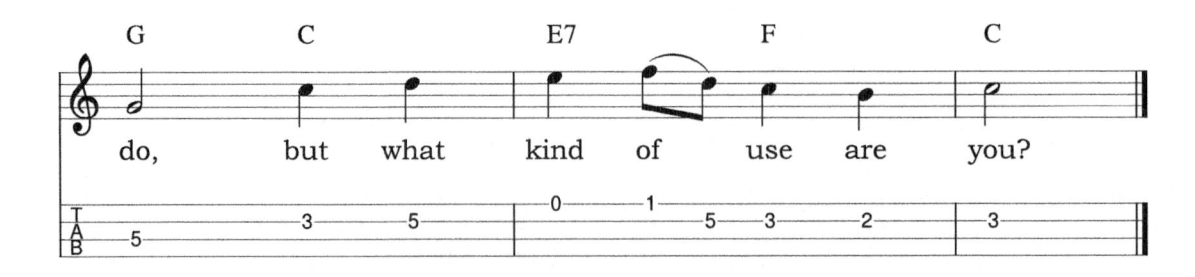

Traditional

Lazy sheep, pray tell me why
In the pleasant field you lie,
Eating grass and daisies white
From the morning till the night?
Every thing can something do,
But what kind of use are you?

Nay, my little master, nay,
Do not serve me so, I pray;
Don't you see the wool that grows
On my back to make your clothes?
Cold, and very cold, you'd be
If you had not wool from me.

True, it seems a pleasant thing,
To nip the daisies in the spring;
But many chilly nights I pass
On the cold and dewy grass,
Or pick a scanty dinner, where
All the common's brown and bare.

Then the farmer comes at last,
When the merry spring is past,
And cuts my woolly coat away,
To warm you in the winter's day:
Little master this is why
In the pleasant fields I lie.

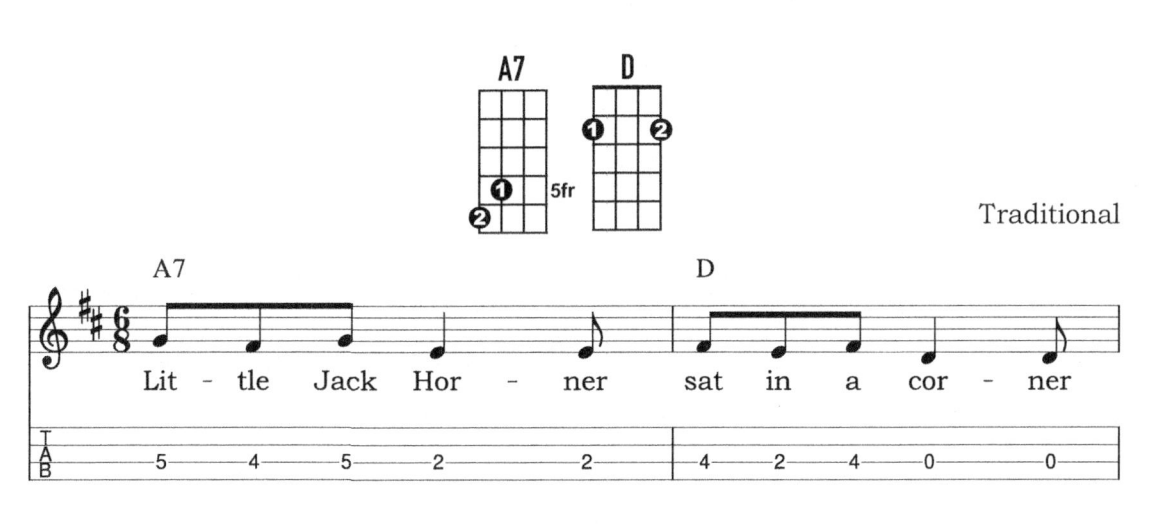

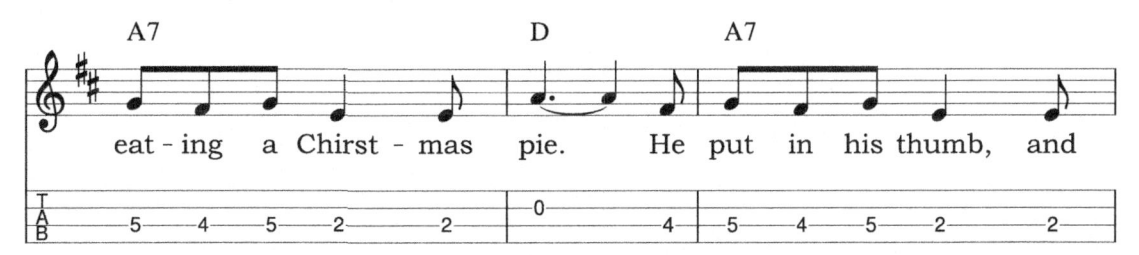

Little Jack Horner

Traditional

Lit - tle Jack Hor - ner sat in a cor - ner eat - ing a Chirst - mas pie. He put in his thumb, and pulled out a plum, and said, "What a good boy am I!".

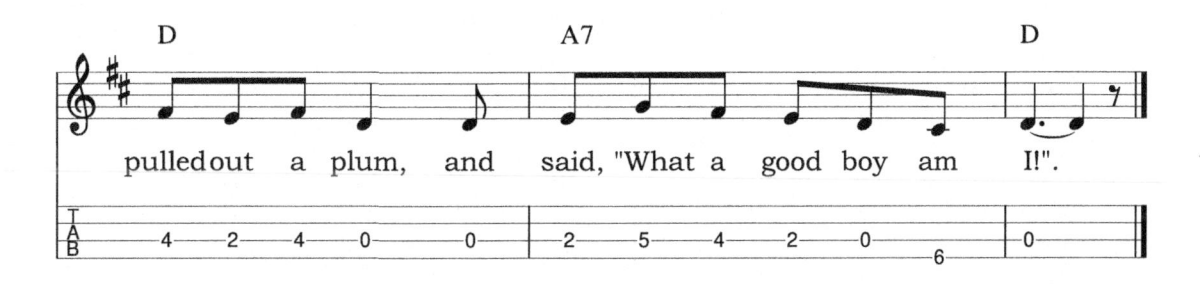

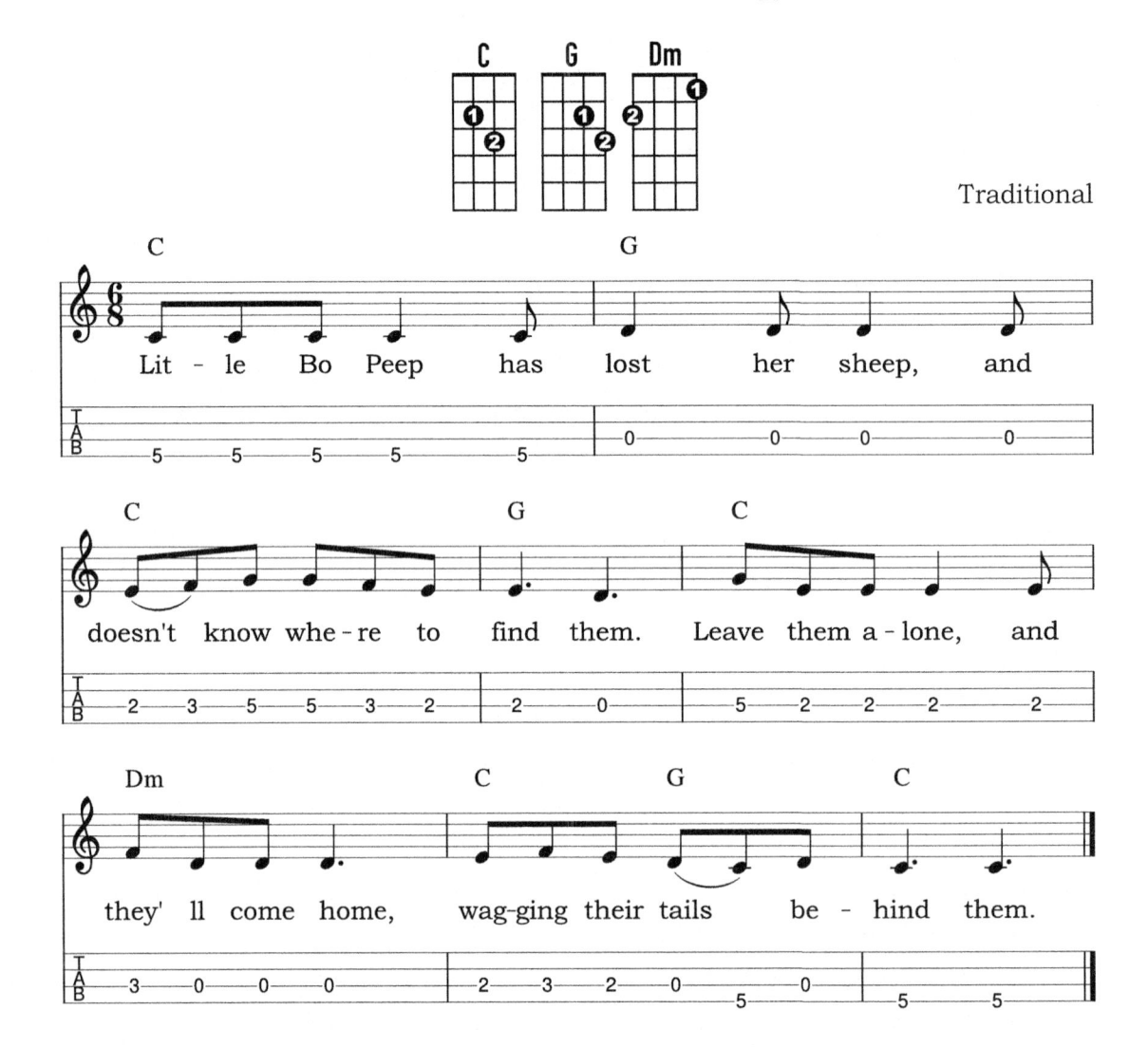

Little Bo-Peep

Traditional

Little Bo-Peep has lost her sheep, and doesn't know where to find them. Leave them alone, and they'll come home, wagging their tails behind them.

Little Bo-Peep has lost her sheep,
And doesn't know where to find them.
Leave them alone,
And they'll come home,
Wagging their tails behind them.

Little Bo-Peep fell fast asleep,
And dreamt she heard them bleating.
But when she awoke,
She found it a joke,
For they were still a-fleeting.

Then up she took her little crook,
Determined for to find them.
She found them indeed,
But it made her heart bleed,
for they'd left their tails behind them.

It happened one day,
As Bo-Peep did stray
Into a meadow hard by,
There she espied their tails side by side,
All hung on a tree to dry.

She heaved a sigh and wiped her eye,
And over the hillocks went rambling,
And tried what she could,
As a shepherdess should,
To tack each again to its lambkin.

Li'l Liza Jane

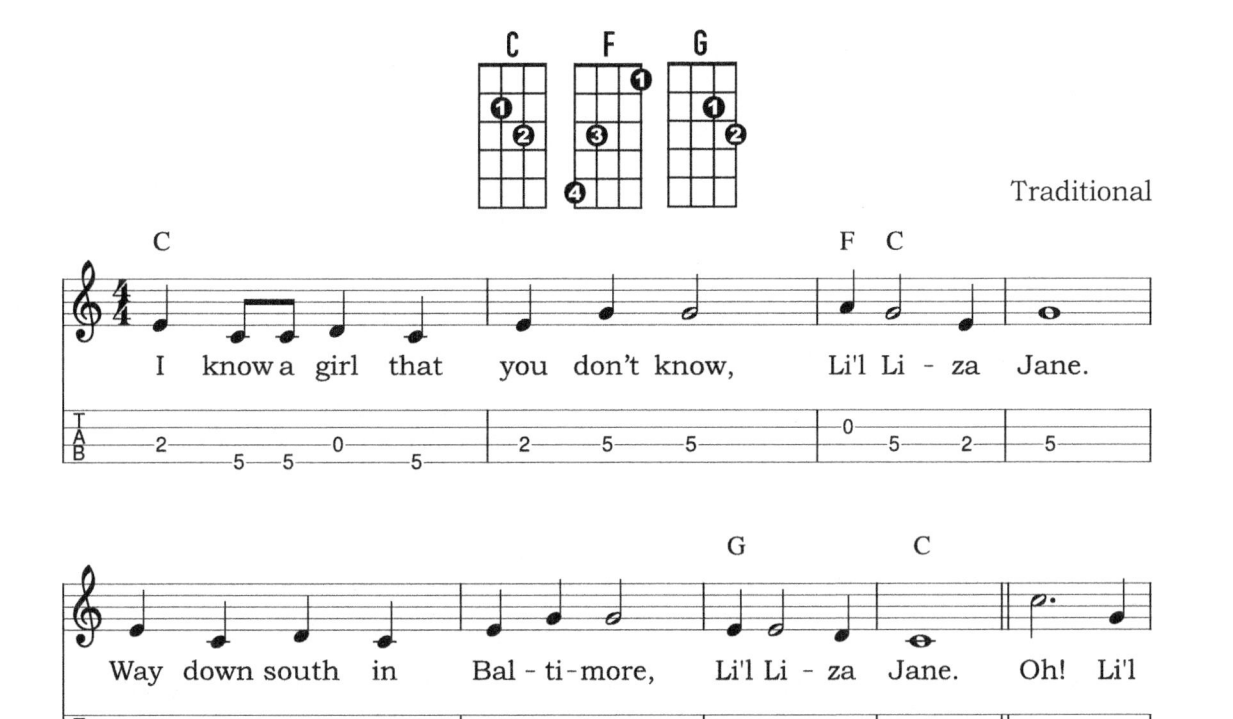

Traditional

I know a girl that you don't know, Li'l Li - za Jane.
Way down south in Bal - ti - more, Li'l Li - za Jane. Oh! Li'l
Li - za, Li'l Li - za Jane. Oh! Li'l Li - za, Li'l Li - za Jane.

Little Miss Muffet

Traditional

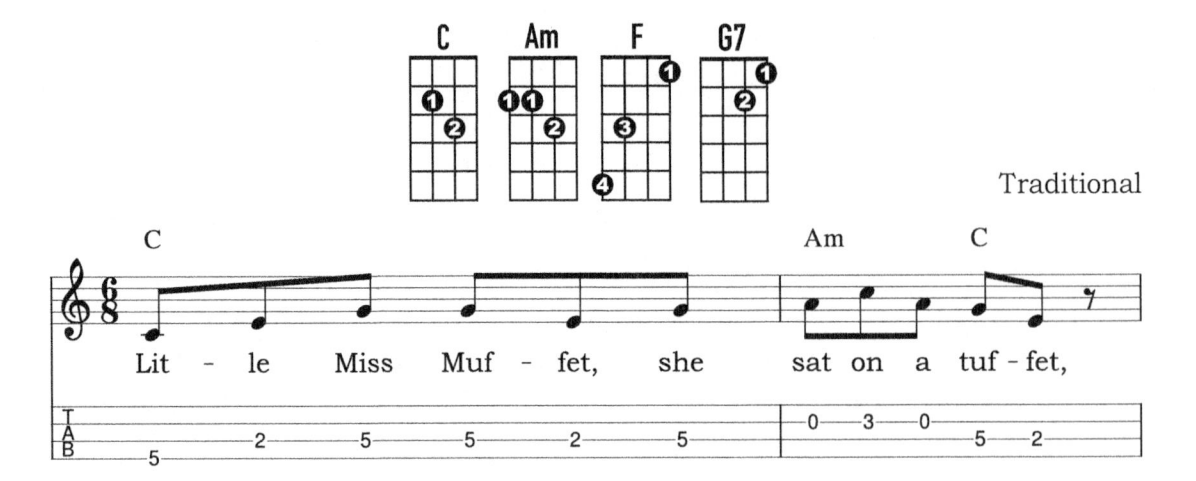

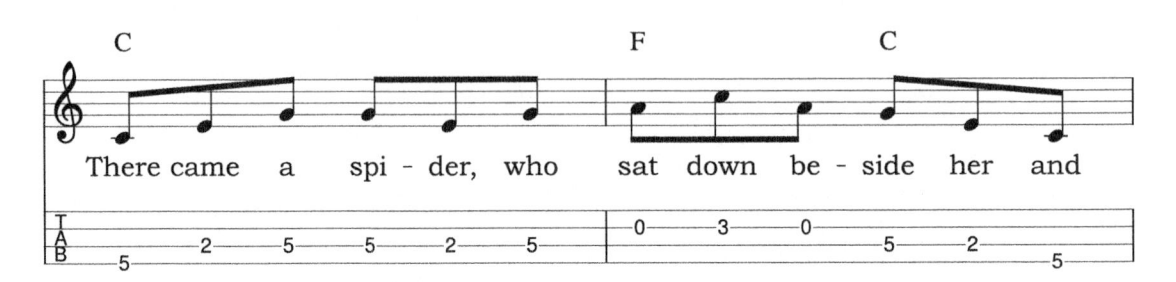

Lit - tle Miss Muf - fet, she sat on a tuf - fet, eat - ing her curds and whey. There came a spi - der, who sat down be - side her and frigh - tened Miss Muf - fet a - way.

Little Polly Flinders

Traditional

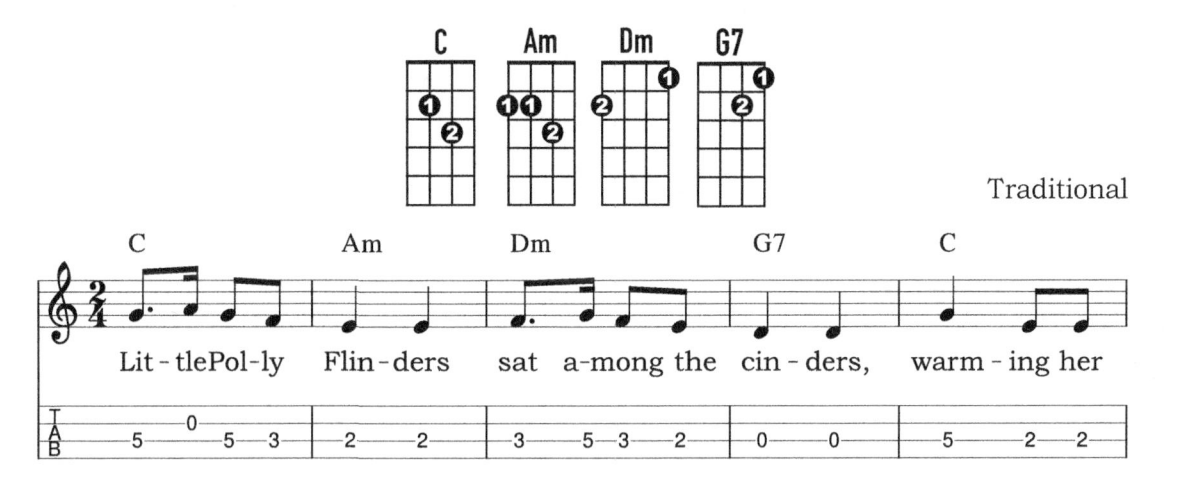

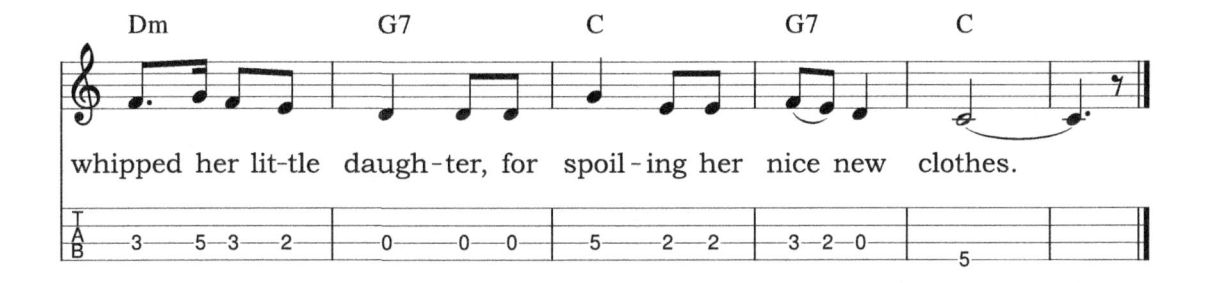

Little Polly Flinders sat among the cinders, warming her pretty little toes! Her mother came and caught her and whipped her little daughter, for spoiling her nice new clothes.

Looby Loo

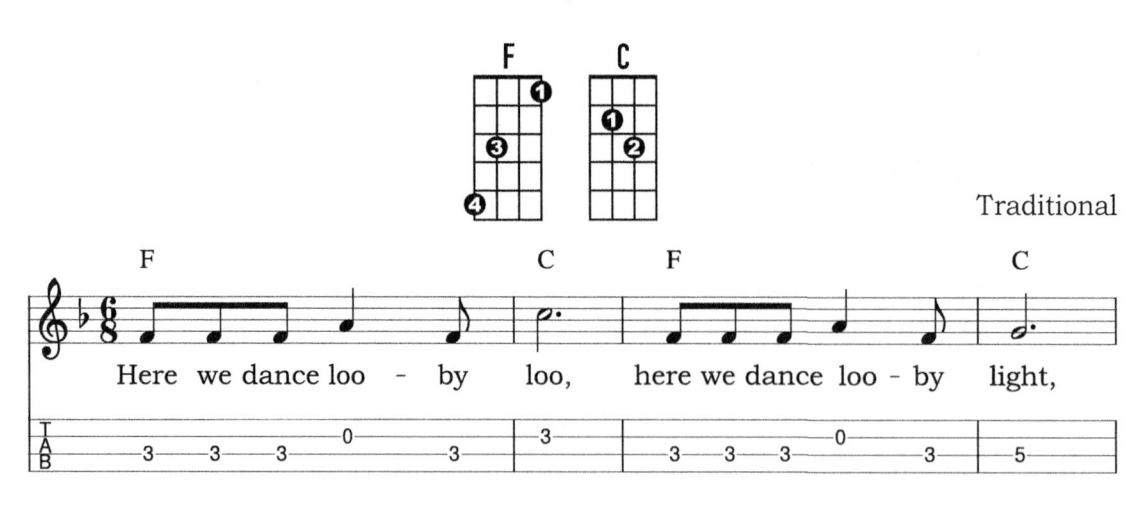

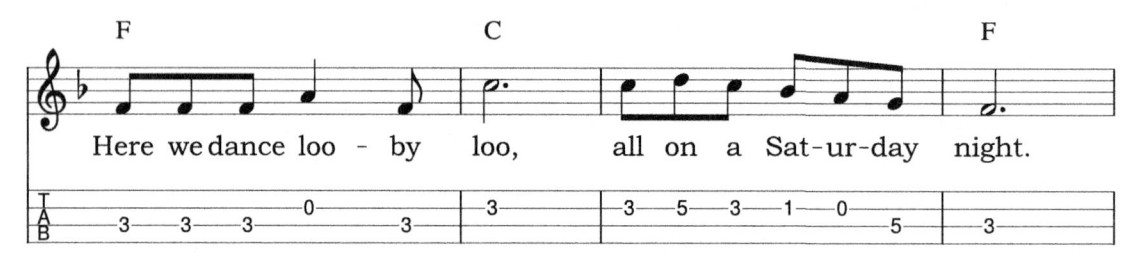

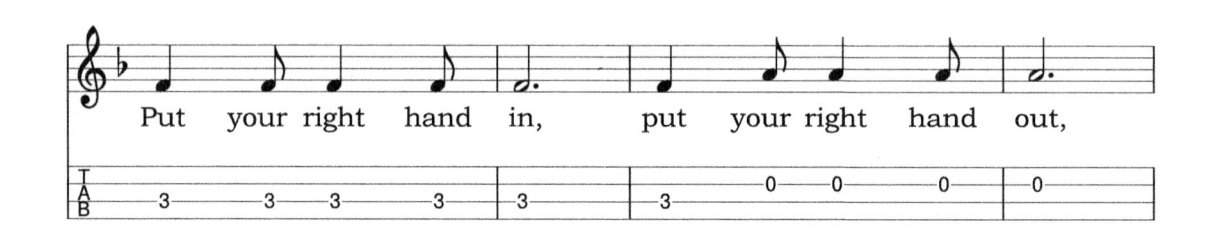

Traditional

Here we dance loo - by loo, here we dance loo - by light,

Here we dance loo - by loo, all on a Sat-ur-day night.

Put your right hand in, put your right hand out,

give your right hand a shake, shake, shake, and turn your-self a - bout.

Here we dance looby loo,
Here we dance looby light,
Here we dance looby loo,
All on a Saturday night.

Put your right hand in.
Put your right hand out.
Give your right hand a shake, shake, shake,
And turn yourself about.

Here we dance looby loo,
Here we dance looby light,
Here we dance looby loo,
All on a Saturday night.

Put your left hand in.
Put your left hand out.
Give your left hand a shake, shake, shake,
And turn yourself about.

Here we dance looby loo,
Here we dance looby light,
Here we dance looby loo,
All on a Saturday night.

Put your right foot in.
Put your right foot out.
Give your right foot a shake, shake, shake,
And turn yourself about.

Here we dance looby loo,
Here we dance looby light,
Here we dance looby loo,
All on a Saturday night.

Put your left foot in.
Put your left foot out.
Give your left foot a shake, shake, shake,
And turn yourself about.

Here we dance looby loo,
Here we dance looby light,
Here we dance looby loo,
All on a Saturday night.

Put your head 'way in,
Put your head 'way out.
You give your head a shake, shake, shake,
And turn yourself about.

Here we dance looby loo,
Here we dance looby light,
Here we dance looby loo,
All on a Saturday night.

Put your whole self in.
Put your whole self out.
Give your self a shake, shake, shake,
And turn yourself about.

Here we dance looby loo,
Here we dance looby light,
Here we dance looby loo,
All on a Saturday night.

London Bridge Is Falling Down

Traditional

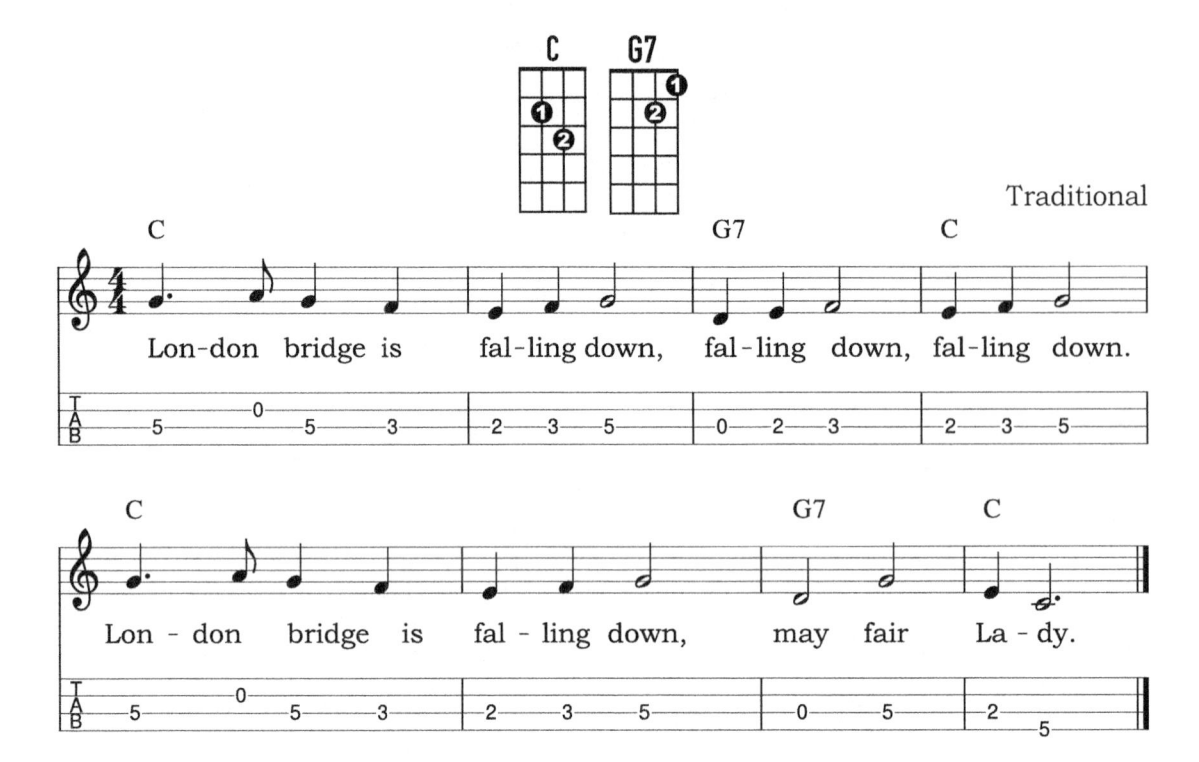

Lon-don bridge is fal-ling down, fal-ling down, fal-ling down.

Lon - don bridge is fal - ling down, may fair La - dy.

Lucy Locket

Traditional

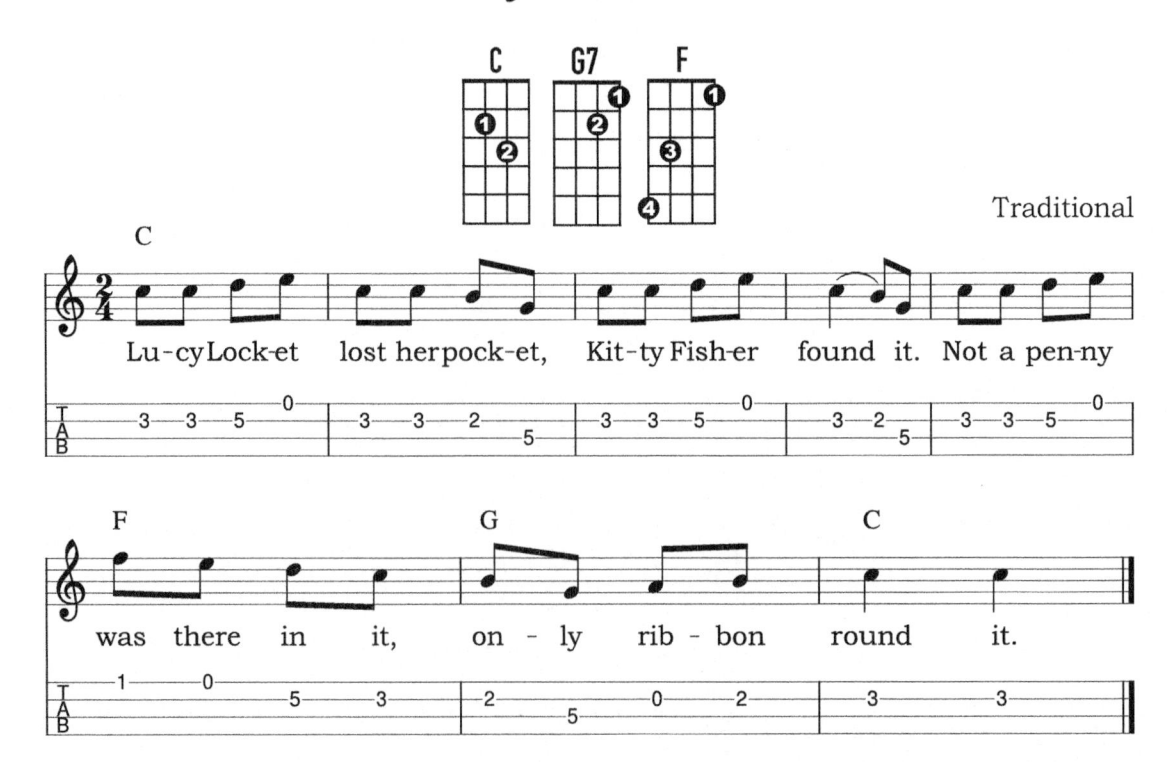

Lu-cy Lock-et lost her pock-et, Kit-ty Fish-er found it. Not a pen-ny

was there in it, on - ly rib - bon round it.

Mary Had a Little Lamb

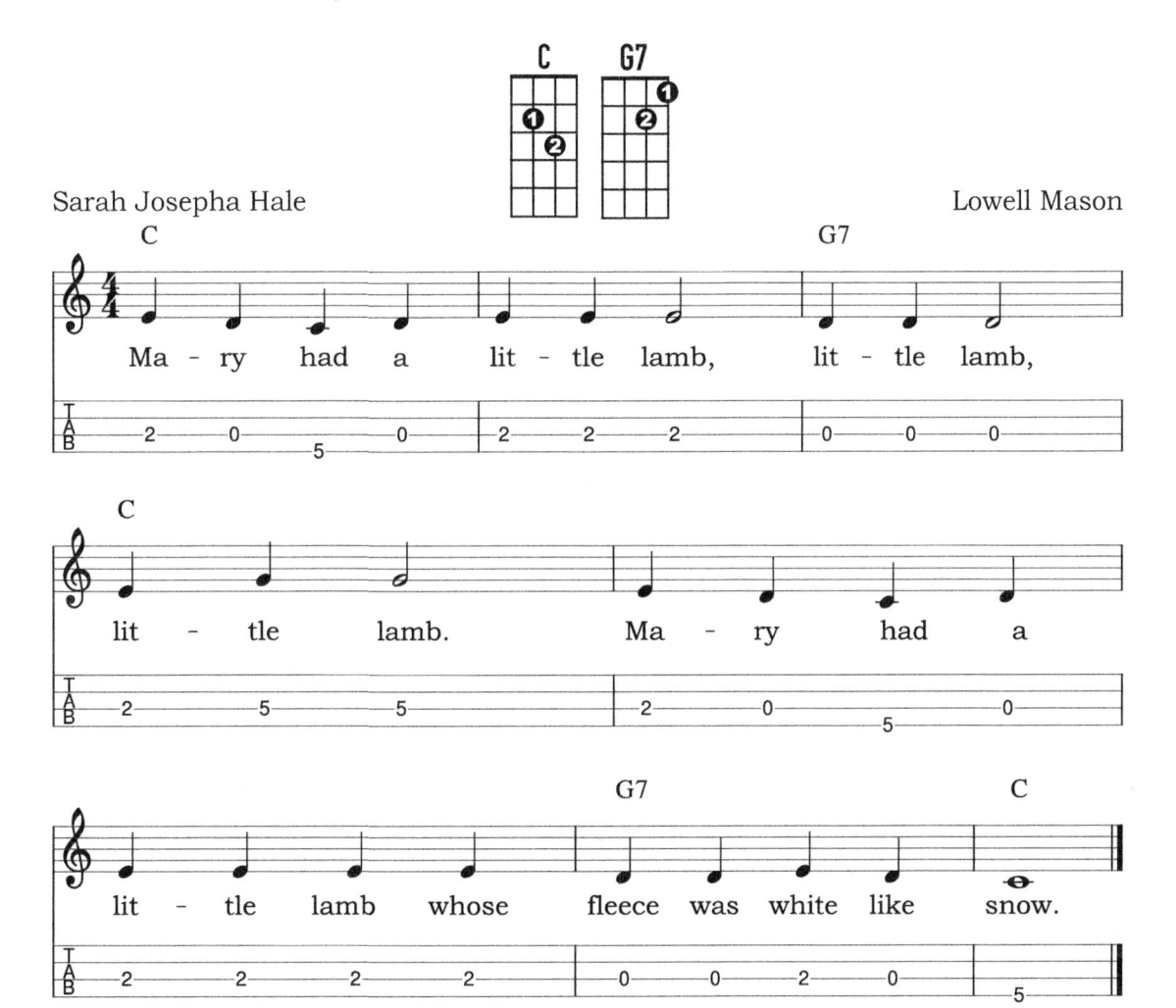

Sarah Josepha Hale

Lowell Mason

Mary had a little lamb,
Little lamb, little lamb,
Mary had a little lamb
Whose fleece was white as snow.

And everywhere that Mary went,
Mary went, Mary went,
Everywhere that Mary went
The lamb was sure to go.

He followed her to school one day,
School one day, school one day,
He followed her to school one day
Which was against the rules.

It made the children laugh and play,
Laugh and play, laugh and play,
It made the children laugh and play,
To see a lamb at school.

And so the teacher turned it out,
Turned it out, turned it out,
And so the teacher turned it out,
But still it lingered near,

He waited patiently about,
Patiently about, patiently about,
He waited patiently about,
Till Mary did appear.

"Why does the lamb love Mary so?
Love Mary so? Love Mary so?
Why does the lamb love Mary so?"
The eager children cried.

"Why, Mary loves the lamb, you know,
Lamb, you know, lamb, you know,
Why, Mary loves the lamb, you know,"
The teacher did reply.

Mary, Mary, Quite Contrary

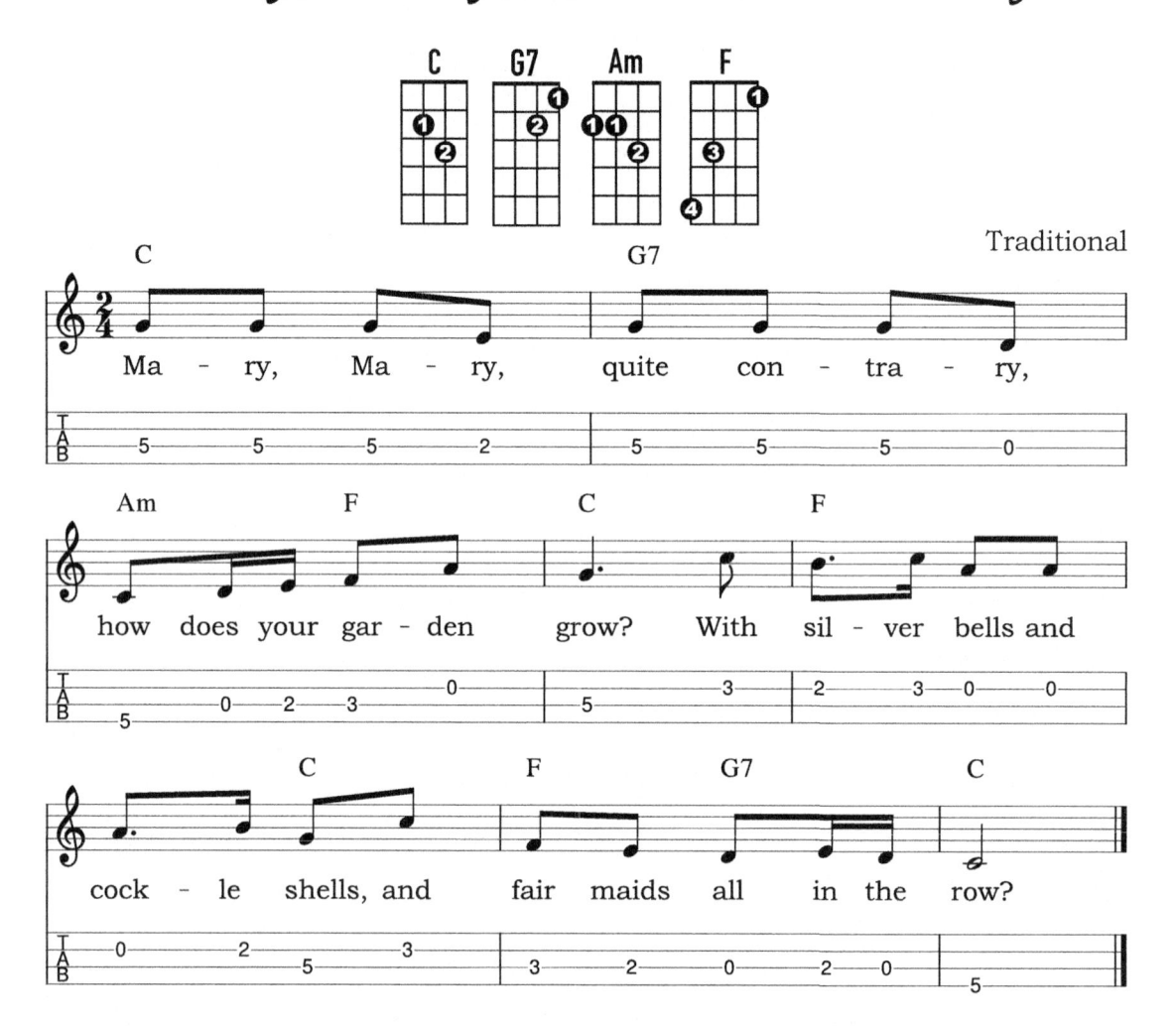

Traditional

Mary, Mary, quite contrary, how does your garden grow? With silver bells and cockle shells, and fair maids all in the row?

Mistress Bond

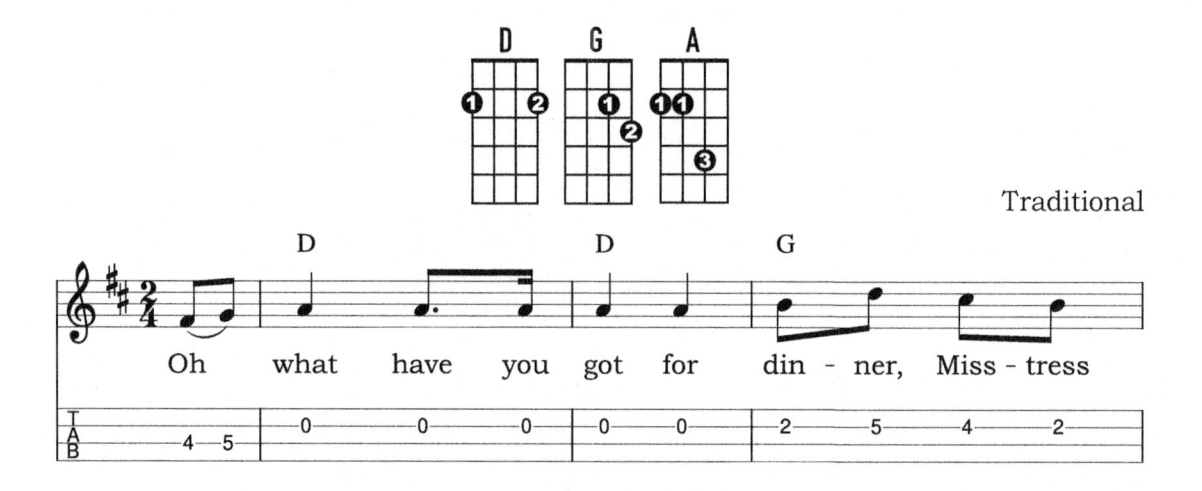

Traditional

Oh what have you got for dinner, Mistress

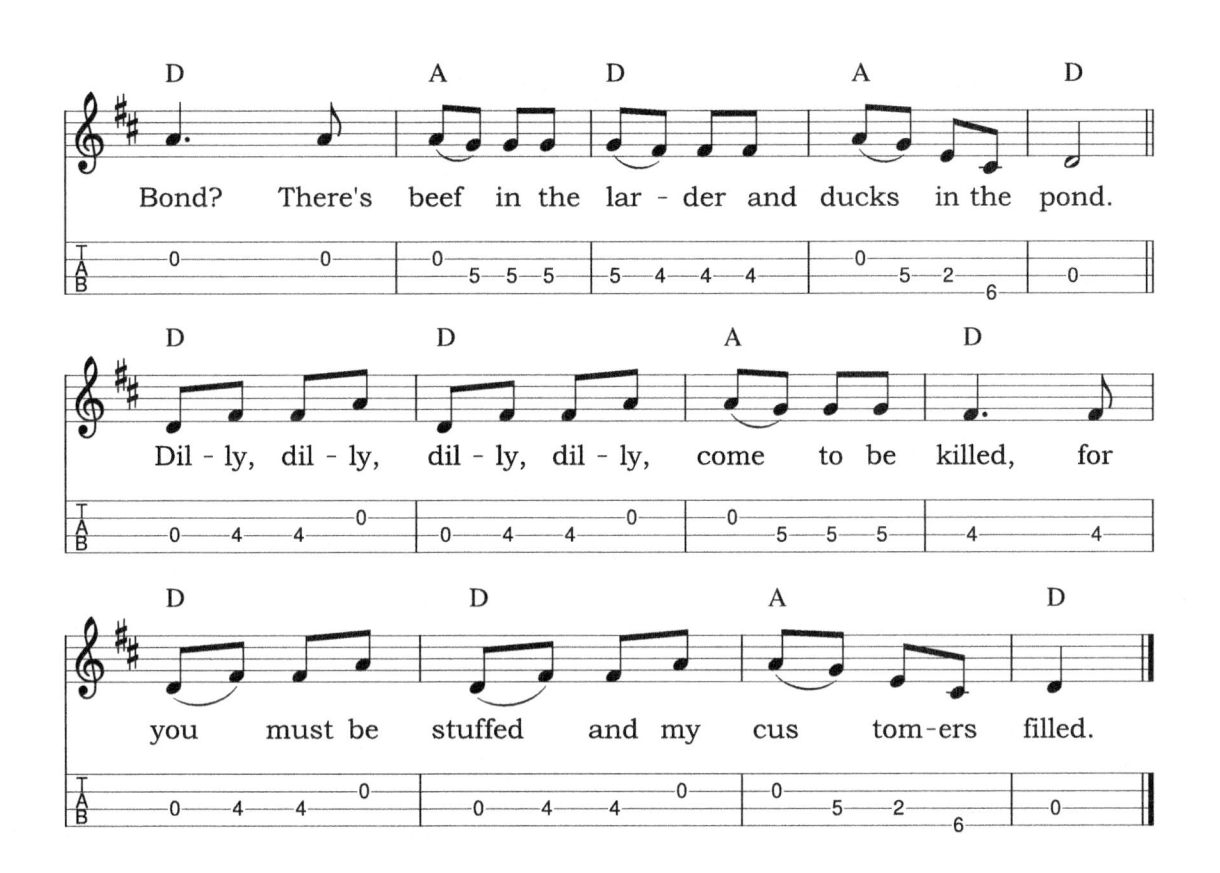

"Oh what have you got for dinner, Mistress Bond?"
"There's beef in the larder and ducks in the pond;"
"Dilly, dilly, dilly, dilly, come to be killed,
For you must be stuff'd and my customers filled!"

"Pray send us the beef in first, Mistress Bond,
And then dress those ducks that are swimming in the pond."
"Dilly, dilly, dilly, dilly, come to be killed,
For you must be stuff'd and my customers filled!".
"John Ostler, go fetch me a duckling or two!"
"Madam," says John Ostler, "I'll try what I can do."
"Dilly, dilly, dilly, dilly, come to be killed,
For you must be stuff'd and my customers filled!"

"I have been to the ducks which are swimming in the pond
But I found they will not come to be killed, Mistress Bond."
"Dilly, dilly, dilly, dilly, come to be killed,
For you must be stuff'd and my customers filled!"

Then away flies Mistress Bond, in a pretty little rage,
With her pockets full of onions and her apron full of sage.
"Dilly, dilly, dilly, dilly, come to be killed,
For you must be stuff'd and my customers filled!"

She cried: "Come, little wag-tails, come to be killed,
For you must be stuffed and my customers filled!"
"Dilly, dilly, dilly, dilly, come to be killed,
For you must be stuff'd and my customers filled!"

My Bonnie Lies over the Ocean

Traditional

My Bon-nie lies o-ver the o-cean, my Bon-nie lies o-ver the sea, my Bon-nie lies o-ver the o-cean, oh, bring back my Bon-nie to me. Bring back, bring back, bring back my Bon-nie to me, to me. Bring back, bring back, oh, bring back my Bon-nie to me.

My Bonnie lies over the ocean,
My Bonnie lies over the sea,
My Bonnie lies over the ocean,
Oh, bring back my Bonnie to me.

Bring back, bring back,
Bring back my Bonnie to me, to me.
Bring back, bring back
Oh, bring back my Bonnie to me.

Oh, blow ye winds over the ocean,
Oh, blow ye winds over the sea,
Oh, blow ye winds over the ocean
and bring back my Bonnie to me.

Bring back, bring back,
Bring back my Bonnie to me, to me.
Bring back, bring back
Oh, bring back my Bonnie to me.

Last night as I lay on my pillow,
Last night as I lay on my bed,
Last night as I lay on my pillow,
I dreamt that my Bonnie was dead.

Bring back, bring back,
Bring back my Bonnie to me, to me.
Bring back, bring back
Oh, bring back my Bonnie to me.

The winds have blown over the ocean,
The winds have blown over the sea,
The winds have blown over the ocean,
And brought back my Bonnie to me.

Bring back, bring back,
Bring back my Bonnie to me, to me.
Bring back, bring back
Oh, bring back my Bonnie to me.

Oh Dear What Can The Matter Be

Traditional

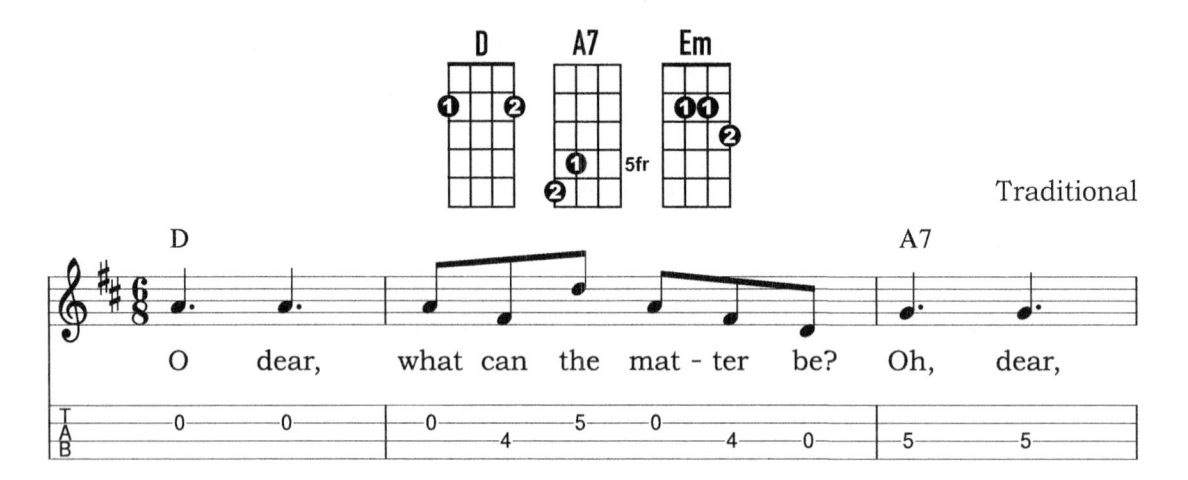

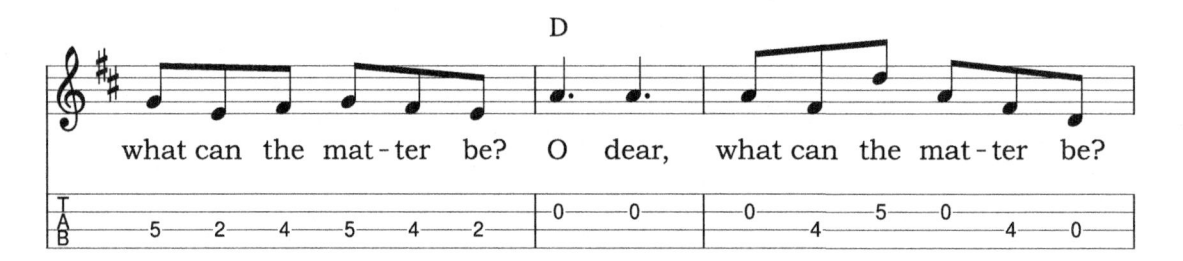

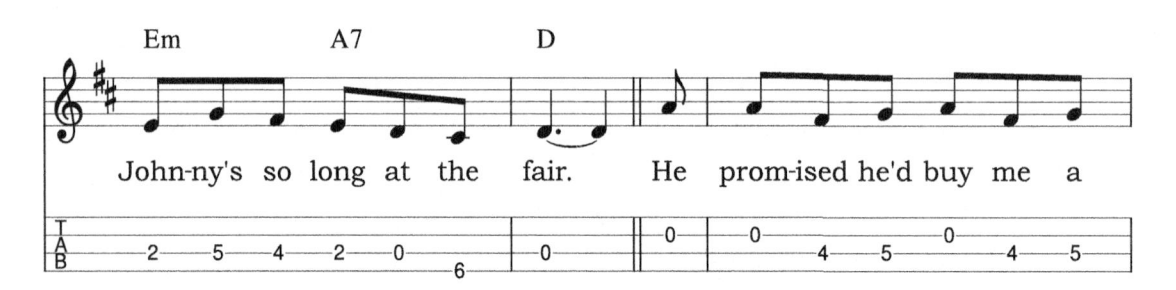

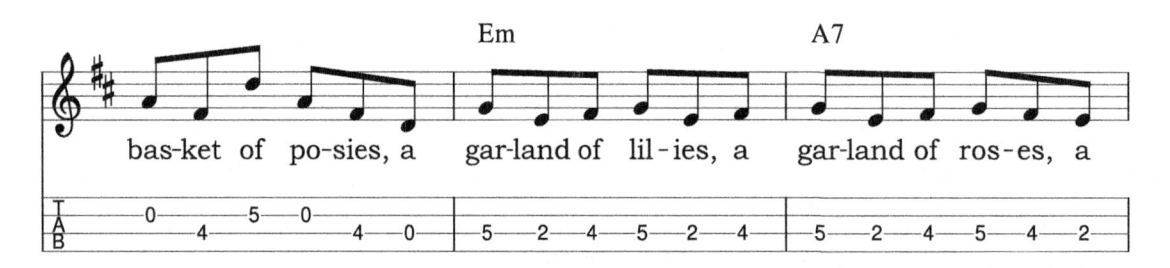

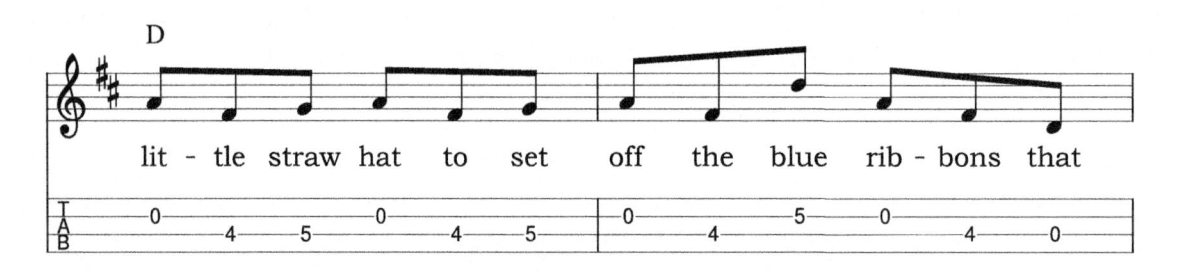

O dear, what can the matter be? Oh, dear, what can the matter be? O dear, what can the matter be? Johnny's so long at the fair. He promised he'd buy me a basket of posies, a garland of lilies, a garland of roses, a little straw hat to set off the blue ribbons that

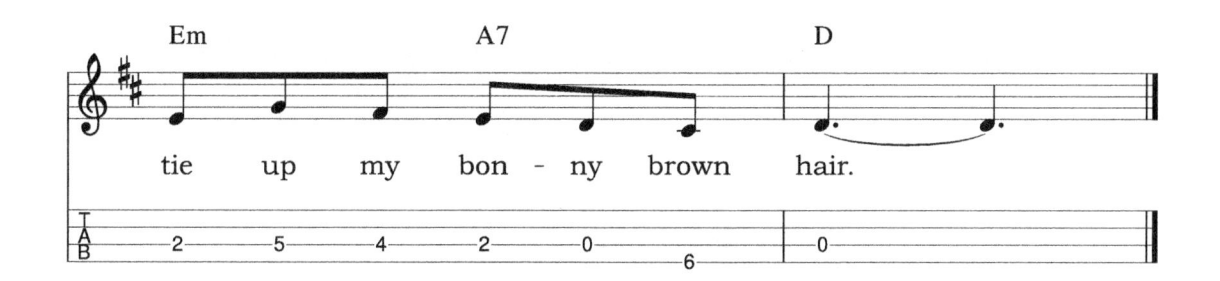

| Em | A7 | D |

tie up my bon - ny brown hair.

Oh Where Has My Little Dog Gone

Septimus Winner

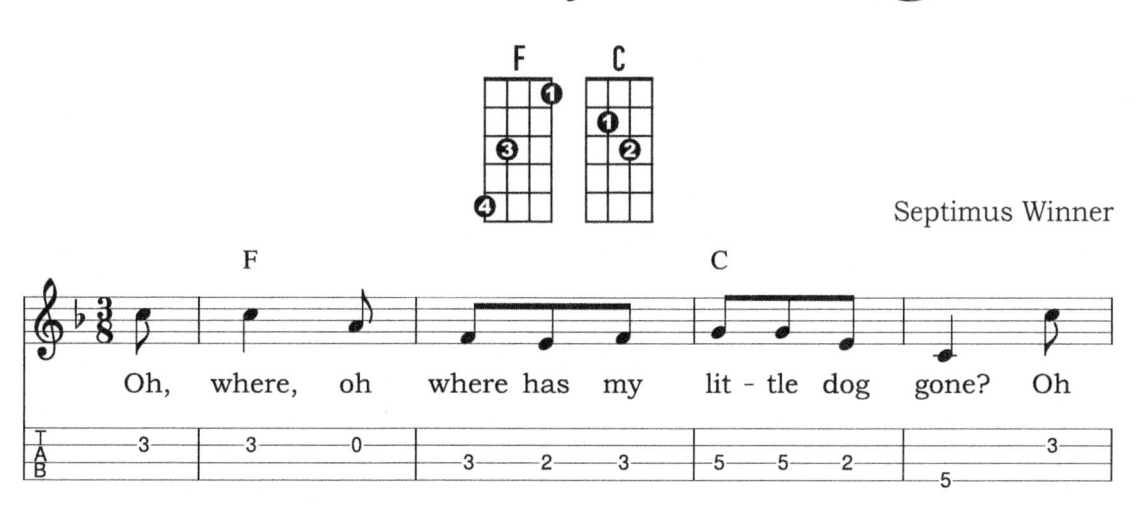

| F | C |

Oh, where, oh where has my lit - tle dog gone? Oh

| F |

where, oh where can he be? With his ears cut short and his

| C | F |

tail cut long. Oh where, oh where can he be?

Oh My Darling, Clementine

Percy Montrose

In a cav-ern, in a can-yon, ex-ca-vat-ing for a mine. Dwelt a min-er for-ty nin-er, and his daugh-ter Clem-en-tine. Oh my dar-ling, oh my dar-ling, oh my dar-ling, Clem-en-tine! Thou art lost and gone for-ev-er, dread-ful sor-ry, Clem-en-tine.

In a cavern, in a canyon,
Excavating for a mine
Dwelt a miner orty-niner,
And his daughter Clementine.

Oh my darling, oh my darling,
Oh my darling, Clementine!
Thou art lost and gone forever
Dreadful sorry, Clementine.

Light she was and like a fairy,
And her shoes were number nine,
Herring boxes, without topses,
Sandals were for Clementine.

Oh my darling, oh my darling,
Oh my darling, Clementine!
Thou art lost and gone forever
Dreadful sorry, Clementine.

Drove she ducklings to the water
Every morning just at nine,
Hit her foot against a splinter,
Fell into the foaming brine.

Oh my darling, oh my darling,
Oh my darling, Clementine!
Thou art lost and gone forever
Dreadful sorry, Clementine.

Ruby lips above the water,
Blowing bubbles, soft and fine,
But, alas, I was no swimmer,
So I lost my Clementine.

Oh my darling, oh my darling,
Oh my darling, Clementine!
Thou art lost and gone forever
Dreadful sorry, Clementine.

How I missed her! How I missed her,
How I missed my Clementine,
But I kissed her little sister,
I forgot my Clementine.

Oh my darling, oh my darling,
Oh my darling, Clementine!
Thou art lost and gone forever
Dreadful sorry, Clementine.

Oh, Susanna

Stephen Foster

I come from Alabama with a banjo on my knee! I'm goin' to Lousiana, my true love for to see. Oh, Susanna! Oh, don't you cry for me! For I come from Alabama with a banjo on my knee,

I came from Alabama,
With my banjo on my knee,
I'm going to Louisiana,
My true love for to see;
It rained all night the day I left,
The weather it was dry,
The sun so hot I froze to death,
Susanna, don't you cry.

Oh! Susanna, Oh don't you cry for me,
For I've come from Alabama
With my banjo on my knee.

I had a dream the other night,
When everything was still;
I thought I saw Susanna,
A coming down the hill;
The buckwheat cake was in her mouth,
The tear was in her eye;
Says I, "I'm coming from the south,
Susanna, don't you cry."

Oh! Susanna, Oh don't you cry for me,
For I've come from Alabama
With my banjo on my knee.

I soon will be in New Orleans,
And then I'll look around,
And when I find Susanna,
I'll fall upon the ground.
But if I do not find her,
Then I will surely die,
And when I'm dead and buried,
Oh, Susanna, don't you cry.

Oh! Susanna, Oh don't you cry for me,
For I've come from Alabama
With my banjo on my knee.

Old King Cole

Traditional

Old King Cole was a mer-ry old soul, and a mer-ry old soul was he. And he called for his pipe, and he called for his bowl, and he called for his fid-dlers three. Eve-ry fid-dler he had a fid-dle, and a ver-y fine fid-dle had he. Oh there's none so rare, as can com-pare with King Cole and his fid-dlers three.

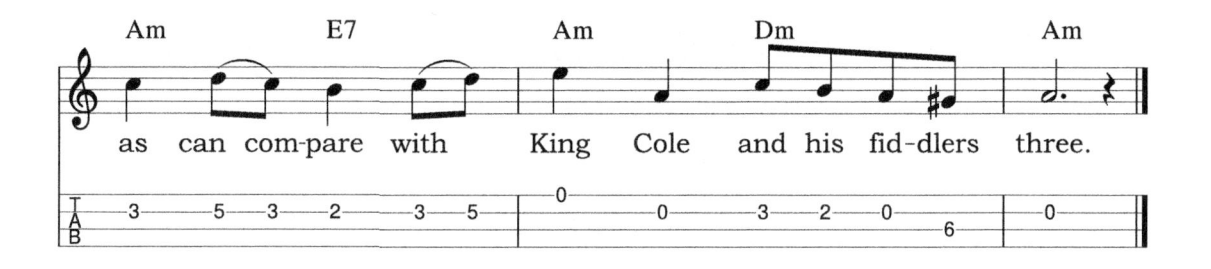

Old MacDonald Had a Farm

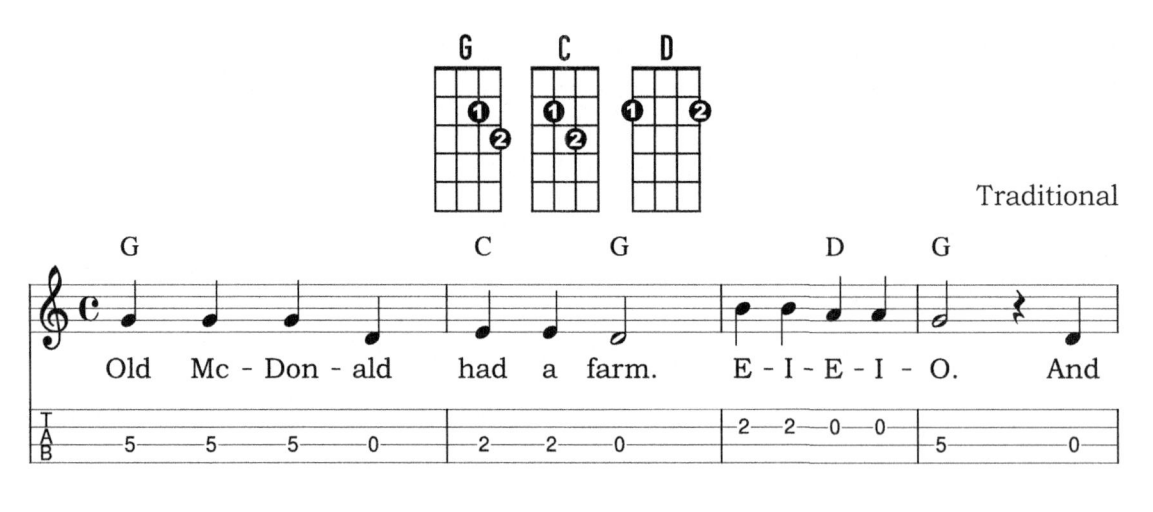

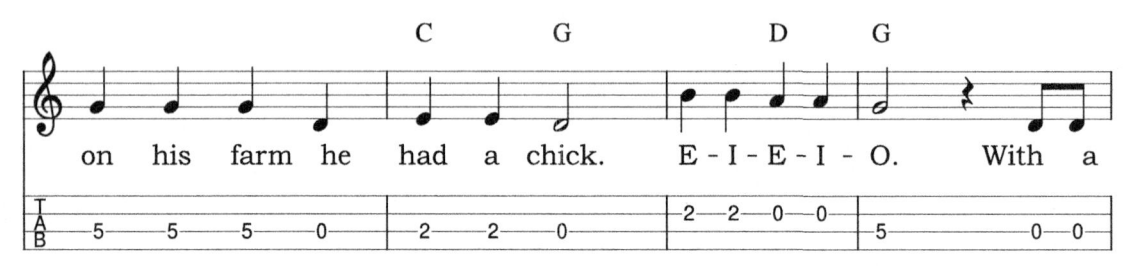

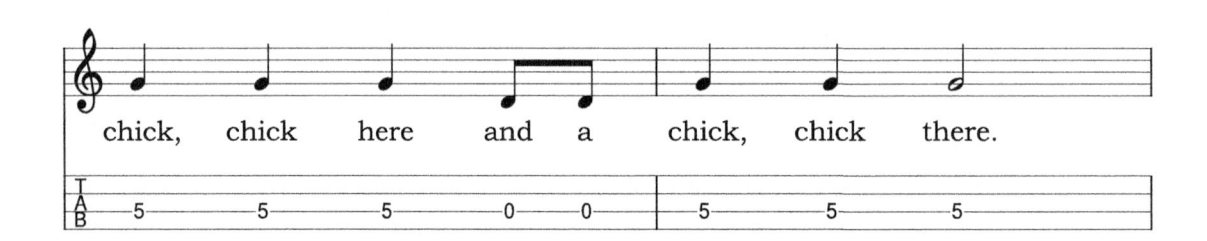

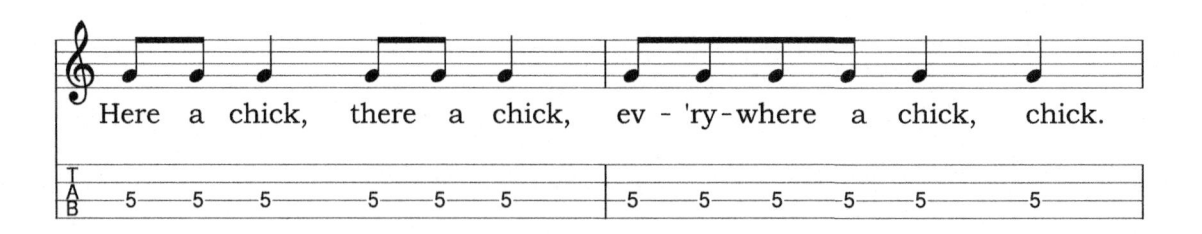

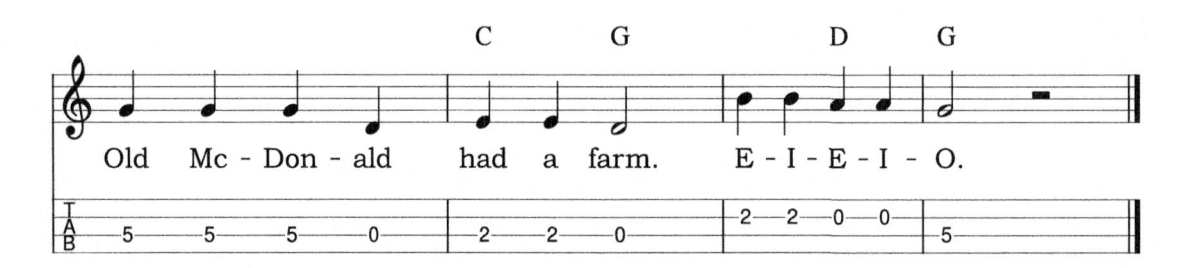

Traditional

G	C G	D G
Old Mc-Don-ald had a farm.	E-I-E-I-O.	And

	C G	D G
on his farm he had a chick.	E-I-E-I-O.	With a

chick, chick here and a chick, chick there.

Here a chick, there a chick, ev-'ry-where a chick, chick.

	C G	D G
Old Mc-Don-ald had a farm.	E-I-E-I-O.	

Old McDonald had a farm.
E-I-E-I-O.
And on his farm he had a chick.
E-I-E-I-O.
With a chick, chick here
and a chick, chick there.
Here a chick, there a chick,
ev'rywhere a chick, chick.
Old McDonald had a farm.
E-I-E-I-O.

Old McDonald had a farm,
E-I-E-I-O.
And on his farm he had a cow,
E-I-E-I-O.
With a "moo-moo" here
and a "moo-moo" there.
Here a "moo" there a "moo"
Everywhere a "moo-moo"
Old McDonald had a farm,
E-I-E-I-O.

Old McDonald had a farm,
E-I-E-I-O.
And on his farm he had a pig,
E-I-E-I-O.
With a "oink" here
and a "oink" there.
Here a "oink" there a "oink"
Everywhere a "oink-oink"
Old McDonald had a farm,
E-I-E-I-O.

Old McDonald had a farm,
E-I-E-I-O.
And on his farm he had a duck,
E-I-E-I-O.
With a "quack-quack" here
And a "quack-quack" there.
Here a "quack", there a "quack"
Everywhere a "quack-quack"
Old MacDonald had a farm,
E-I-E-I-O.

Old McDonald had a farm,
E-I-E-I-O.
And on his farm he had a horse,
E-I-E-I-O.
With a "neigh-neigh" here
And a "neigh-neigh" there.
Here a "neigh", there a "neigh"
Everywhere a "neigh-neigh"
Old MacDonald had a farm,
E-I-E-I-O.

Old McDonald had a farm,
E-I-E-I-O.
And on his farm he had a sheep,
E-I-E-I-O.
With a "baa-baa" here
And a "baa-baa" there.
Here a "baa", there a "baa"
Everywhere a "baa-baa"
Old MacDonald had a farm,
E-I-E-I-O.

Old McDonald had a farm,
E-I-E-I-O.
And on his farm he had a dog,
E-I-E-I-O.
With a "woof-woof" here
And a "woof-woof" there.
Here a "woof", there a "woof"
Everywhere a "woof-woof"
Old MacDonald had a farm,
E-I-E-I-O.

Old McDonald had a farm,
E-I-E-I-O.
And on his farm he had a hen
E-I-E-I-O.
With a "cluck-cluck" here
And a "cluck-cluck" there.
Here a "cluck", there a "cluck"
Everywhere a "cluck-cluck"
Old MacDonald had a farm,
E-I-E-I-O.

Old Woman Who Lived in a Shoe

Traditional

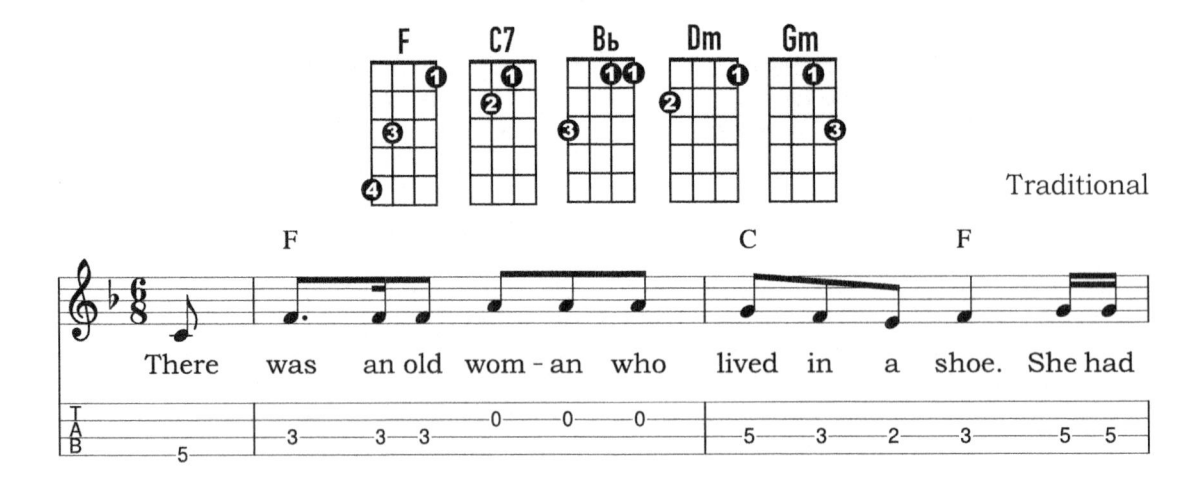

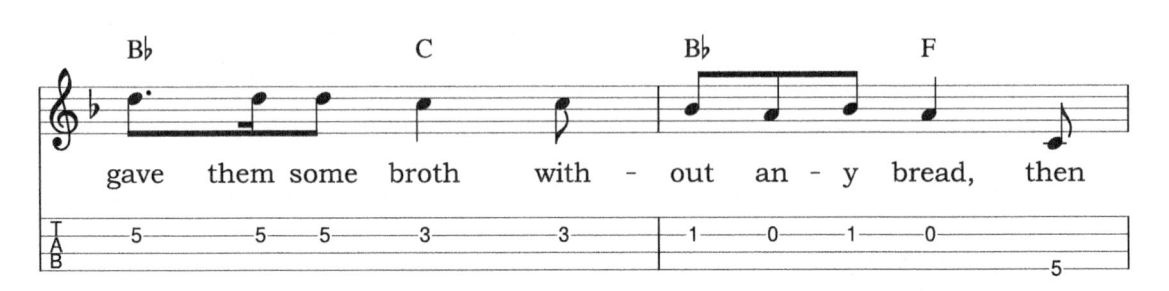

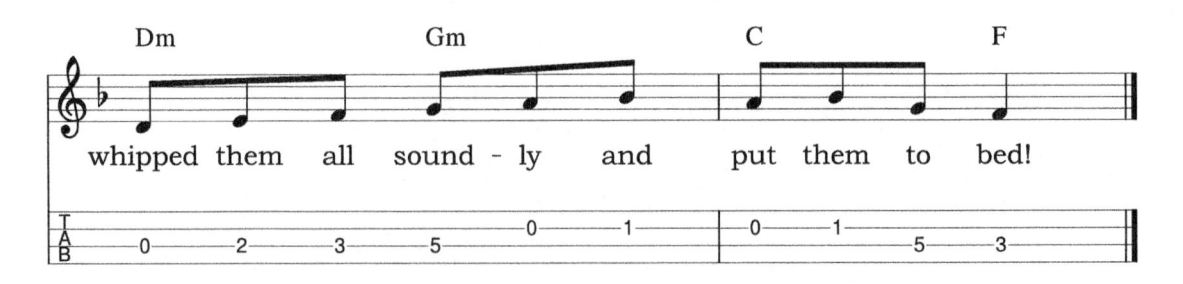

There was an old wom-an who lived in a shoe. She had so man-y chil-dren, did-n't know what to do. She gave them some broth with-out an-y bread, then whipped them all sound-ly and put them to bed!

On Top of Old Smoky

Traditional

On top of Old Smok-y, All cov-ered with snow, I lost my true lov-er For cour-ting too slow.

On top of old smokey
All covered with snow
I lost my true lover
For courting too slow

For courting's a pleasure
And parting's a grief.
And a false hearted lover
Is worse than a thief.

For a thief will just rob you
And take all you save,
But a false hearted lover
Will lead you to the grave.

And the grave will decay you
And turn you to dust.
Not one girl in a hundred
A poor boy can trust.

They'll hug you and kiss you
And tell you more lies.
Than cross lines on a railroad
Or stars in the skies.

So come all your maidens
And listen to me,
Never place your affections
On a green willow tree.

For the leaves they will wither
And the roots they will die.
You'll all be forsaken
And never know why.

Over in the Meadow

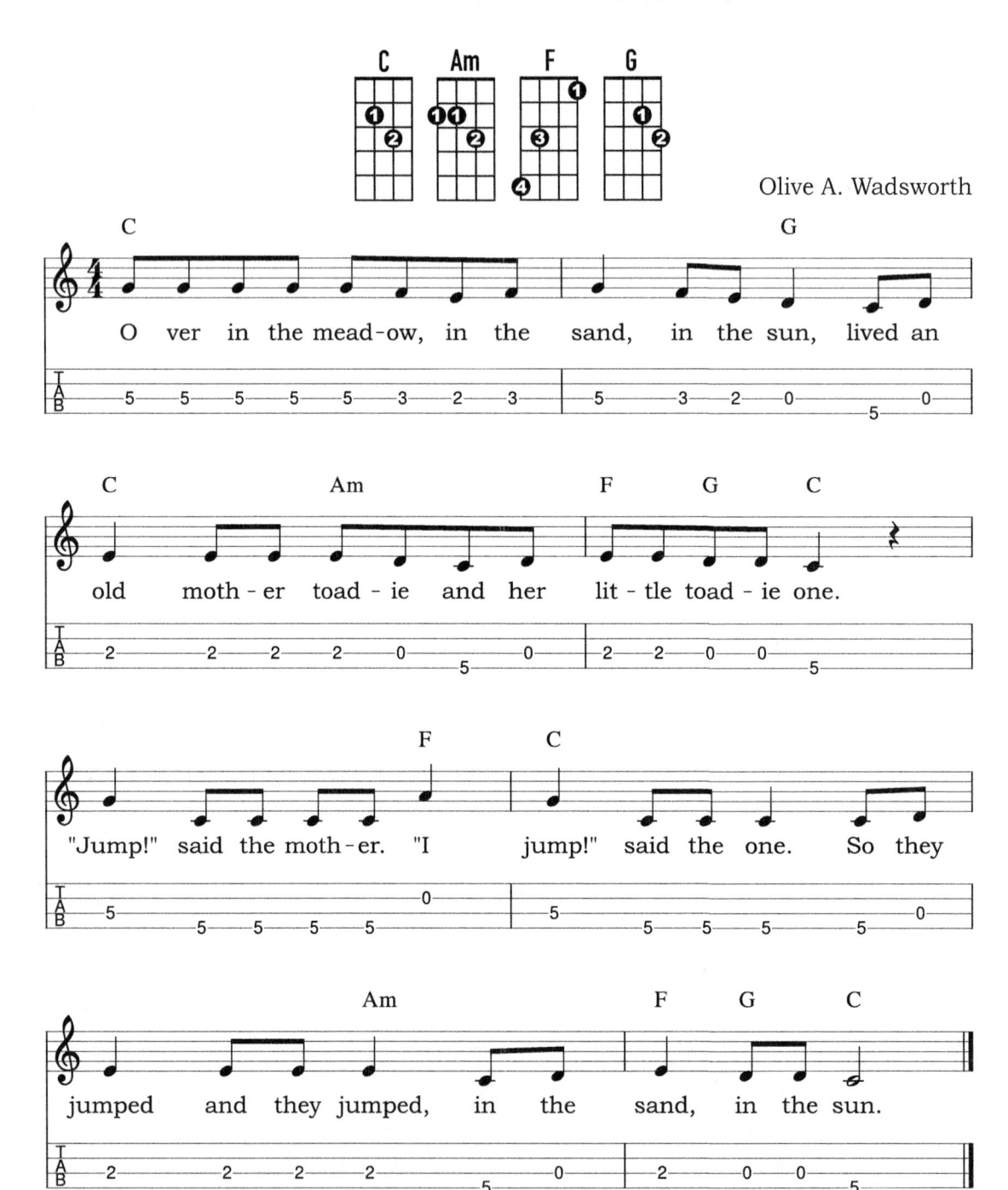

Olive A. Wadsworth

C | O ver in the mead-ow, in the sand, G | in the sun, lived an

C | old moth-er toad-ie Am | and her F G C | lit-tle toad-ie one.

"Jump!" said the moth-er. "I F C | jump!" said the one. So they

jumped and they jumped, Am | in the sand, F G C | in the sun.

Over in the meadow,
In the sand, in the sun,
Lived an old mother toadie
And her little toadie one.
"Jump!" said the mother;
"I jump!" said the one.
So they jumped and they jumped,
In the sand in the sun.

Over in the meadow,
Where the stream runs blue,
Lived an old mother fish
And her little fishes two.
"Swim!" said the mother;
"We swim!" said the two.
So they swam and they swam,
Where the stream runs blue.

Over in the meadow,
In a hole in a tree,
Lived an old mother bird
And her little birdies three.
"Sing!" said the mother;
"We sing!" said the three.
So they sang and they sang,
In their home in a tree.

Over in the meadow,
In a snug beehive,
Lived a mother honey bee
And her little honies five.
"Buzz!" said the mother;
"We buzz!" said the five.
So they buzzed and they buzzed,
In their snug beehive.

Over in the meadow,
In the grass soft and even,
Lived a mother cricket
And her little crickets seven.
"Chirp!" said the mother;
"We chirp!" said the seven.
So they chirped cheery notes,
In the grass soft and even.

Over in the meadow,
Where the cool pools shine,
Lived a green mother frog
And her little froggies nine.
"Croak!" said the mother;
"We croak!" said the nine.
So they croaked and they croaked,
Where the cool pools shine.

One, Two, Three, Four, Five

Traditional

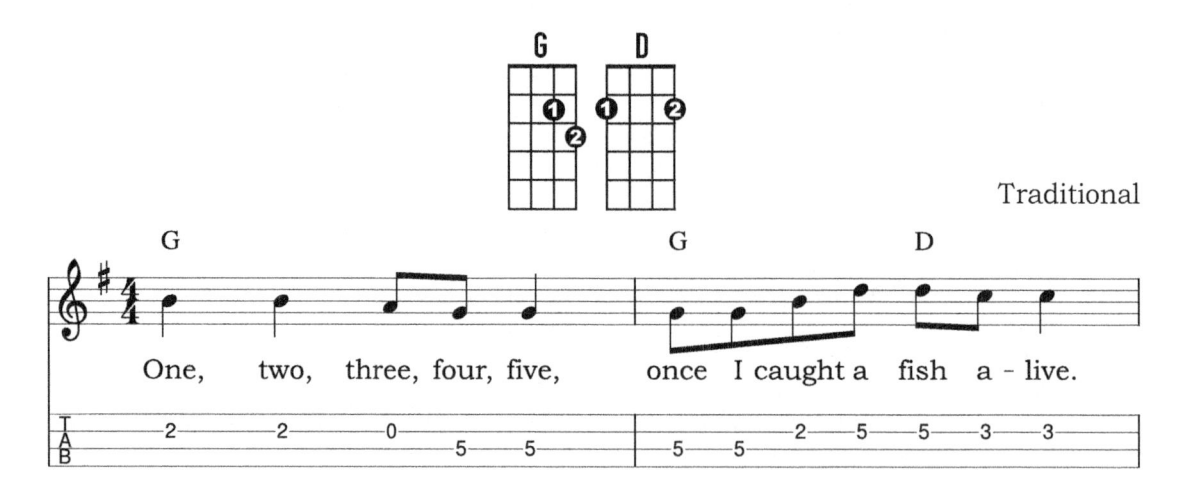

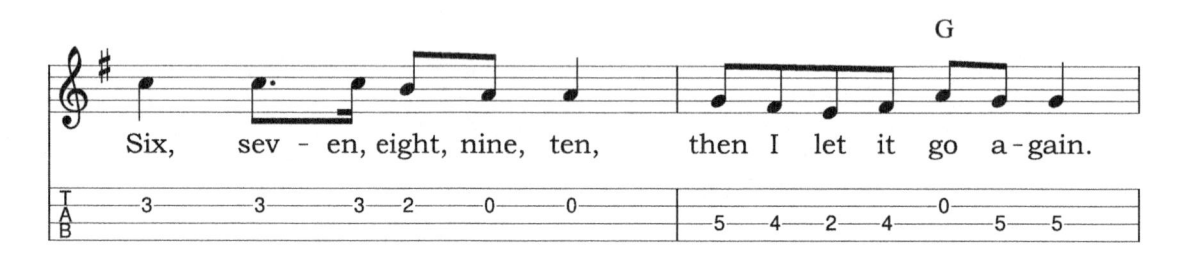

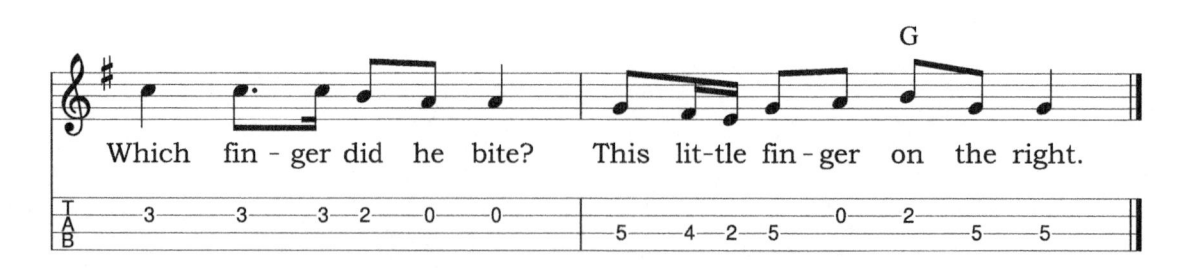

One, two, three, four, five, once I caught a fish a - live.

Six, sev - en, eight, nine, ten, then I let it go a - gain.

Why did I let it go? Be - cause he bit my fin - ger so!

Which fin - ger did he bite? This lit - tle fin - ger on the right.

Pat-a-cake

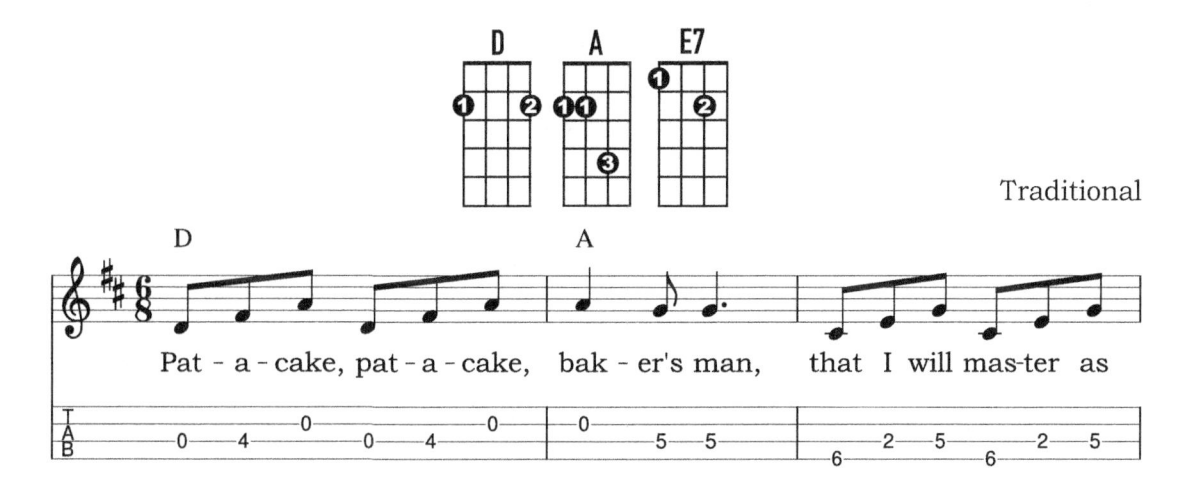

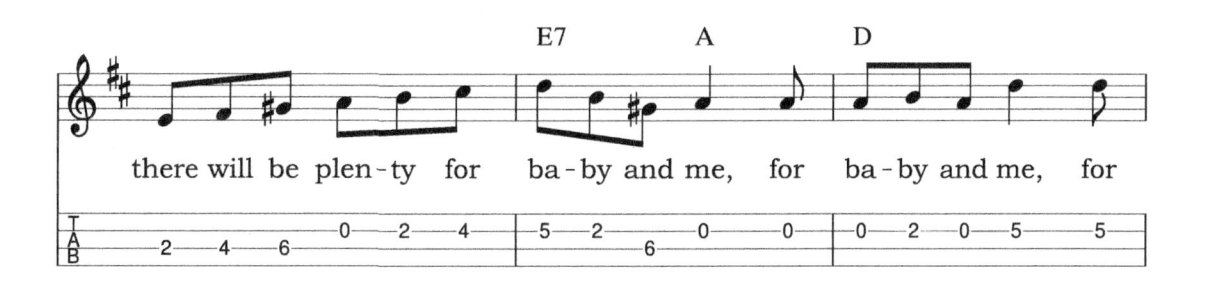

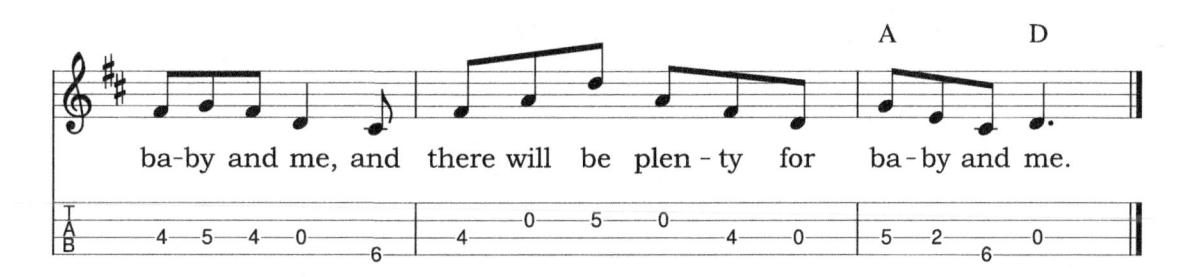

Traditional

Pat - a - cake, pat - a - cake, bak - er's man, that I will mas-ter as quick as I can. Prick it and nick it and mark it with T, and there will be plen-ty for ba-by and me, for ba-by and me, for ba-by and me, and there will be plen-ty for ba-by and me.

Pop! Goes the Weasel

Traditional

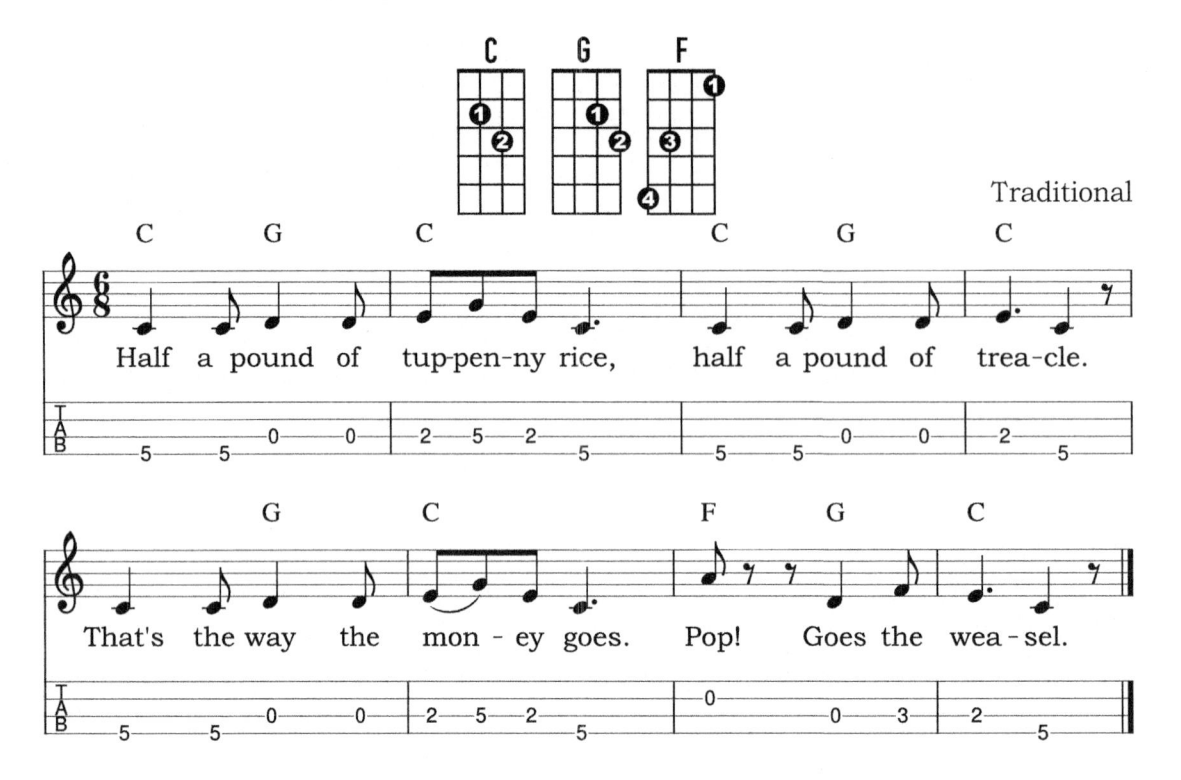

Half a pound of tup-pen-ny rice, half a pound of trea-cle.
That's the way the mon-ey goes. Pop! Goes the wea-sel.

Half a pound of tuppenny rice,
Half a pound of treacle.
That's the way the money goes,
Pop! goes the weasel.

Every night when I go out,
The monkey's on the table,
Take a stick and knock it off,
Pop! goes the weasel.

Up and down the City road,
In and out the Eagle,
That's the way the money goes,
Pop goes the weasel.

Polly, Put the Kettle On

Traditional

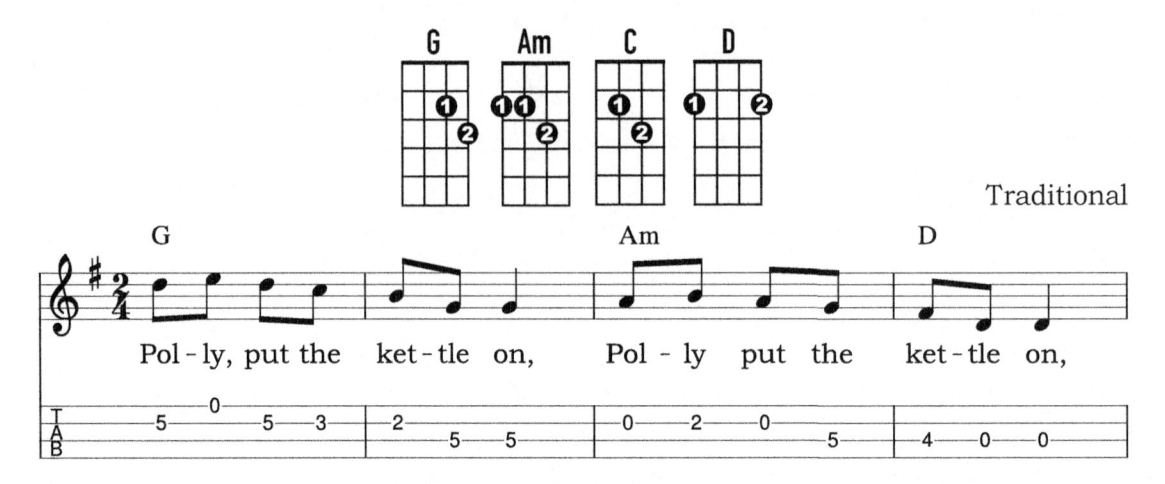

Pol-ly, put the ket-tle on, Pol-ly put the ket-tle on,

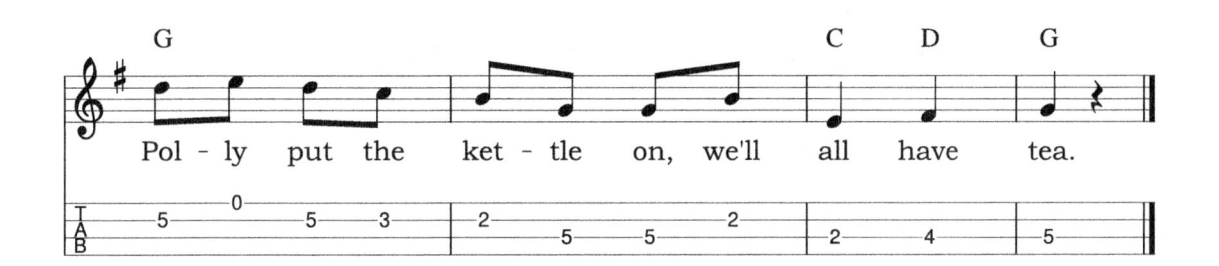

Rock-a-bye Baby

Traditional

Rock-a-bye ba - by, on the tree top, when the wind blows, the cra - dle will rock. When the bought breaks, the cra - dle will fall, and down will come ba - by, cra - dle and all!

Rain, Rain Go Away

Traditional

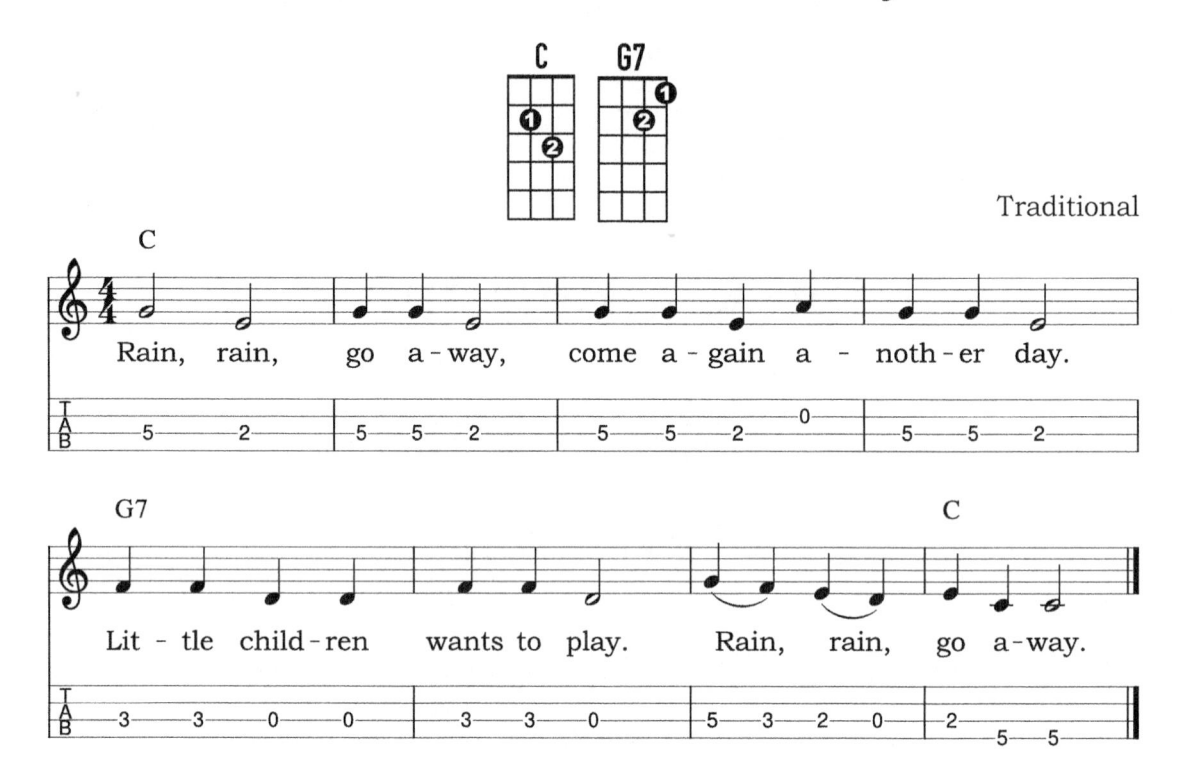

Rain, rain, go a-way, come a-gain a-noth-er day.
Lit-tle child-ren wants to play. Rain, rain, go a-way.

Ring a Ring o' Roses

Traditional

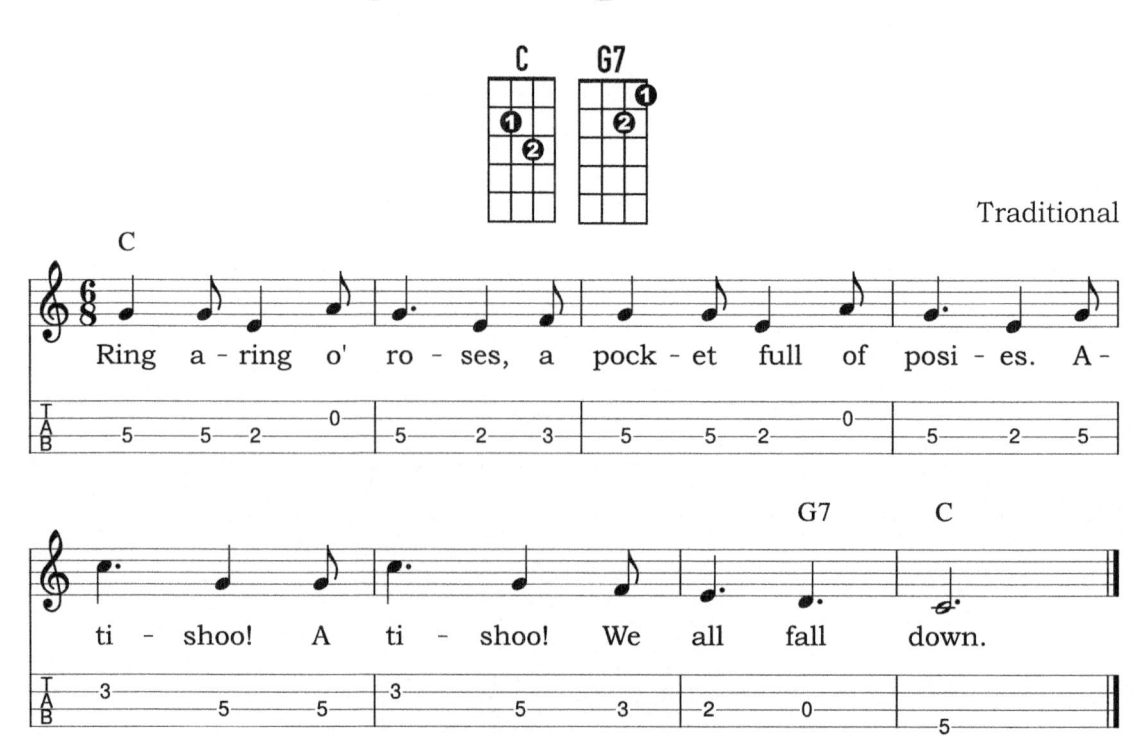

Ring a-ring o' ro-ses, a pock-et full of posi-es. A-
ti-shoo! A ti-shoo! We all fall down.

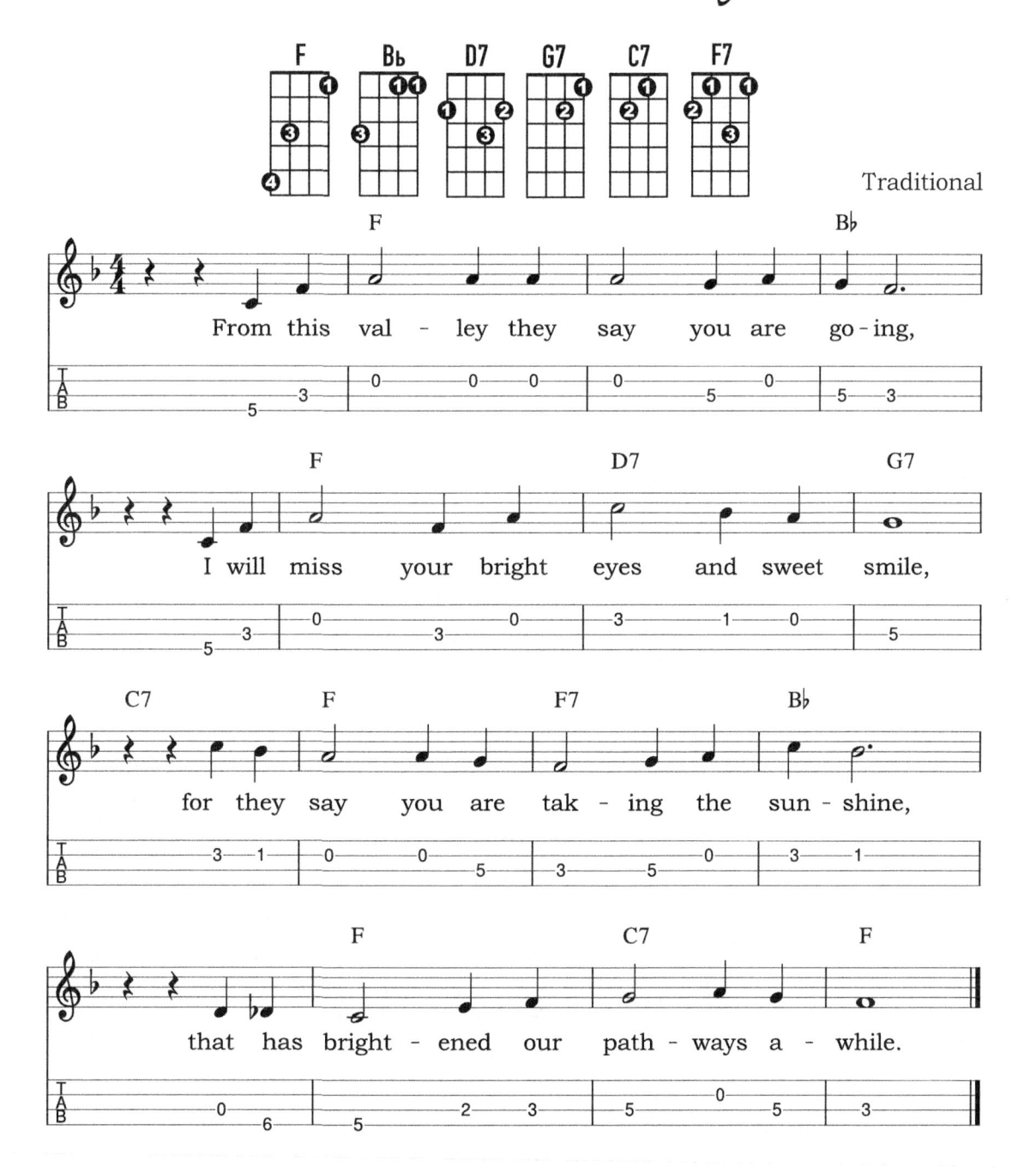

Red River Valley

Traditional

From this valley they say you are going,
I will miss your bright eyes and sweet smile,
for they say you are tak - ing the sun - shine,
that has bright - ened our path - ways a - while.

From this valley they say you are going.
We will miss your bright eyes and sweet smile,
For they say you are taking the sunshine
That has brightened our pathway a while.

So come sit by my side if you love me.
Do not hasten to bid me adieu.
Just remember the Red River Valley,
And the cowboy that has loved you so true.

Row, Row, Row Your Boat

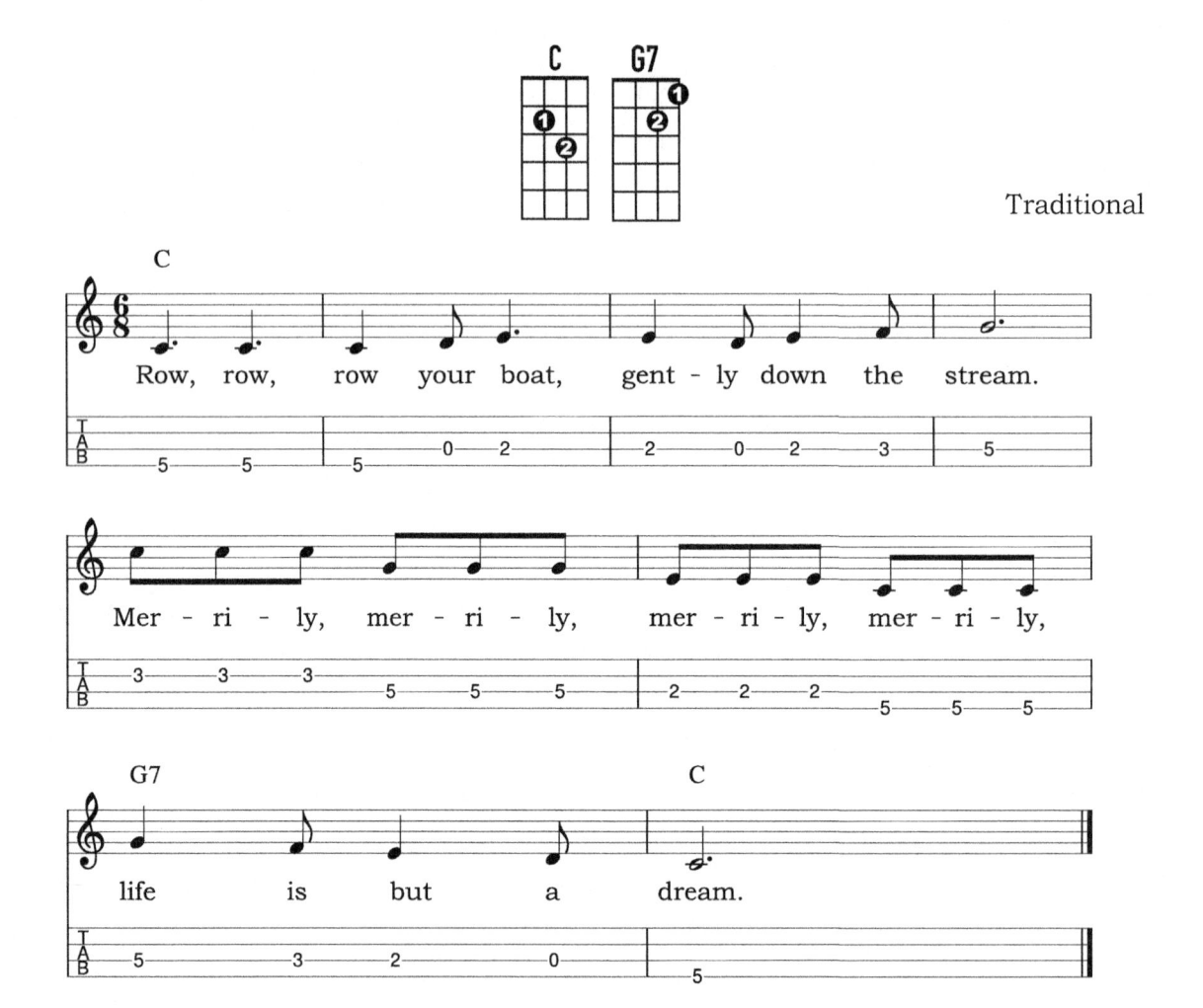

Traditional

Row, row, row your boat, gent - ly down the stream.
Mer - ri - ly, mer - ri - ly, mer - ri - ly, mer - ri - ly,
life is but a dream.

Rub-a-dub-dub

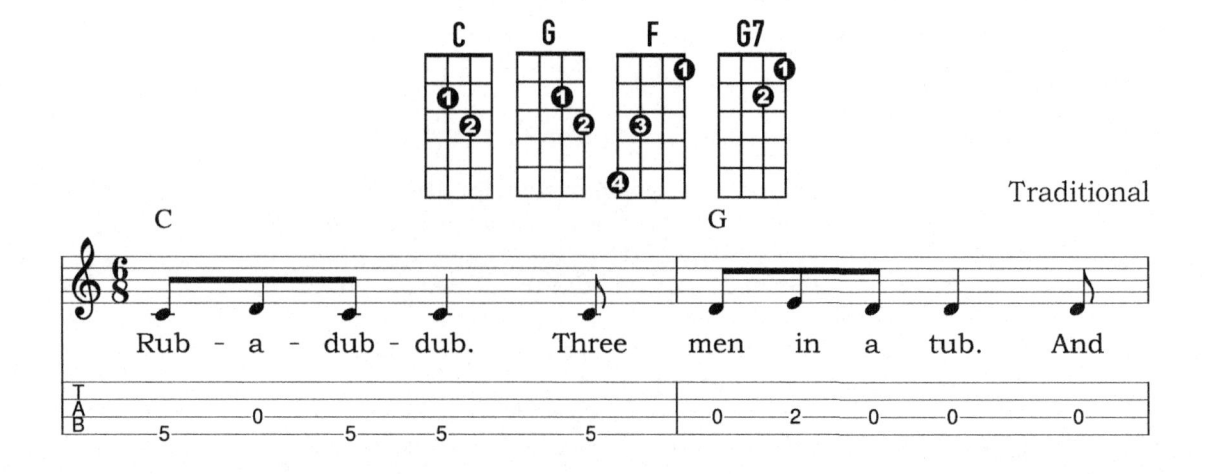

Traditional

Rub - a - dub - dub. Three men in a tub. And

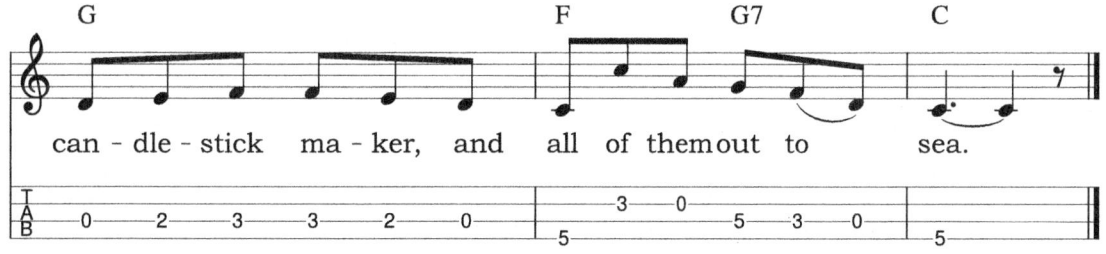

C			G	C

who do you think they be? The but-cher, the ba-ker, the

G		F	G7	C

can-dle-stick ma-ker, and all of them out to sea.

See Saw Margery Daw

C

Traditional

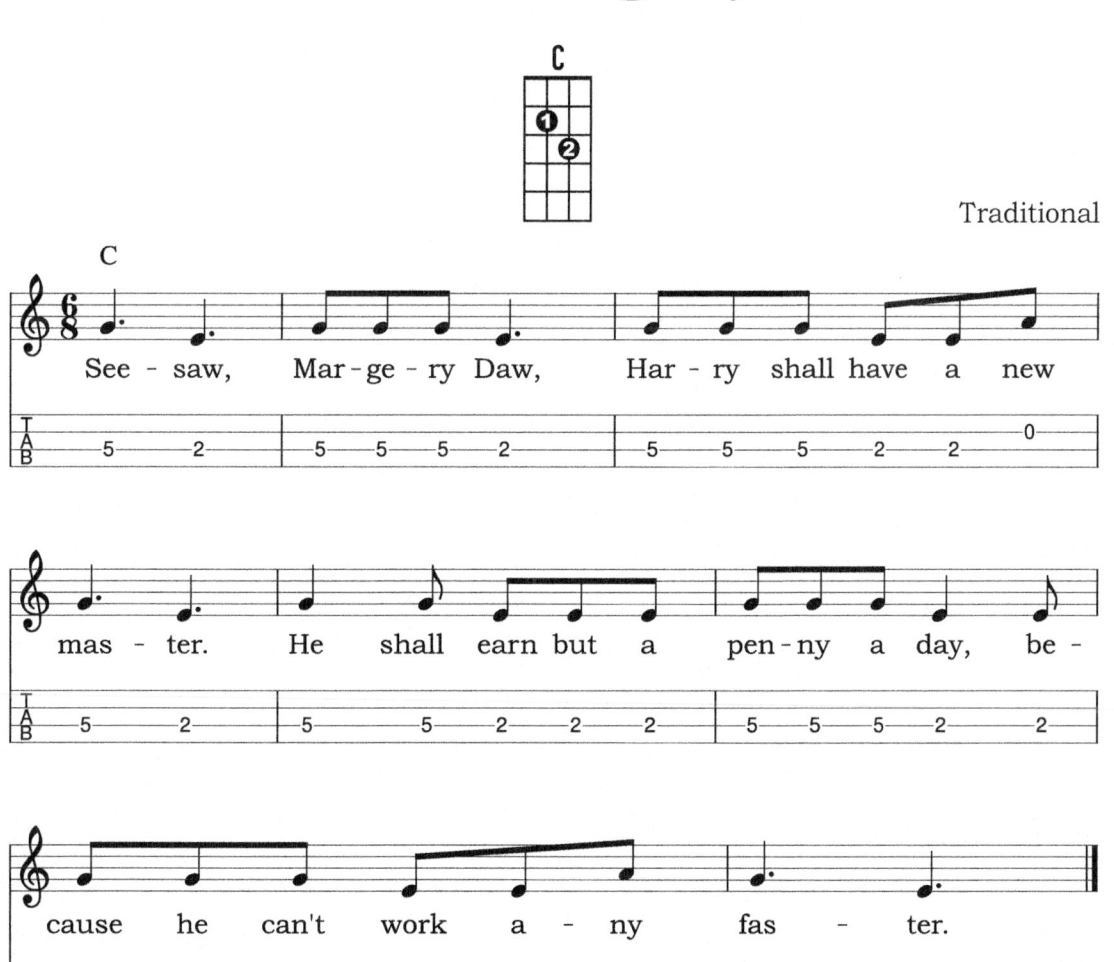

C

See - saw, Mar-ge-ry Daw, Har-ry shall have a new

mas - ter. He shall earn but a pen-ny a day, be-

cause he can't work a - ny fas - ter.

She'll Be Coming 'Round the Mountain

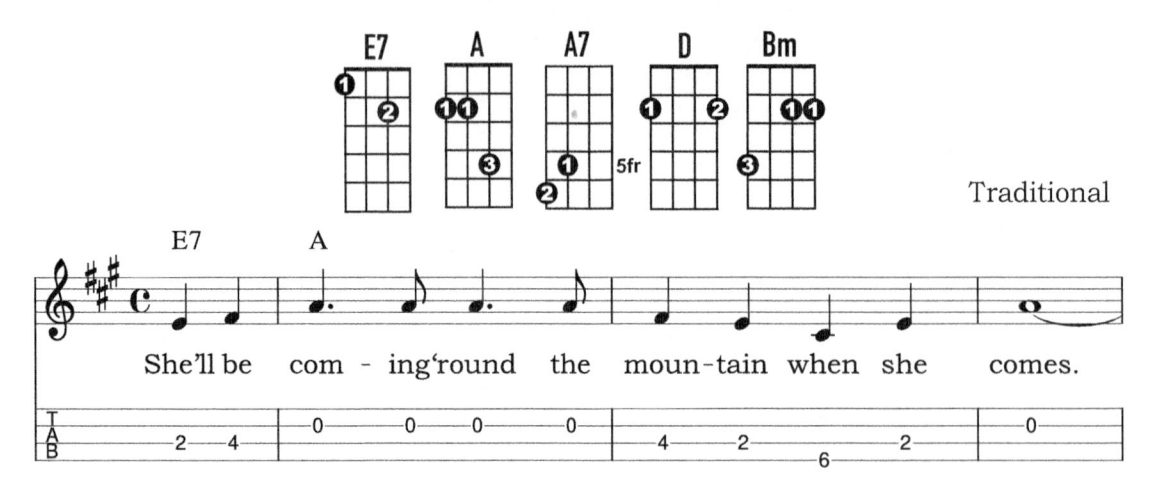

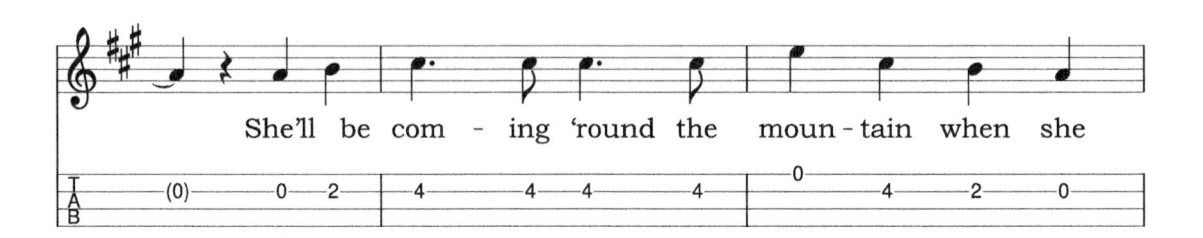

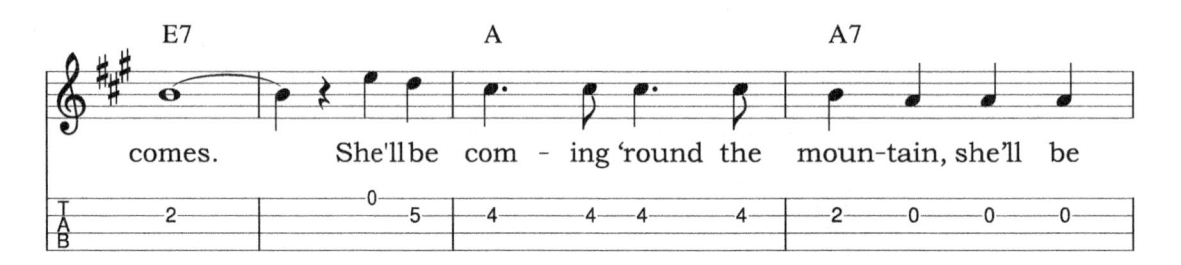

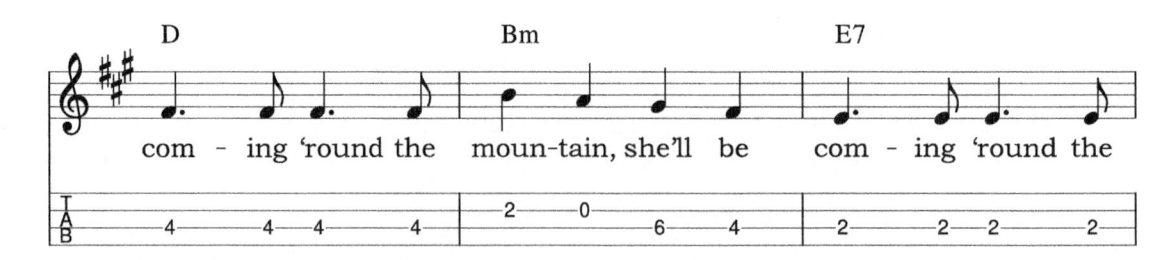

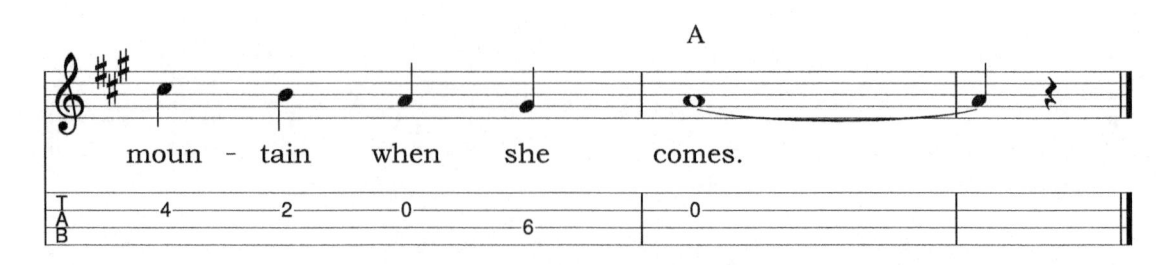

Traditional

She'll be coming 'round the mountain when she comes.
She'll be coming 'round the mountain when she comes.
She'll be coming 'round the mountain,
she'll be coming 'round the mountain,
she'll be coming 'round the mountain when she comes.

She'll be driving six white horses when she comes.
She'll be driving six white horses when she comes.
She'll be driving six white horses,
she'll be driving six white horses,
she'll be driving six white horses when she comes.

Oh, we'll all go out to meet her when she comes.
Oh, we'll all go out to meet her when she comes.
Oh, we'll all go out to meet her,
Oh, we'll all go out to meet her,
Oh, we'll all go out to meet her when she comes.

Oh, we'll all have chicken and dumplings when she comes.
Oh, we'll all have chicken and dumplings when she comes.
Oh we'll all have chicken and dumplings,
Oh, we'll all have chicken and dumplings,
Oh, we'll all have chicken and dumplings when she comes.

We'll be singing "Hallelujah" when she comes.
We'll be singing "Hallelujah" when she comes.
We'll be singing "Hallelujah,
"We'll be singing "Hallelujah,
"We'll be singing "Hallelujah" when she comes.

Ride a Cock Horse to Banbury Cross

Traditional

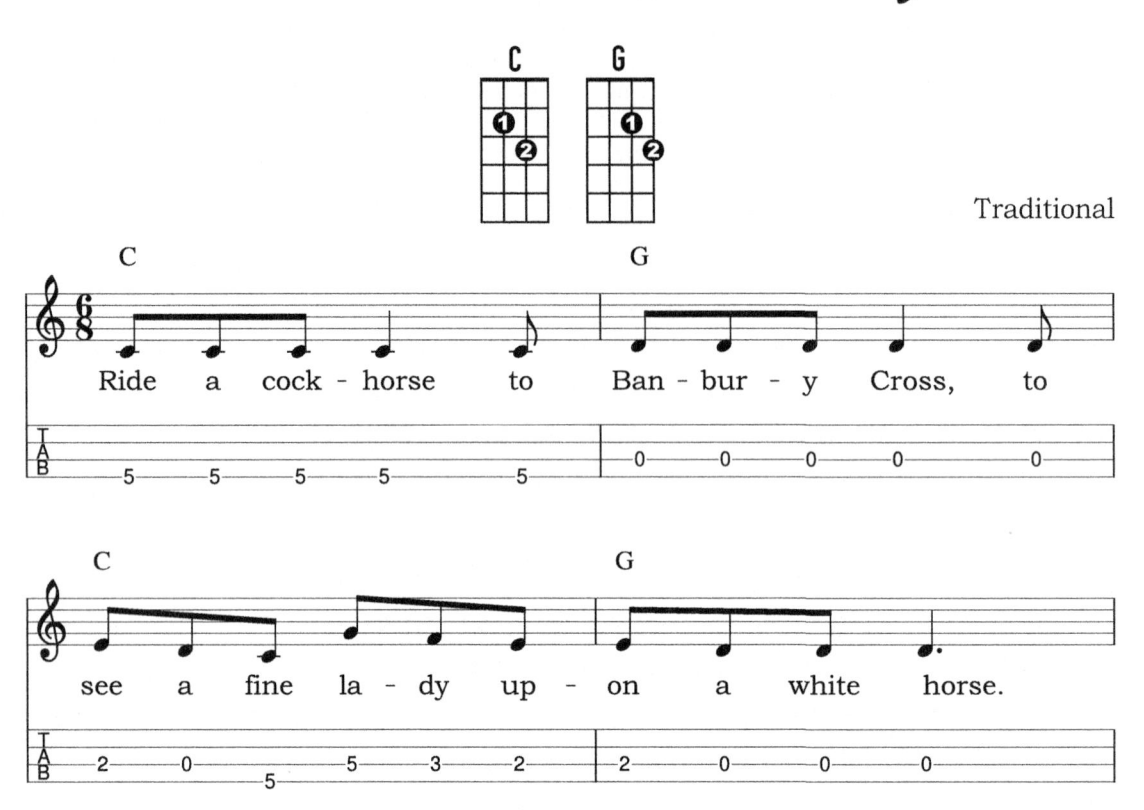

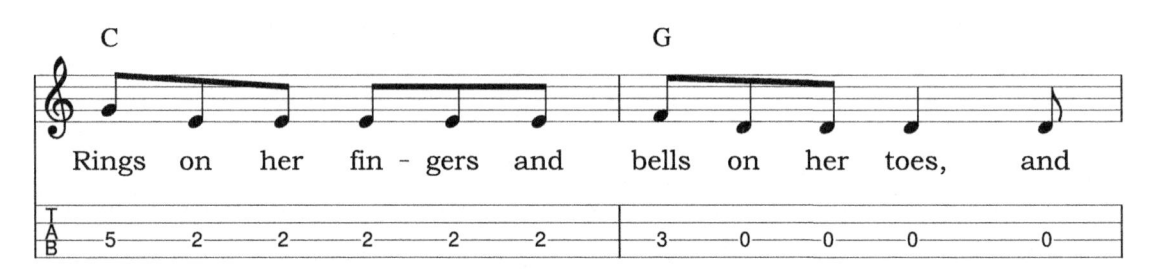

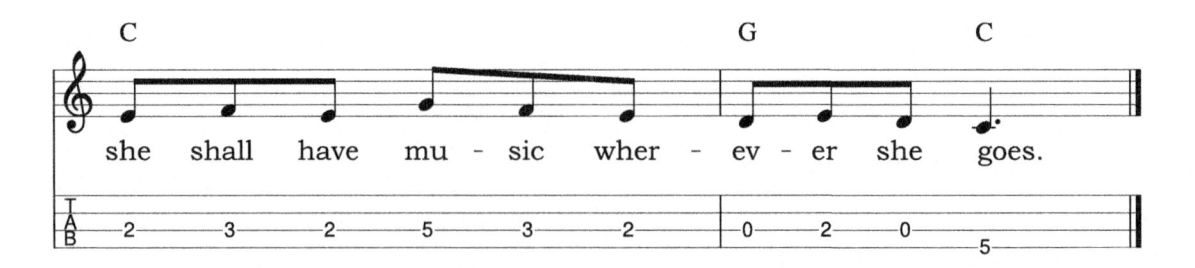

Ride a cock-horse to Banbury Cross, to see a fine lady upon a white horse. Rings on her fingers and bells on her toes, and she shall have music wherever she goes.

Silent Night

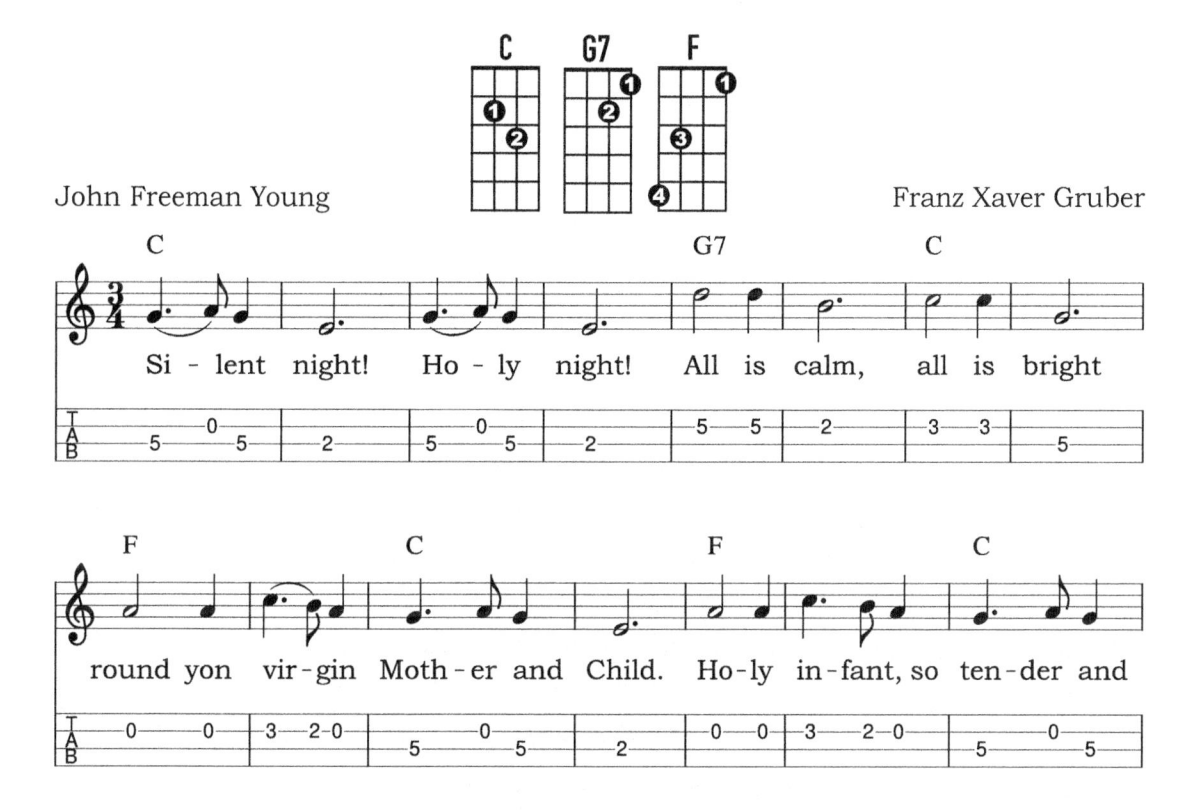

John Freeman Young
Franz Xaver Gruber

Si-lent night! Ho-ly night! All is calm, all is bright round yon vir-gin Moth-er and Child. Ho-ly in-fant, so ten-der and mild, sleep in heav-en-ly, peace. Sleep in heav-en-ly peace!

Silent night! Holy night!
All is calm, all is bright
Round yon virgin Mother and child!
Holy infant, so tender and mild,
Sleep in heavenly peace!
Sleep in heavenly peace!

Silent night! Holy night!
Shepherds quake at the sight!
Glories stream from heaven afar,
Heavenly hosts sing Alleluia!
Christ the Saviour is born!
Christ the Saviour is born!

Silent night! Holy night!
Son of God, love's pure light
Radiant beams from thy holy face
With the dawn of redeeming grace,
Jesus, Lord, at thy birth!
Jesus, Lord, at thy birth!

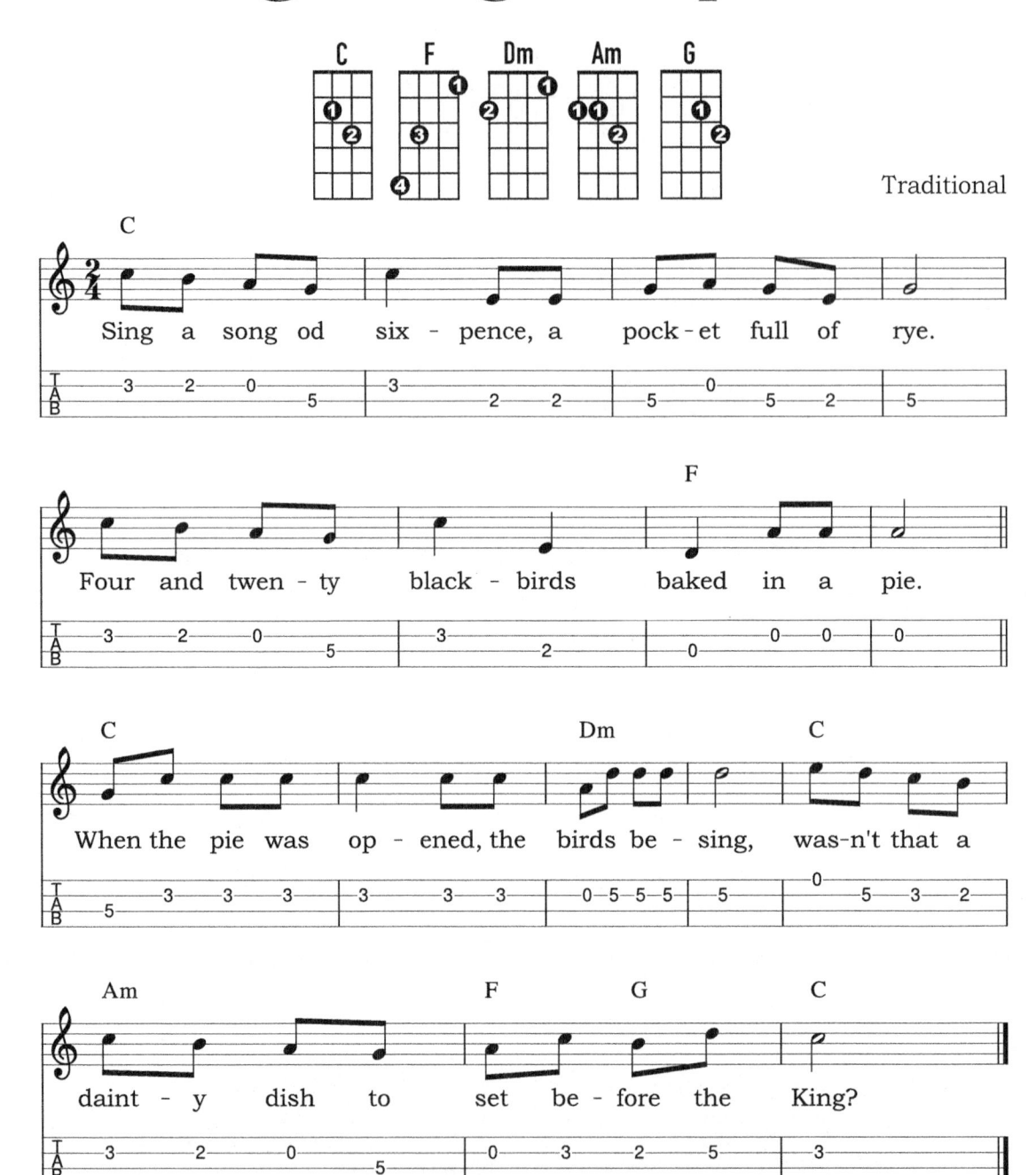

Sing a Song of Sixpence

Traditional

Sing a song od six - pence, a pock - et full of rye.
Four and twen - ty black - birds baked in a pie.
When the pie was op - ened, the birds be - sing, was-n't that a
daint - y dish to set be - fore the King?

Sing a song of sixpence,
A pocket full of rye.
Four and twenty blackbirds,
Baked in a pie.
When the pie was opened
The birds began to sing;
Wasn't that a dainty dish,
To set before the king.

The king was in his counting house,
Counting out his money;
The queen was in the parlour,
Eating bread and honey.
The maid was in the garden,
Hanging out the clothes,
When down came a blackbird
And pecked off her nose.

Skip to My Lou

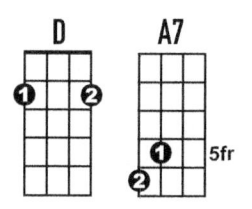

Traditional

Skip, skip, skip to my Lou, skip, skip, skip to my Lou,
skip, skip, skip to my Lou, skip to my Lou, my dar - ling.

Skip, skip, skip to my Lou,
Skip, skip, skip to my Lou,
Skip, skip, skip to my Lou,
Skip to my Lou, my darlin'.

Lou, Lou skip to my Lou,
Lou, Lou skip to my Lou,
Lou, Lou skip to my Lou,
Skip to my Lou my darlin'.

Fly in the buttermilk, shoo, fly, shoo.
Fly in the buttermilk, shoo, fly, shoo.
Fly in the buttermilk, shoo, fly, shoo.
Skip to my Lou, my darlin'.

Lou, Lou skip to my Lou,
Lou, Lou skip to my Lou,
Lou, Lou skip to my Lou,
Skip to my Lou my darlin'.

There's a little red wagon, paint it blue.
There's a little red wagon, paint it blue.
There's a little red wagon, paint it blue.
Skip to my Lou, my darlin'.

Lou, Lou skip to my Lou,
Lou, Lou skip to my Lou,
Lou, Lou skip to my Lou,
Skip to my Lou my darlin'.

I lost my partner, what'll I do?
I lost my partner, what'll I do?
I lost my partner, what'll I do?
Skip to my Lou, my darlin'.

Lou, Lou skip to my Lou,
Lou, Lou skip to my Lou,
Lou, Lou skip to my Lou,
Skip to my Lou my darlin'.

I'll get another, as pretty as you.
I'll get another, as pretty as you.
I'll get another, as pretty as you.
Skip to my Lou, my darlin'.

Lou, Lou skip to my Lou,
Lou, Lou skip to my Lou,
Lou, Lou skip to my Lou,
Skip to my Lou my darlin'.

Skidamarink

Felix F. Feist   Al Piantadosi

Skid-a-ma-rink a dink a dink, skid-a-ma-rink a doo. I love you! Skid-a-ma-rink a dink adink, skid-a-ma-rink a doo. I love you! I love you in the morn-ing, and in the af-ter-noon. I love you in the eve-ning, and un-der-neath the moon. Oh, skid-a-ma-rink a dink adink, skid-a-ma-rink a doo. I love you!

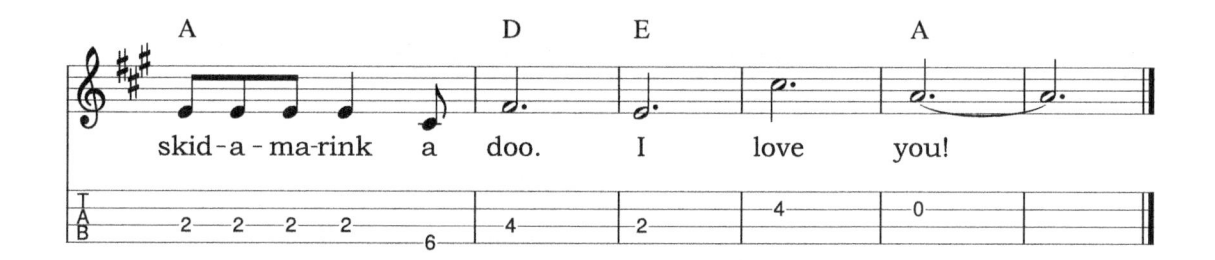

Sur le Pont d'Avignon

Traditional

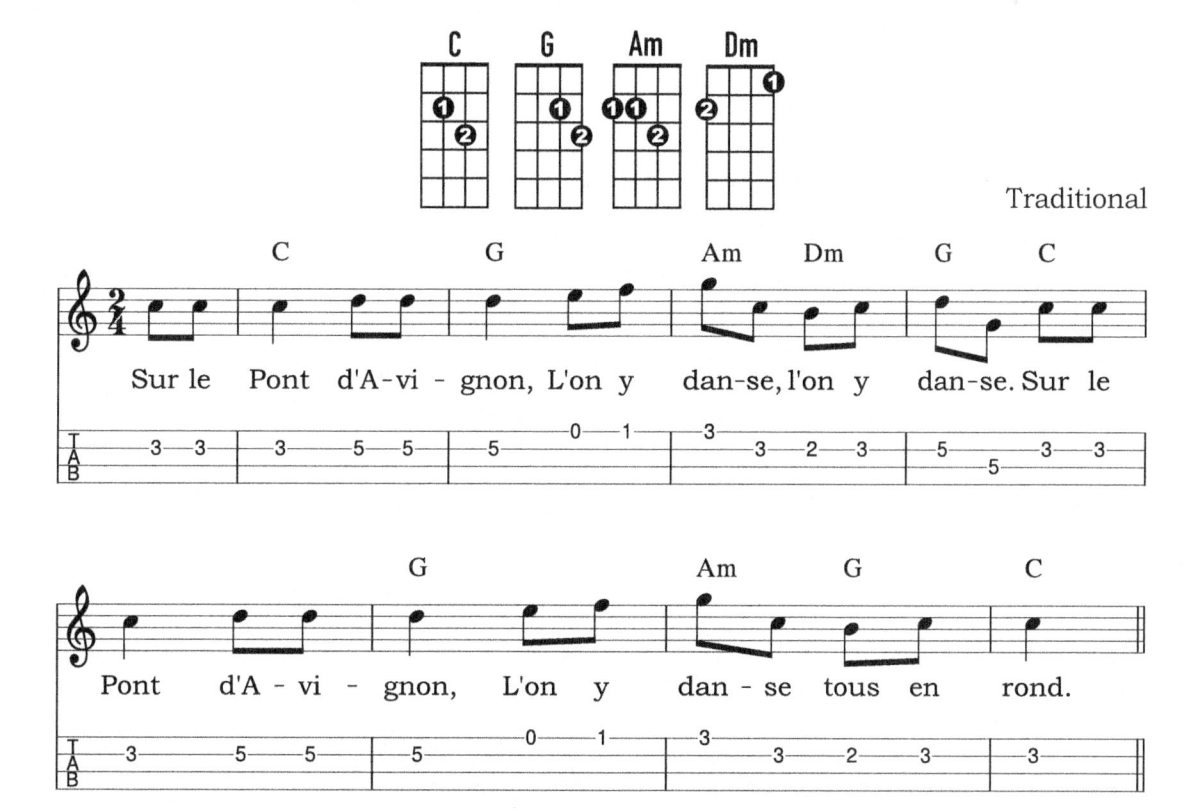

Sur le Pont d'A-vi-gnon, L'on y dan-se, l'on y dan-se. Sur le Pont d'A-vi-gnon, L'on y dan-se tous en rond.

Sur le Pont d'Avignon
L'on y danse, l'on y danse
Sur le Pont d'Avignon
L'on y danse tous en rond.

On the bridge of Avignon
We're all dancing, we're all dancing
On the bridge of Avignon
We all dance in circles.

Sleep, Baby, Sleep

Traditional

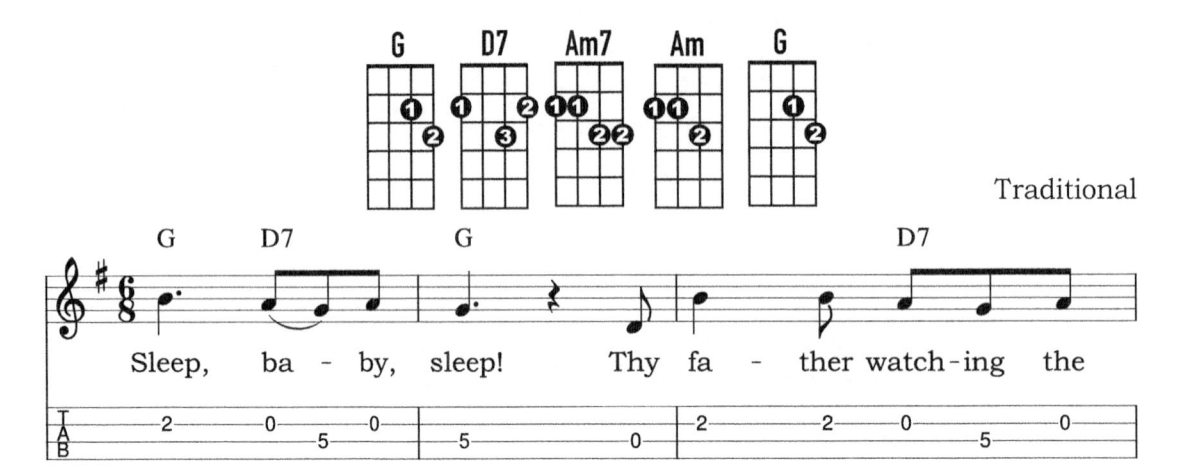

Sleep, ba - by, sleep! Thy fa - ther watch-ing the sheep. Thy mo - ther sha-king the dream - land tree, and down fall pleas - ant dreams fot thee. Sleep, ba-by, sleep.

Sleep, baby, sleep!
Thy father watches the sheep;
Thy mother is shaking the dream-land tree,
And down falls a little dream on thee:
Sleep, baby, sleep!

Sleep, baby, sleep.
The large stars are the sheep,
The wee stars are the lambs, I guess,
The fair moon is the shepherdess:
Sleep, baby, sleep!

The A.B.C.

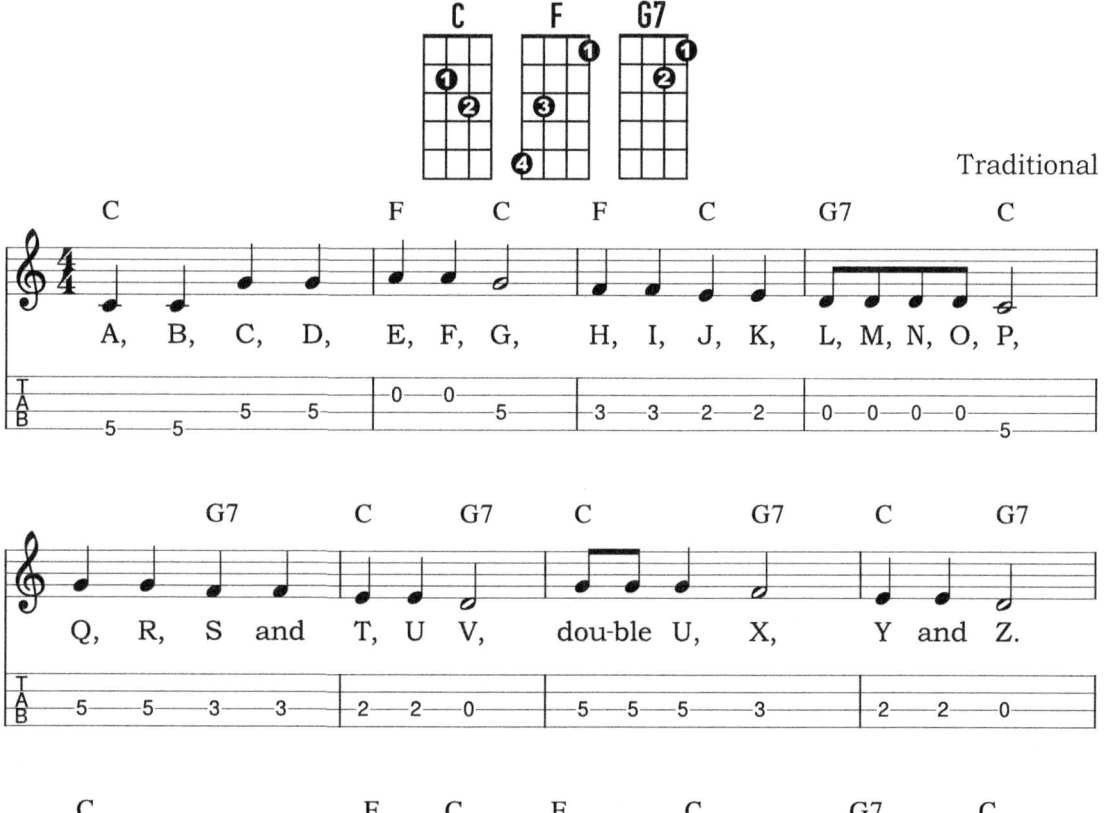

Traditional

A, B, C, D, E, F, G, H, I, J, K, L, M, N, O, P,

Q, R, S and T, U V, dou-ble U, X, Y and Z.

Now I know my A B Cs, won't you sing a - long with me?

Swing Low Sweet Chariot

Traditional

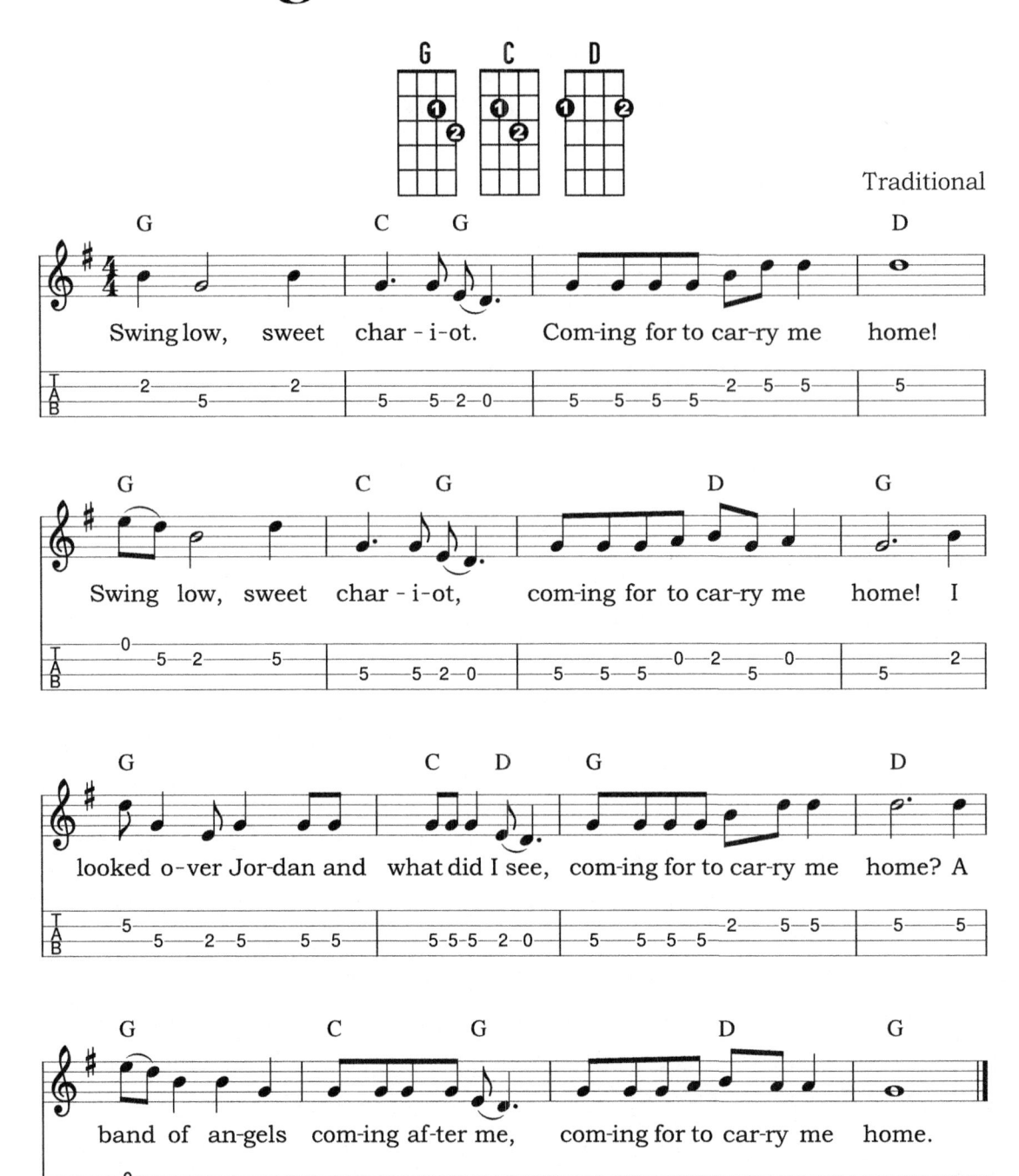

*Swing low, sweet chariot,
Coming for to carry me home.
Swing low, sweet chariot,
Coming for to carry me home.*

*I looked over Jordan, and what did I see,
Coming for to carry me home.
A band of angels coming after me,
Coming for to carry me home. Oh,*

Chorus

If you get there before I do,
Coming for to carry me home.
Tell all my friends I'm coming too,
Coming for to carry me home. Oh,

Chorus

The brightest day that ever I saw
Coming for to carry me home.
When Jesus washed my sins away,
Coming for to carry me home. Oh,

Chorus

I'm sometimes up and sometimes down,
Coming for to carry me home.
But still my soul feels heavenly bound,
Coming for to carry me home. Oh,

Chorus

Ten Little Teddy Bears

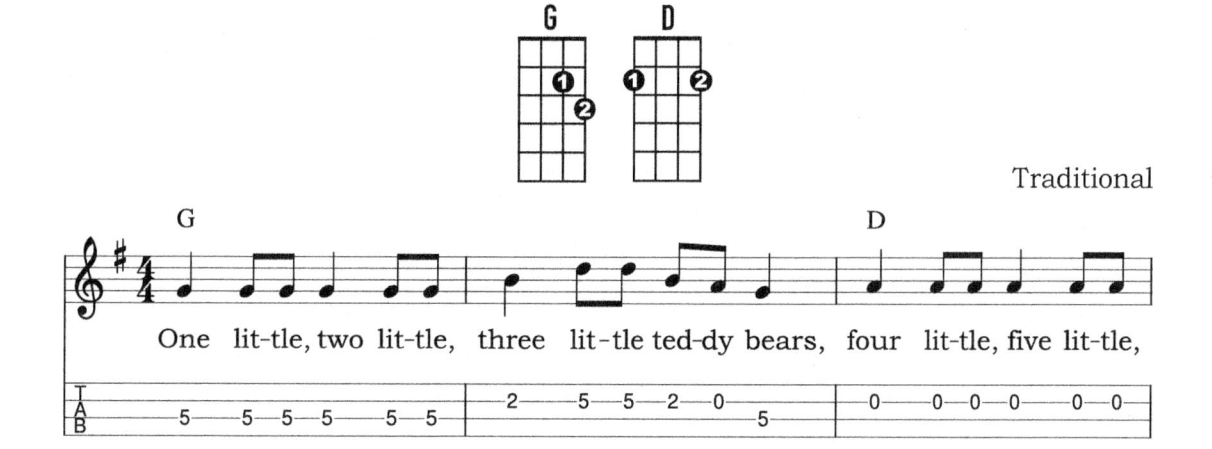

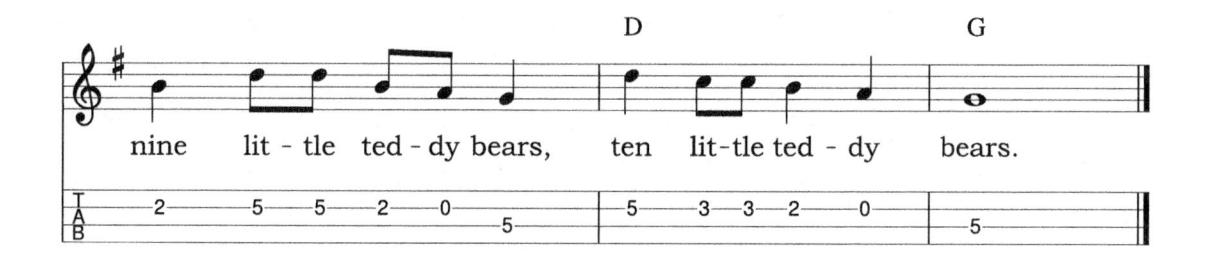

Traditional

One little, two little, three little teddy bears, four little, five little, six little teddy bears, seven little, eight little, nine little teddy bears, ten little teddy bears.

The Bear Went Over the Mountain

Traditional

The Farmer in the Dell

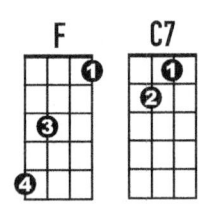

Traditional

The farmer in the dell, the farmer in the dell. Hi-ho, the derry-o. The farmer in the dell.

The farmer in the dell,
The farmer in the dell.
Hi-ho, the derry-o.
The farmer in the dell.

The farmer takes the wife,
The farmer takes the wife.
Hi-ho, the derry-o.
The farmer takes the wife.

The wife takes the child,
The wife takes the child.
Hi-ho, the derry-o.
The wife takes the child.

The child takes the nurse,
The child takes the nurse.
Hi-ho, the derry-o.
The child takes the nurse.

The nurse takes the cow,
The nurse takes the cow.
Hi-ho, the derry-o.
The nurse takes the cow.

The cow takes the dog,
The cow takes the dog.
Hi-ho, the derry-o.
The cow takes the dog.

The dog takes the cat,
The dog takes the cat.
Hi-ho, the derry-o.
The dog takes the cat.

The cat takes the mouse,
The cat takes the mouse.
Hi-ho, the derry-o.
The cat takes the mouse.

The mouse takes the cheese,
The mouse takes the cheese.
Hi-ho, the derry-o.
The mouse takes the cheese.

The cheese stands alone,
The cheese stands alone.
Hi-ho, the derry-o.
The cheese stands alone.

The King Of France

Traditional

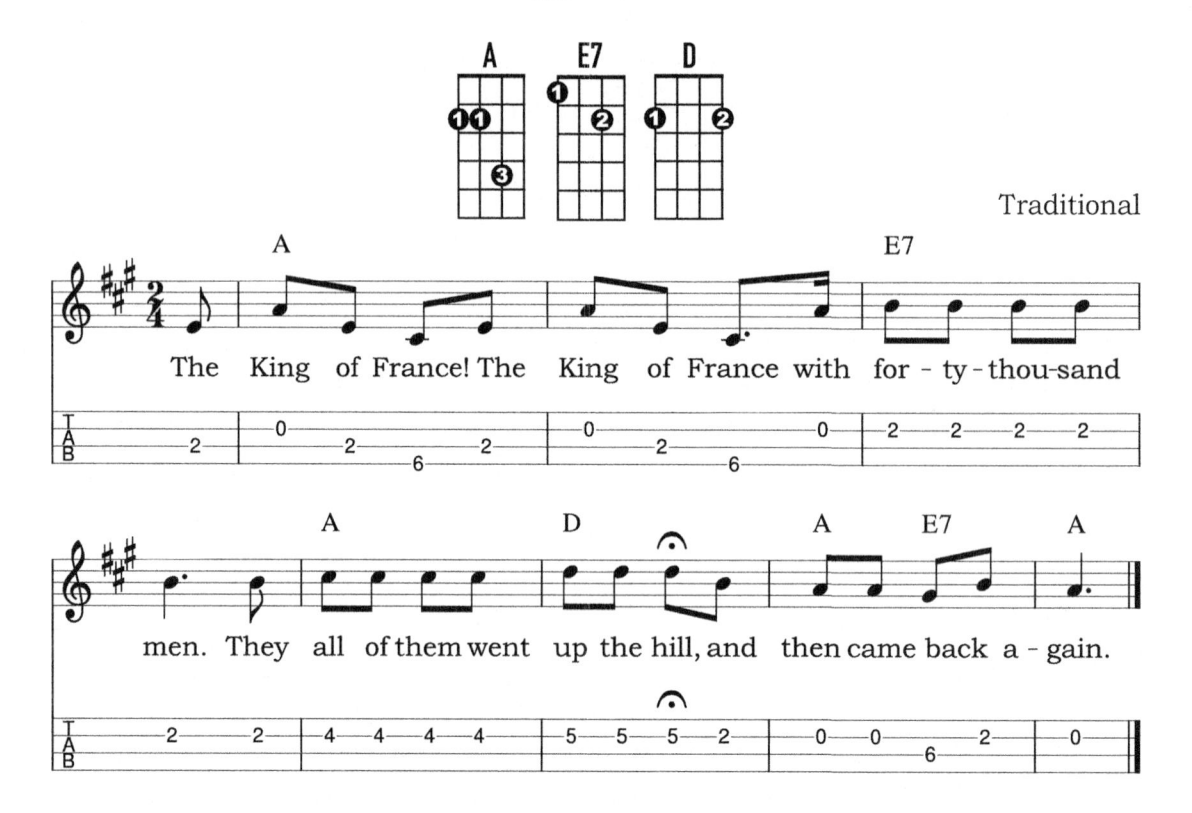

The King of France! The King of France with for-ty-thou-sand men. They all of them went up the hill, and then came back a-gain.

98

The Muffin Man

Traditional

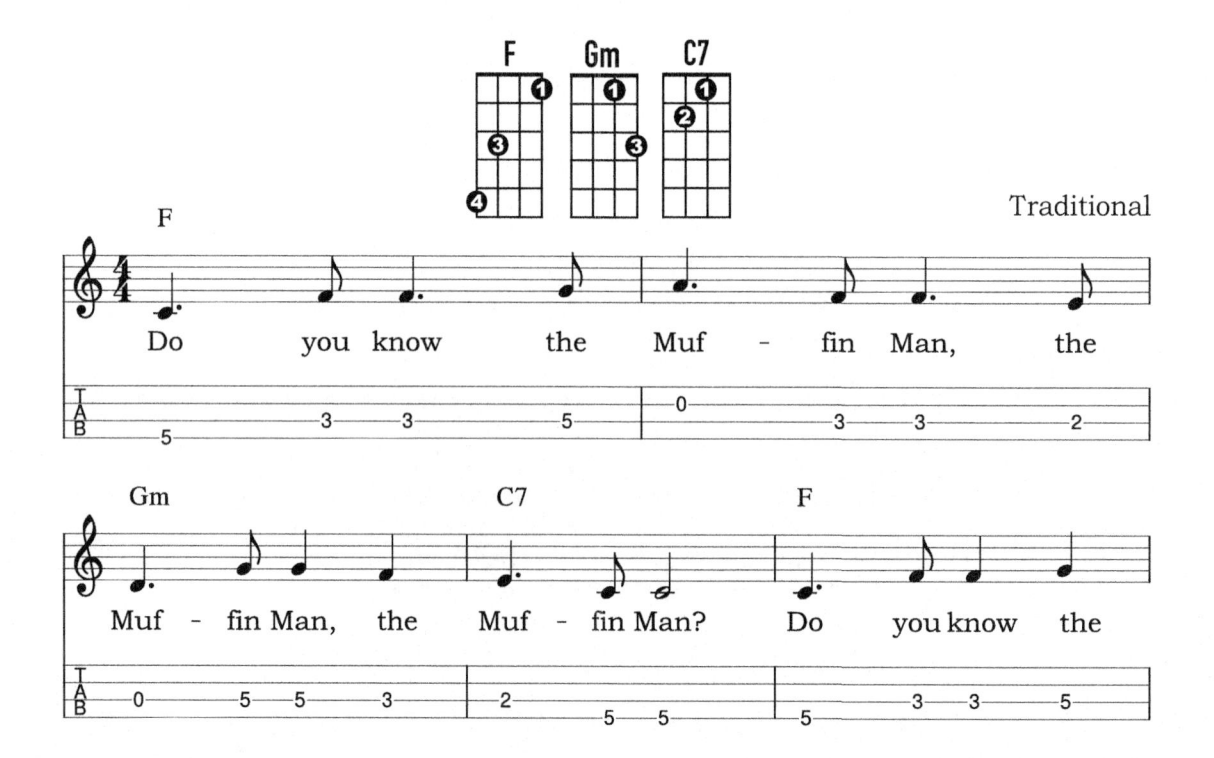

Do you know the Muf-fin Man, the Muf-fin Man, the Muf-fin Man? Do you know the

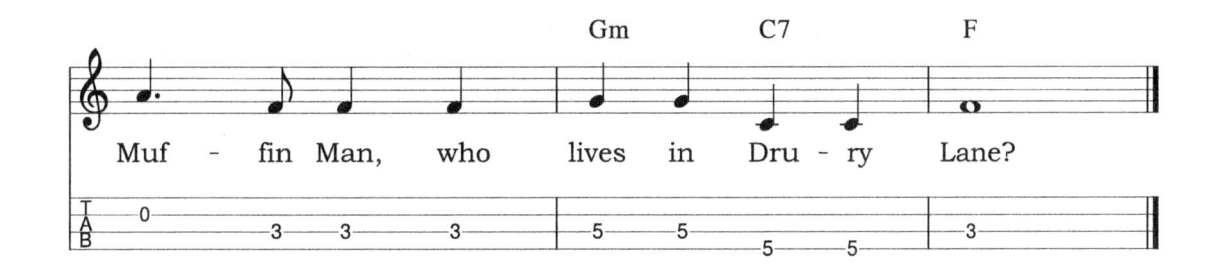

Muf - fin Man, who lives in Dru - ry Lane?

Do you know the muffin man,
The muffin man, the muffin man?
Do you know the muffin man,
Who lives on Drury Lane?

Yes, I know the muffin man,
The muffin man, the muffin man.
Yes, I know the muffin man,
Who lives on Drury Lane.

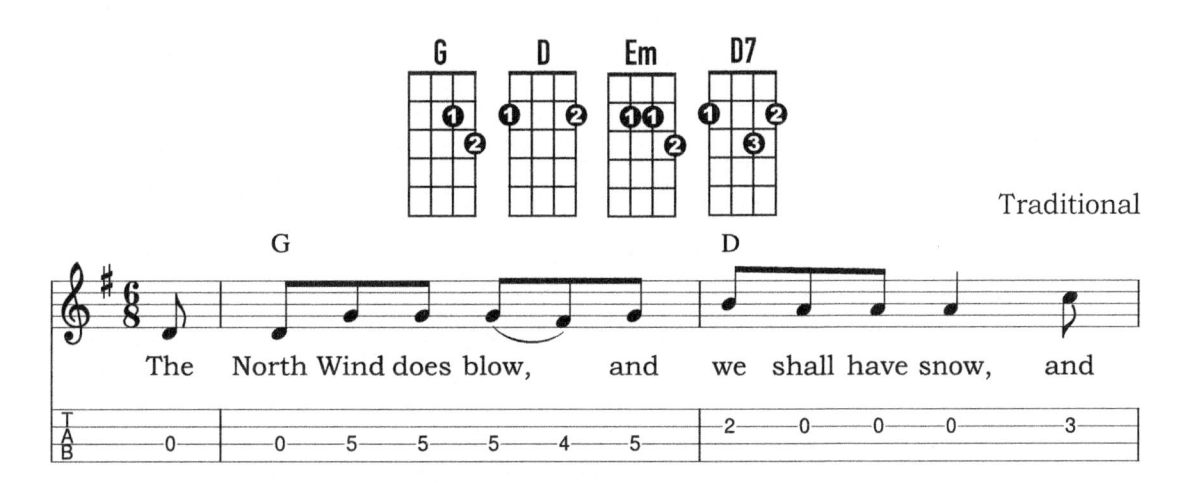

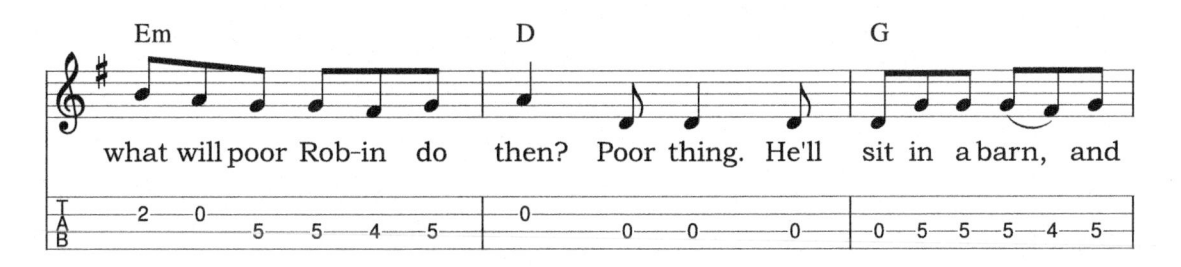

The North Wind Does Blow

Traditional

The North Wind does blow, and we shall have snow, and what will poor Rob-in do then? Poor thing. He'll sit in a barn, and keep him-self warm, and hide his head un-der his wing. Poor thing.

The Riddle Song

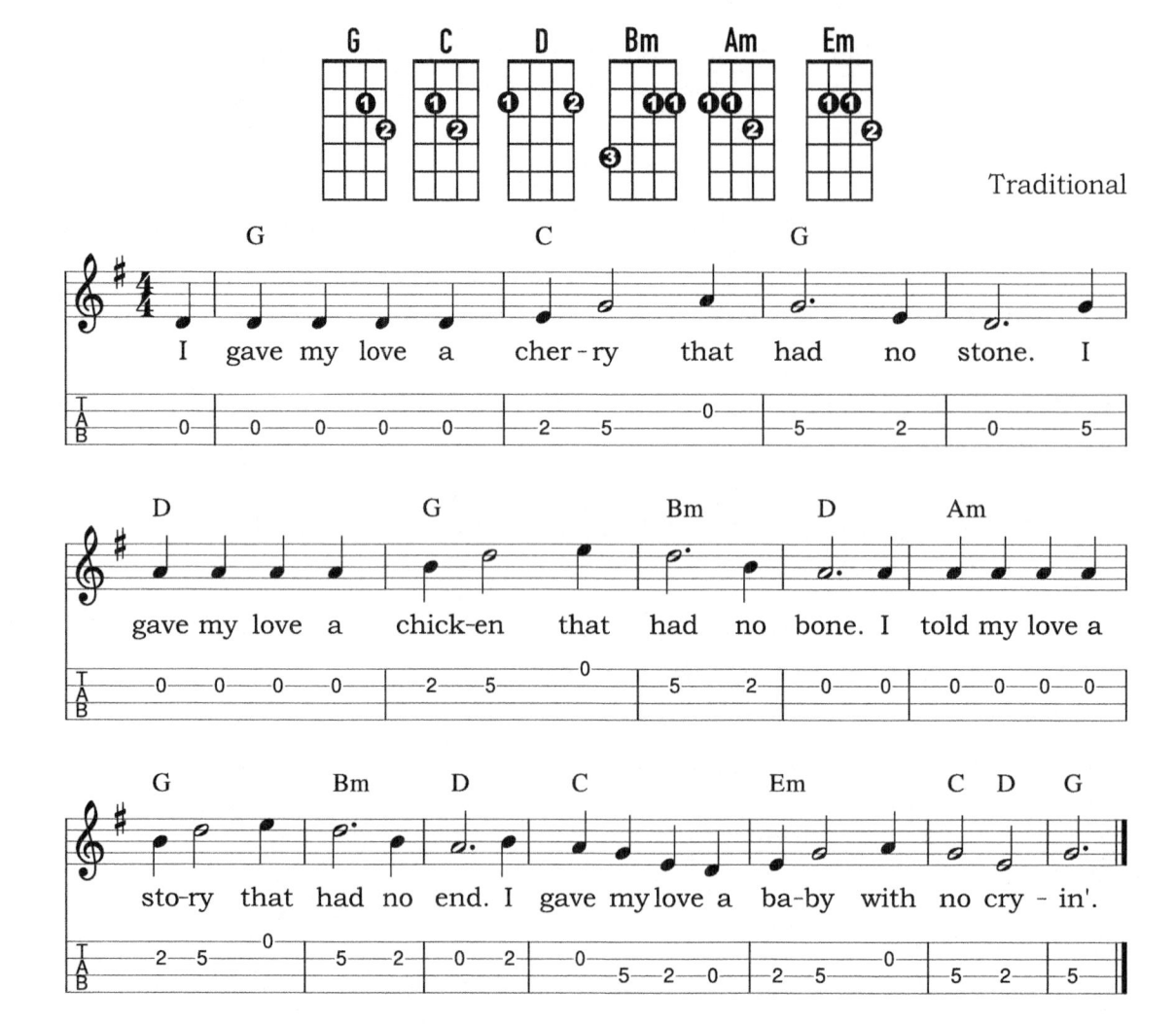

Traditional

I gave my love a cherry that had no stone. I gave my love a chicken that had no bone. I told my love a story that had no end. I gave my love a baby with no cry-in'.

I gave my love a cherry
That had no stone.
I gave my love a chicken
That had no bone.
I told my love a story
That had no end.
I gave my love a baby
With no cryin'.

A cherry when it's bloomin'
It has no stone.
A chicken when it's pippin'
It has no bone.
The story of I love you
It has no end.
A baby when it's sleeping
It's not cryin'.

How can there be a cherry
That has no stone?
And how can there be a chicken
That has no bone?
And how can there be a story
That has no end?
And how can there be a baby
With no cryin'?

I gave my love a cherry
That had no stone.
I gave my love a chicken
That had no bone.
I told my love a story
That had no end.
I gave my love a baby
With no cryin'.

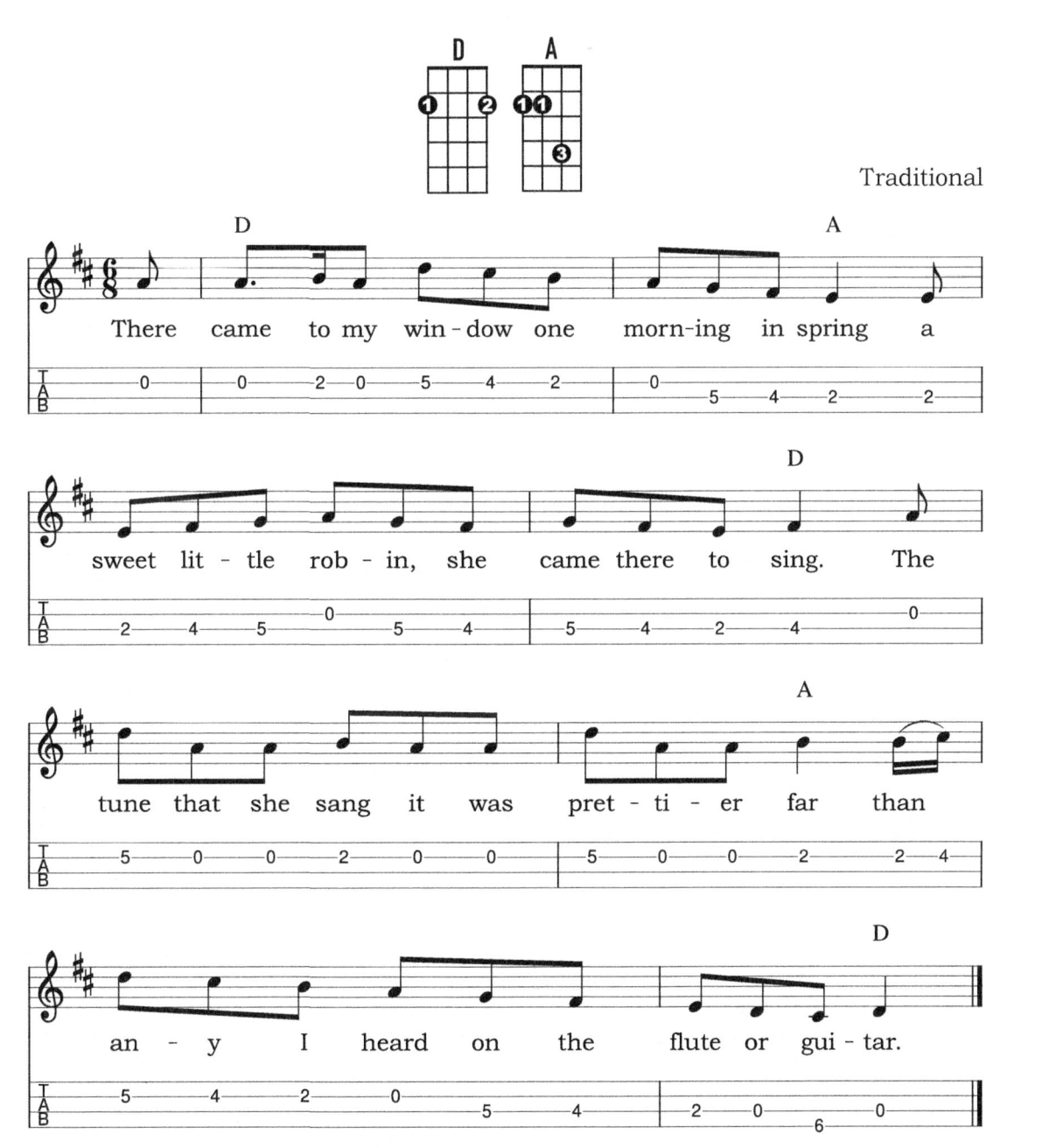

There Came To My Window

Traditional

There came to my window one morning in spring a
sweet little robin, she came there to sing. The
tune that she sang it was pretier far than
any I heard on the flute or guitar.

There came to my window one morning in spring
A sweet little robin, she came there to sing,
The tune that she sang it was prettier far
Than any I heard on the flute or guitar.

Her wings she was spreading to soar far away,
Then resting a moment seem'd sweetly to say:
"Oh happy, how happy the world seems to be,
Awake, little girl, and be happy with me!"

This Old Man

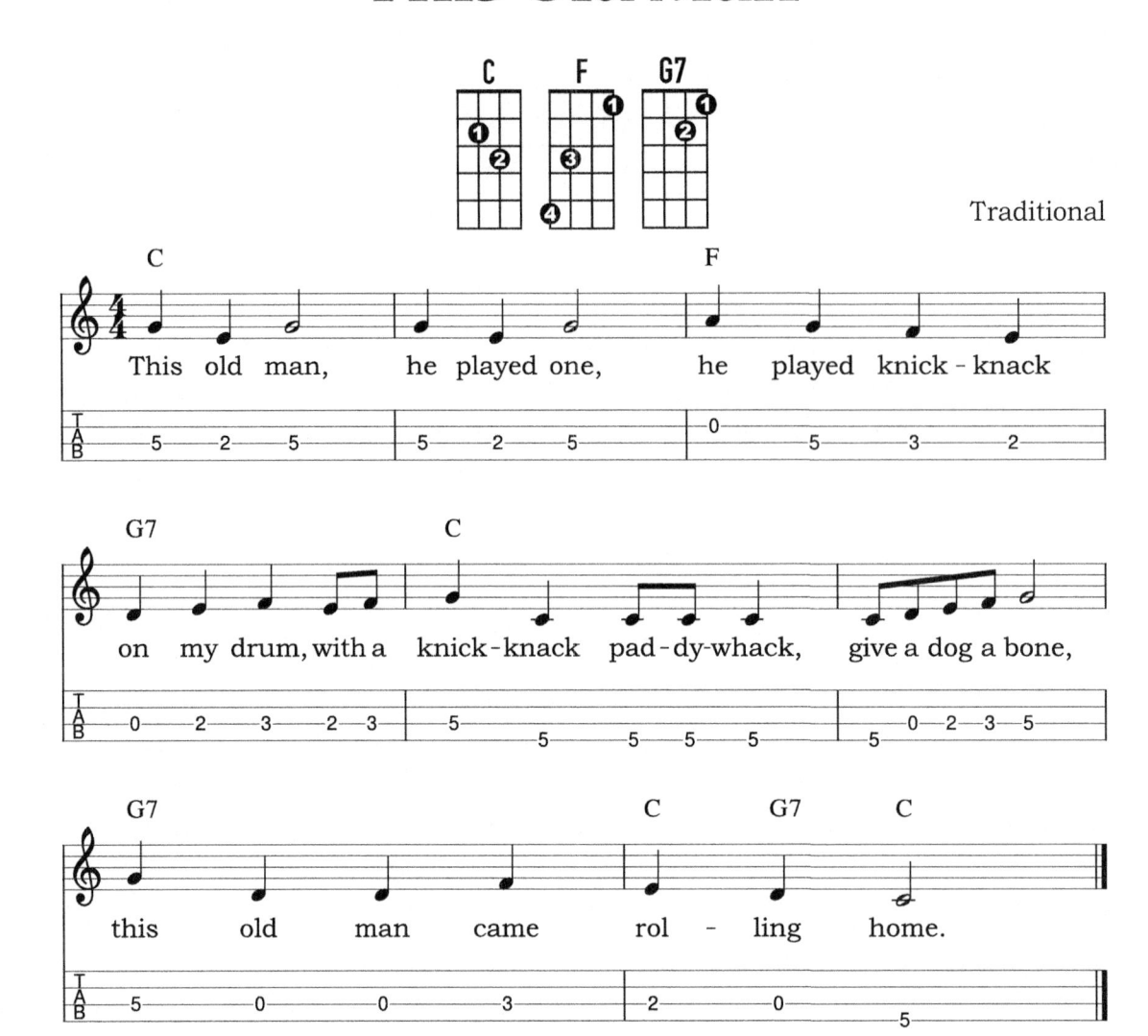

Traditional

This old man, he played one, he played knick-knack on my drum, with a knick-knack pad-dy-whack, give a dog a bone, this old man came rol-ling home.

This old man, he played one,
He played knick-knack on my thumb;
With a knick-knack paddywhack,
Give a dog a bone,
This old man came rolling home.

This old man, he played two,
He played knick-knack on my shoe;
With a knick-knack paddywhack,
Give a dog a bone,
This old man came rolling home.

This old man, he played three,
He played knick-knack on my knee;
With a knick-knack paddywhack,
Give a dog a bone,
This old man came rolling home.

This old man, he played four,
He played knick-knack on my door;
With a knick-knack paddywhack,
Give a dog a bone,
This old man came rolling home.

This old man, he played five,
He played knick-knack on my hive;
With a knick-knack paddywhack,
Give a dog a bone,
This old man came rolling home.

This old man, he played six,
He played knick-knack with my sticks;
With a knick-knack paddywhack,
Give a dog a bone,
This old man came rolling home.

This old man, he played seven,
He played knick-knack up in heaven;
With a knick-knack paddywhack,
Give a dog a bone,
This old man came rolling home.

This old man, he played eight,
He played knick-knack on my gate;
With a knick-knack paddywhack,
Give a dog a bone,
This old man came rolling home.

This old man, he played nine,
He played knick-knack on my spine;
With a knick-knack paddywhack,
Give a dog a bone,
This old man came rolling home.

This old man, he played ten,
He played knick-knack once again;
With a knick-knack paddywhack,
Give a dog a bone,
This old man came rolling home.

Tom, Tom, the Piper's Son

Traditional

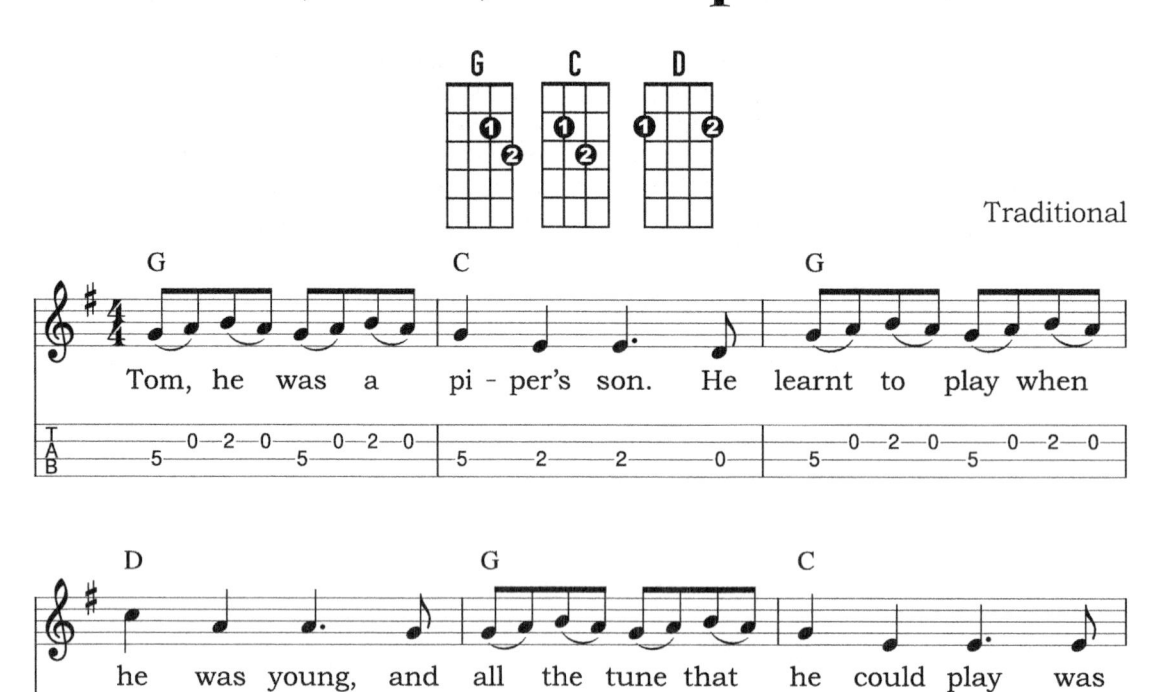

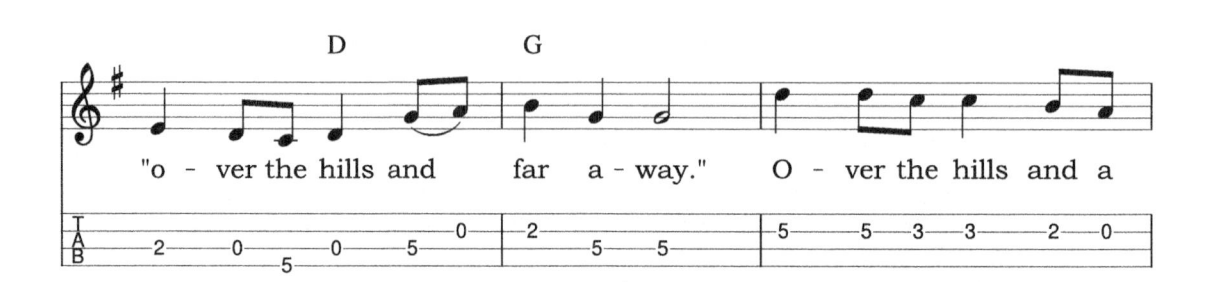

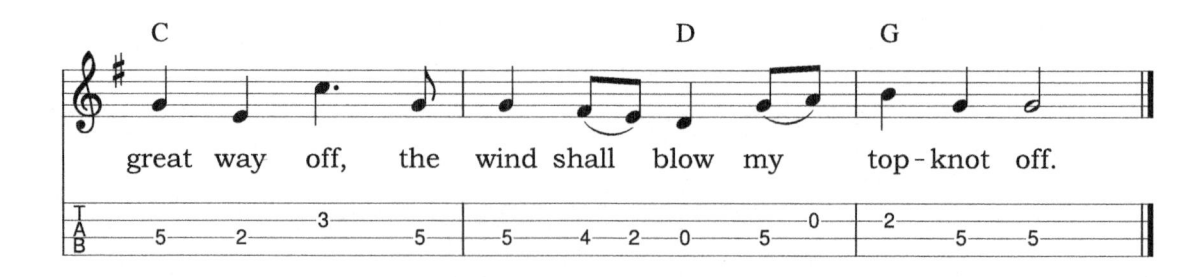

Tom, he was a piper's son. He learnt to play when he was young, and all the tune that he could play was "o-ver the hills and far a-way." O-ver the hills and a great way off, the wind shall blow my top-knot off.

Tom, he was a piper's son,
He learnt to play when he was young,
And all the tune that he could play
Was 'over the hills and far away'.
Over the hills and a great way off,
The wind shall blow my top-knot off.

Tom with his pipe made such a noise,
That he pleased both the girls and boys,
They all stopped to hear him play,
'Over the hills and far away'.
Over the hills and a great way off,
The wind shall blow my top-knot off.

Tom with his pipe did play with such skill
That those who heard him could never keep still;
As soon as he played they began for to dance,
Even the pigs on their hind legs would after him prance.
Over the hills and a great way off,
The wind shall blow my top-knot off.

As Dolly was milking her cow one day,
Tom took his pipe and began to play.
So Dolly and the cow danced 'The Cheshire Round',
Till the pail was broken and the milk ran on the ground.
Over the hills and a great way off,
The wind shall blow my top-knot off.

He met old Dame Trot with a basket of eggs,
He used his pipe and she used her legs;
She danced about till the eggs were all broke,
She began for to fret, but he laughed at the joke.
Over the hills and a great way off,
The wind shall blow my top-knot off.

Tom saw a cross fellow was beating an ass,
Heavy laden with pots, pans, dishes, and glass;
He took out his pipe and he played them a tune,
And the poor donkey's load was lightened full soon.
Over the hills and a great way off,
The wind shall blow my top-knot off.

Three Craws

Traditional

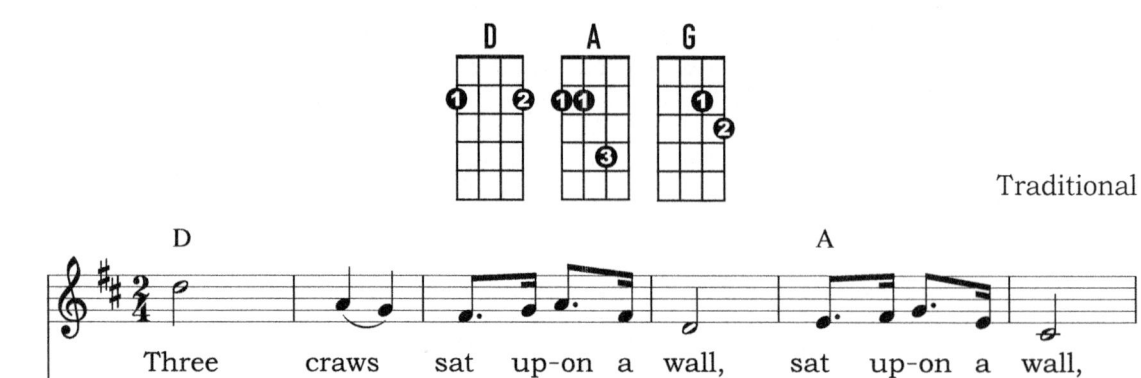

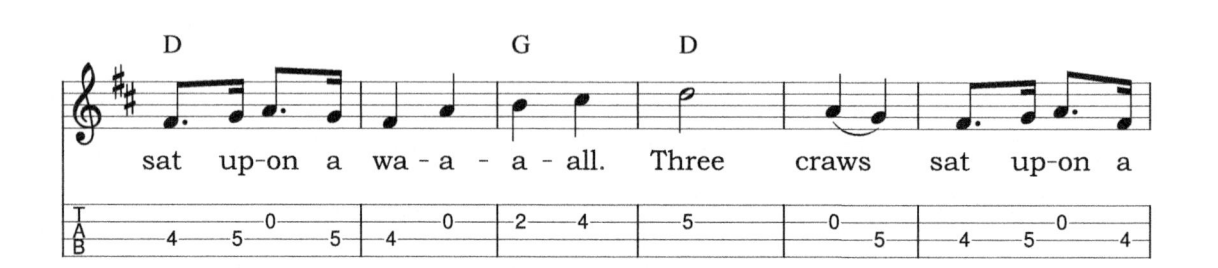

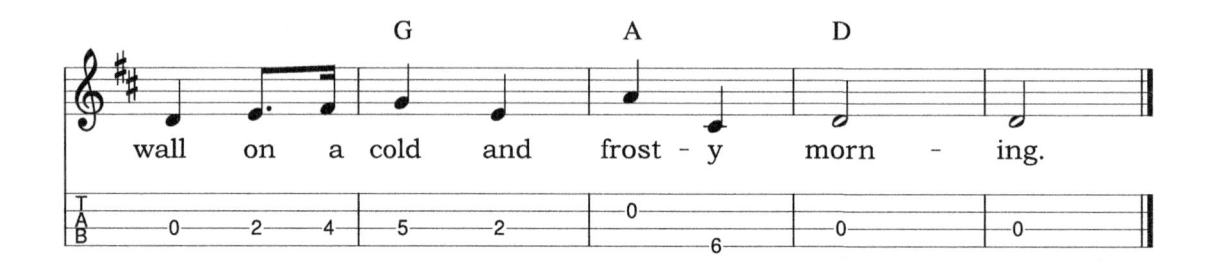

Three craws sat upon a wall, sat upon a wall, sat upon a wa-a-a-all. Three craws sat upon a wall on a cold and frost-y morn-ing.

Three crows sat upon a wall,
Sat upon a wall,
Sat upon a wall.
Three crows sat upon a wall
On a cold and frosty morning.

The first crow was crying for his mother,
Crying for his mother,
Crying for his mother.
The first crow was crying for his mother
On a cold and frosty morning.

The second crow was crying for his father,
Crying for his father,
Crying for his father.
The second crow was crying for his father
On a cold and frosty morning.

The third crow couldn't fly at all,
Couldn't fly at all,
Couldn't fly at all.
The third crow couldn't fly at all
On a cold and frosty morning.

Three Little Kittens

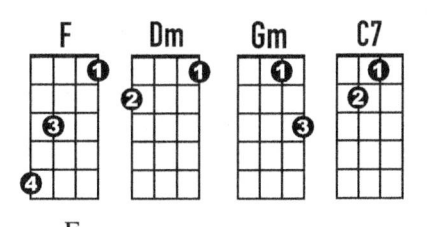

Traditional

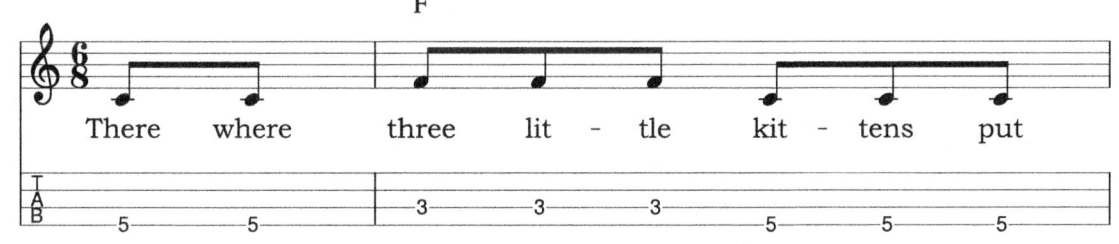

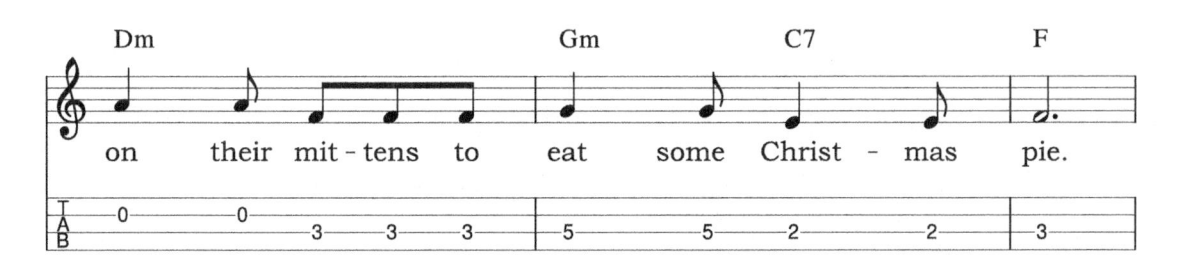

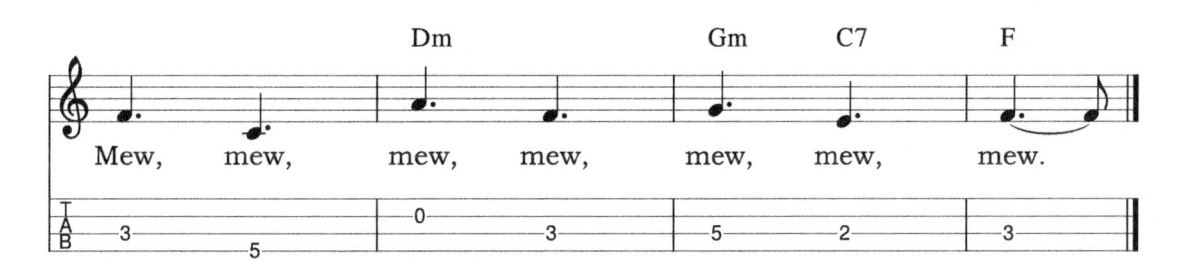

There were three little kittens
Put on their mittens
To eat some Christmas pie.
Mew, mew, mew, mew, mew, mew, mew.

These three little kittens
They lost their mittens,
And all began to cry.
Mew, mew, mew, mew, mew, mew, mew.

"Go, go, naughty kittens,
And find your mittens,
Or you shan't have any pie."
Mew, mew, mew, mew, mew, mew, mew.

These three little kittens
They found their mittens,
And joyfully they did cry.
Mew, mew, mew, mew, mew, mew, mew.

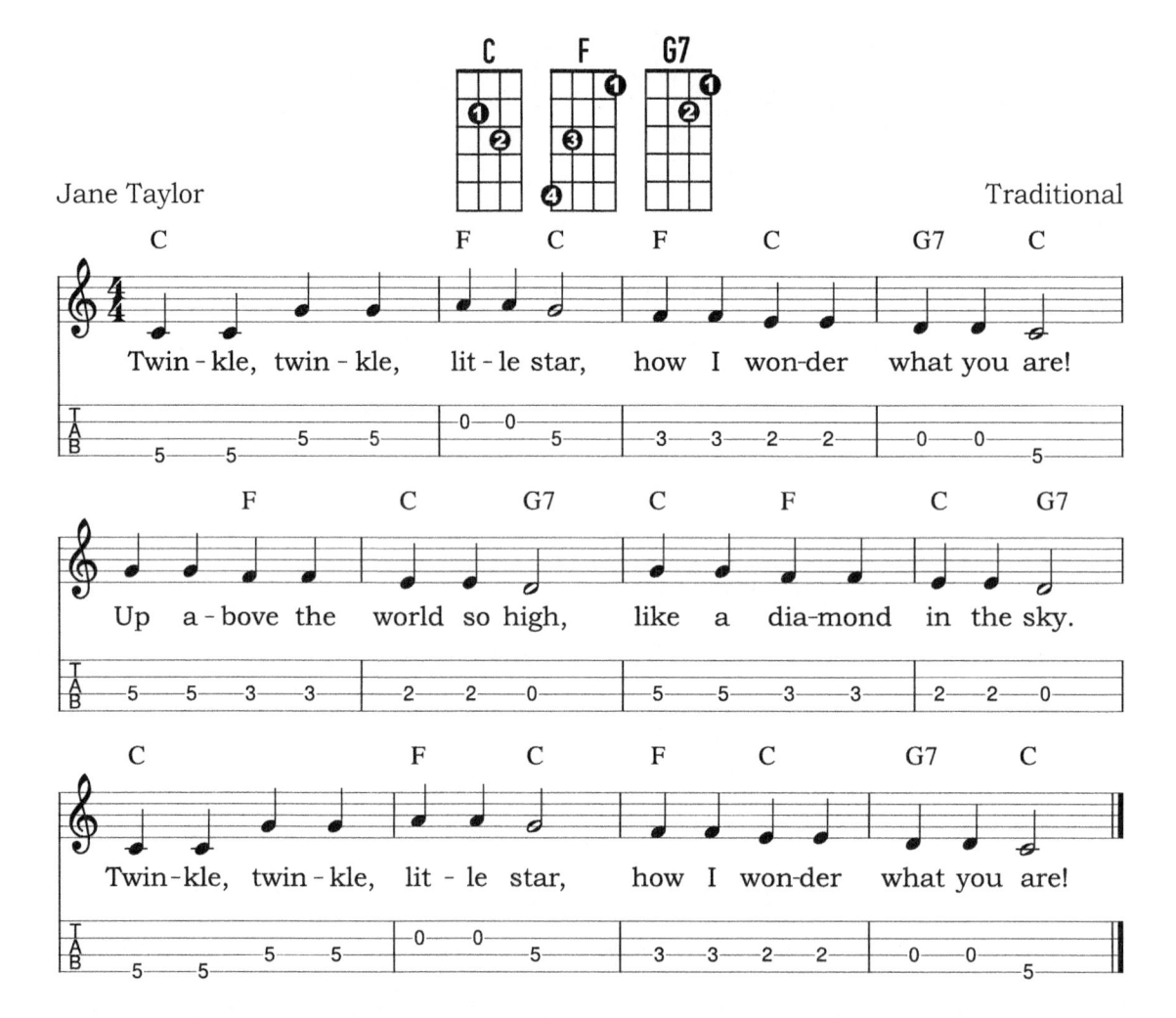

Twinkle, Twinkle, Little Star

Jane Taylor
Traditional

Twin-kle, twin-kle, lit-le star, how I won-der what you are!
Up a-bove the world so high, like a dia-mond in the sky.
Twin-kle, twin-kle, lit-le star, how I won-der what you are!

Twinkle, twinkle, little star,
How we wonder what you are.
Up above the world so high,
Like a diamond in the sky.
Twinkle, twinkle, little star,
How we wonder what you are.

When the blazing sun is gone,
When he nothing shines upon,
Then you show your little light,
Twinkle, twinkle, all the night.
Twinkle, twinkle, little star,
How we wonder what you are.

Then the traveler in the dark,
Thanks you for your tiny spark,
He could not see which way to go,
If you did not twinkle so.
Twinkle, twinkle, little star,
How we wonder what you are.

In the dark blue sky you keep,
And often through my curtains peep,
For you never shut your eye,
Till the sun is in the sky.
Twinkle, twinkle, little star,
How we wonder what you are.

As your bright and tiny spark,
Lights the traveler in the dark,
Though I know not what you are,
Twinkle, twinkle, little star.
Twinkle, twinkle, little star,
How we wonder what you are.

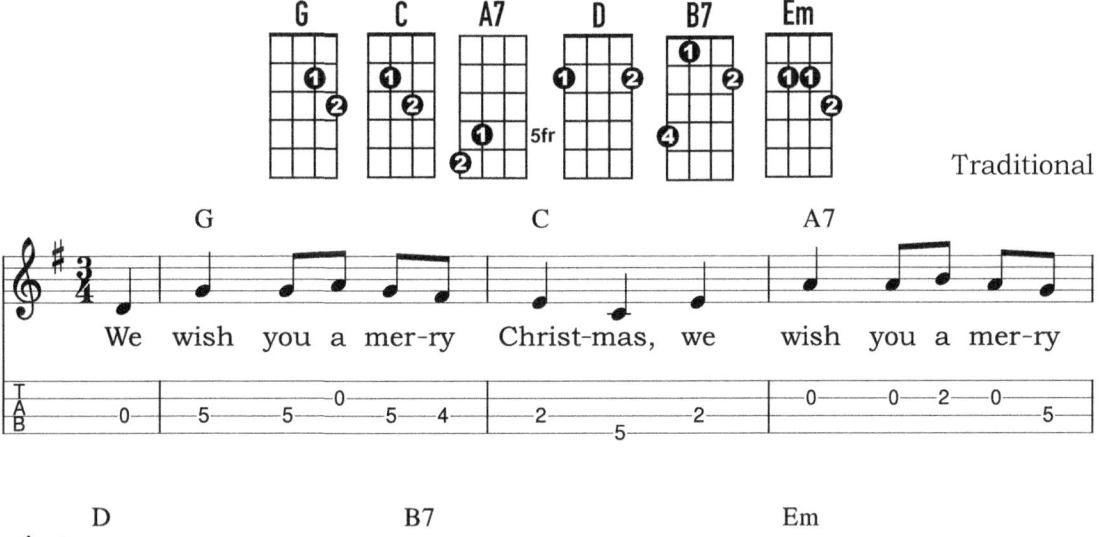

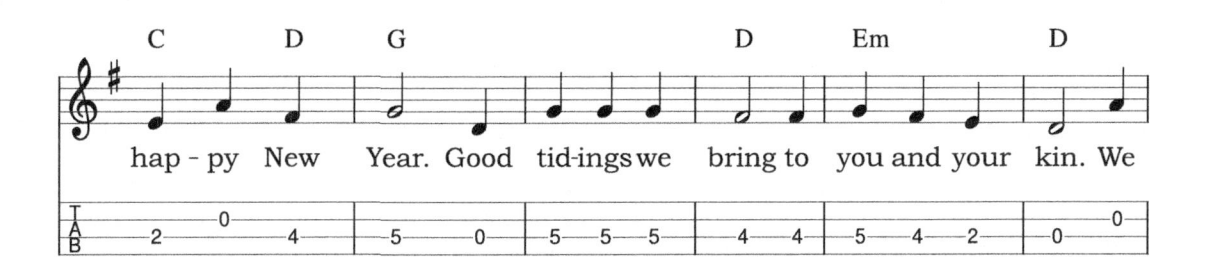

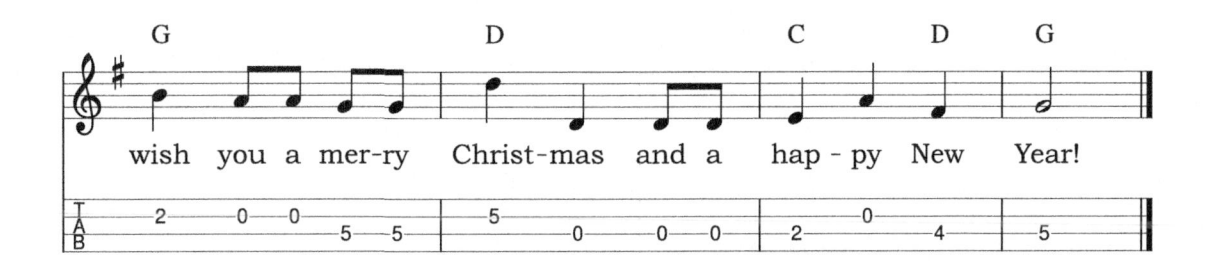

We wish you a merry Christmas

Traditional

Wee Willie Winki

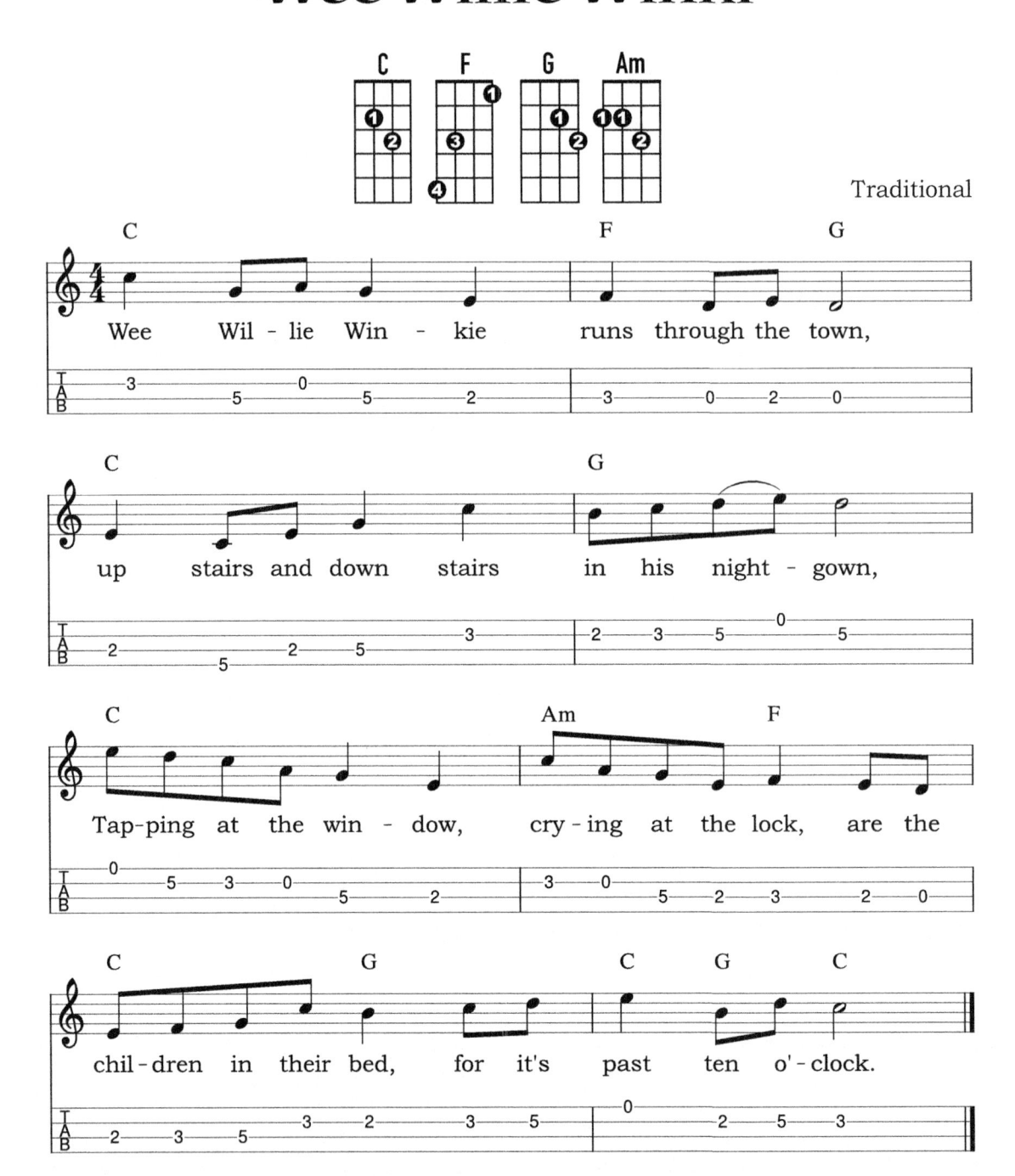

Traditional

Wee Willie Winkie runs through the town,
Up stairs and down stairs in his night-gown,
Tapping at the window, crying at the lock,
Are the children in their bed, for it's past ten o'clock?

Hey, Willie Winkie, are you coming in?
The cat is singing purring sounds to the sleeping hen,
The dog's spread out on the floor, and doesn't give a cheep,
But here's a wakeful little boy who will not fall asleep!

Anything but sleep, you rogue! glowering like the moon,'
Rattling in an iron jug with an iron spoon,
Rumbling, tumbling round about, crowing like a cock,
Shrieking like I don't know what, waking sleeping folk.

Hey, Willie Winkie – the child's in a creel!
Wriggling from everyone's knee like an eel,
Tugging at the cat's ear, and confusing all her thrums
Hey, Willie Winkie – see, there he comes!"

Weary is the mother who has a dusty child,
A small short sturdy child, who can't run on his own,
Who always has a battle with sleep before he'll close an eye
But a kiss from his rosy lips gives strength anew to me.

When the Boat Comes In

Traditional

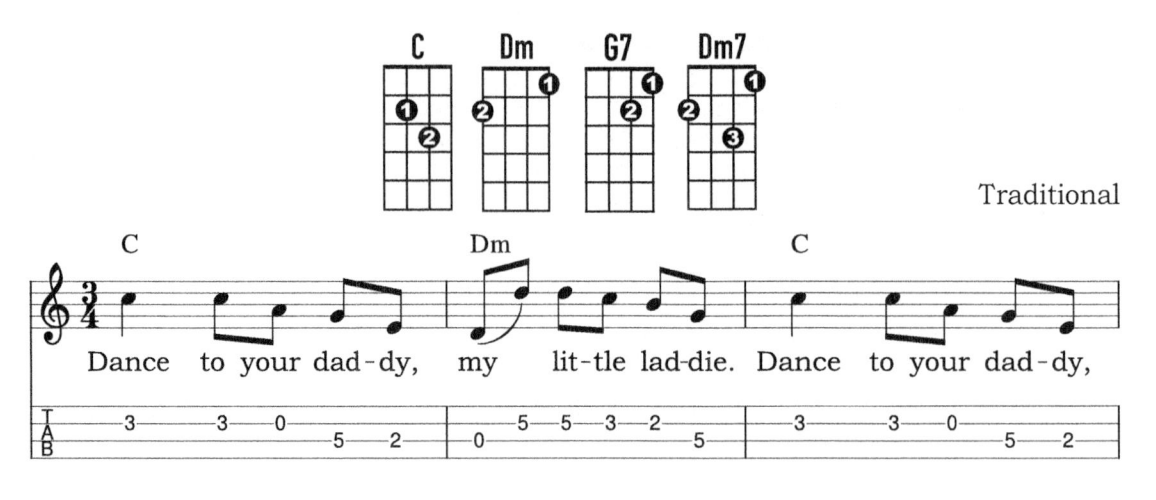

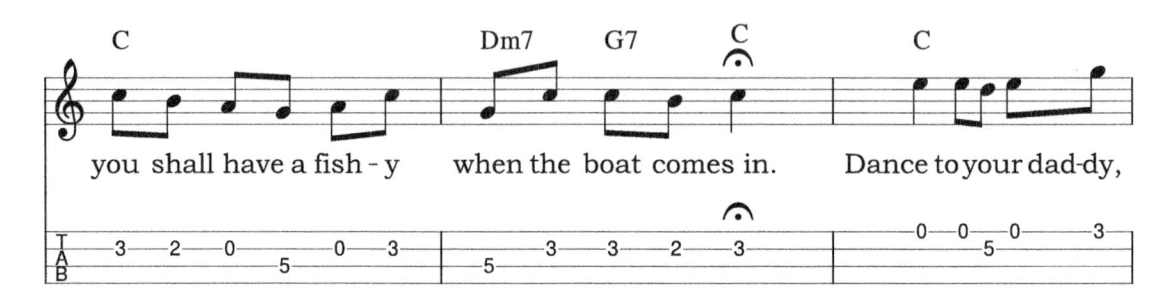

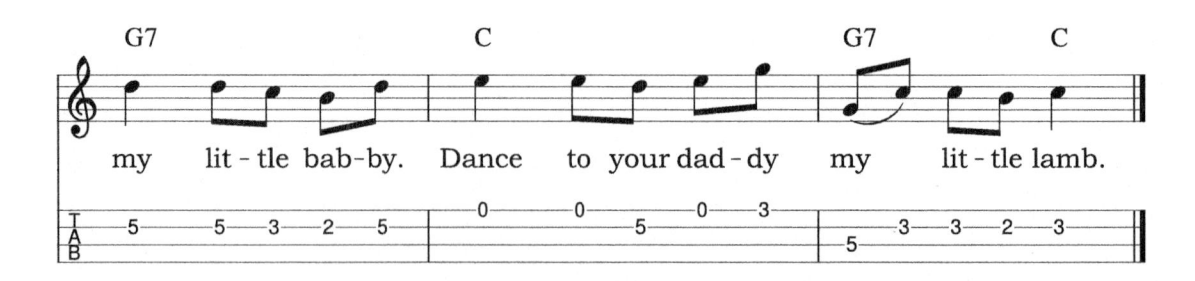

Dance to your dad-dy, my lit-tle lad-die. Dance to your dad-dy, my lit-tle man. You shall have a fish-y on a lit-tle dish-y, you shall have a fish-y when the boat comes in. Dance to your dad-dy, my lit-tle bab-by. Dance to your dad-dy my lit-tle lamb.

When the Saints Go Marching In

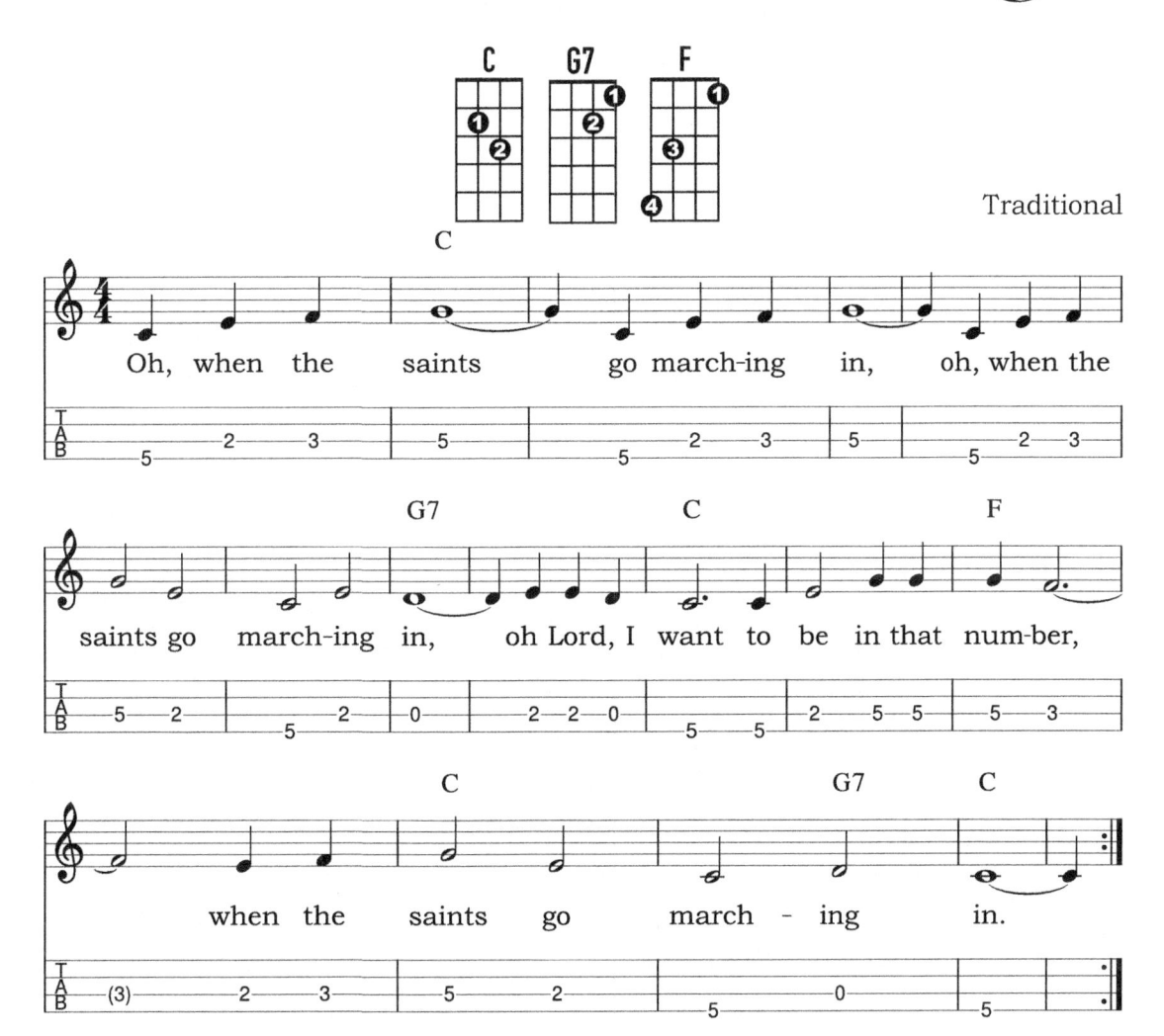

Traditional

Oh, when the saints go marching in, oh, when the saints go marching in, oh Lord, I want to be in that number, when the saints go marching in.

Oh, when the saints go marching in,
Oh, when the saints go marching in,
Oh Lord I want to be in that number,
When the saints go marching in.

Oh, when the drums begin to bang,
Oh, when the drums begin to bang,
Oh Lord I want to be in that number,
When the saints go marching in.

Oh, when the stars fall from the sky,
Oh, when the stars fall from the sky,
Oh Lord I want to be in that number,
When the saints go marching in.

Oh, when the moon turns red with blood,
Oh, when the moon turns red with blood,
Oh Lord I want to be in that number,
When the saints go marching in.

Oh, when the trumpet sounds its call,
Oh, when the trumpet sounds its call,
Oh Lord I want to be in that number,
When the saints go marching in.

Oh, when the horsemen begin to ride,
Oh, when the horsemen begin to ride,
Oh Lord I want to be in that number,
When the saints go marching in.

Oh, brother Charles you are my friend,
Oh, brother Charles you are my friend,
Yea, you gonna be in that number,
When the saints go marching in.

Oh, when the saints go marching in,
Oh, when the saints go marching in,
Oh Lord I want to be in that number,
When the saints go marching in.

Yankee Doodle

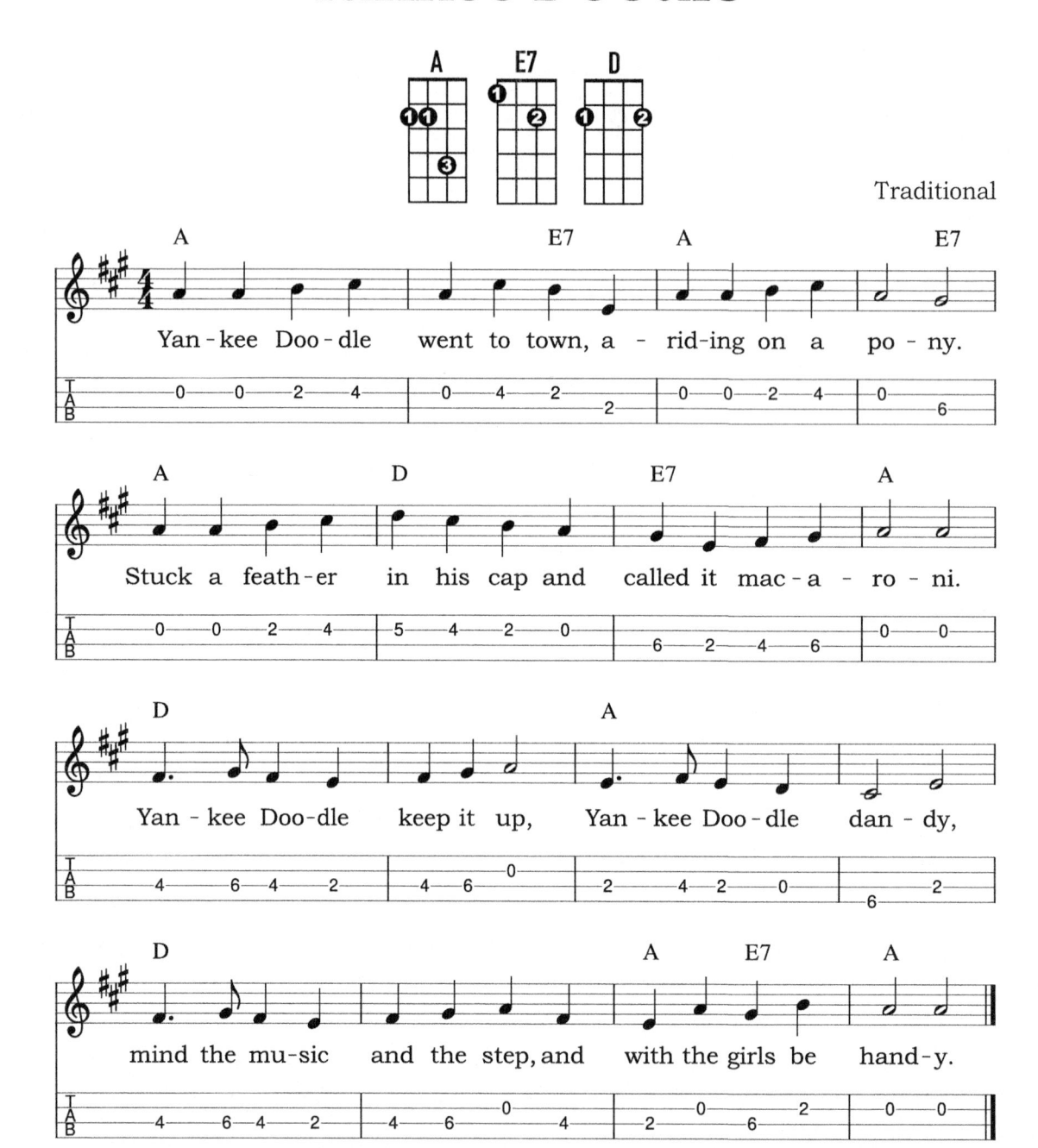

Traditional

Yankee Doodle went to town
A-riding on a pony,
Stuck a feather in his cap
And called it macaroni.

Yankee Doodle keep it up,
Yankee Doodle dandy,
Mind the music and the step,
And with the girls be handy.

Father and I went down to camp,
Along with Captain Gooding,[a]
And there we saw the men and boys
As thick as hasty pudding.

Yankee Doodle keep it up,
Yankee Doodle dandy,
Mind the music and the step,
And with the girls be handy.

And there we saw a thousand men
As rich as Squire David,
And what they wasted every day,
I wish it could be savèd.

Chorus

The 'lasses they eat every day,
Would keep a house a winter;
They have so much, that I'll be bound,
They eat it when they've a mind to.

Chorus

And there I see a swamping gun
Large as a log of maple,
Upon a deuced little cart,
A load for father's cattle.

Chorus

And every time they shoot it off,
It takes a horn of powder,
And makes a noise like father's gun,
Only a nation[c] louder.

Chorus

I went as nigh to one myself
As 'Siah's underpinning;
And father went as nigh again,
I thought the deuce was in him.

Chorus

Cousin Simon grew so bold,
I thought he would have cocked it;
It scared me so I shrinked it off
And hung by father's pocket.

Chorus

And Cap'n Davis had a gun,
He kind of clapt his hand on't
And stuck a crooked stabbing iron
Upon the little end on't

Chorus

And there I see a pumpkin shell
As big as mother's basin,
And every time they touched it off
They scampered like the nation.

Chorus

I see a little barrel too,
The heads were made of leather;
They knocked on it with little clubs
And called the folks together.

Chorus

And there was Cap'n Washington,
And gentle folks about him;
They say he's grown so 'tarnal proud
He will not ride without 'em.

Chorus

He got him on his meeting clothes,
Upon a slapping stallion;
He sat the world along in rows,
In hundreds and in millions.

Chorus

The flaming ribbons in his hat,
They looked so tearing fine, ah,
I wanted dreadfully to get
To give to my Jemima.

Chorus

I see another snarl of men
A-digging graves, they told me,
So 'tarnal long, so 'tarnal deep,
They 'tended they should hold me.

Chorus

It scared me so, I hooked it off,
Nor stopped, as I remember,
Nor turned about till I got home,
Locked up in mother's chamber.

Chorus

Peter Upclaire
Guitar
Songbook
for Beginners
ONLINE MP3
45
Oldies and
Goldies
American
Songs with
Tabs and
Chords

Guitar
Songbook
for Beginners
Peter Upclaire
ONLINE MP3
100
Timeless
Folk and
Children
Songs
with Tabs
and
Chords

Peter Upclaire
3 Chord
Guitar
Songbook
ONLINE MP3
50
Timeless
Children
Songs
with
Tabs and
Chords
C
G7
F

Peter Upclaire
Ukulele
Songbook
for Beginners
ONLINE MP3
45 Oldies and
Goldies American
Songs with Tabs
and Chords

Ukulele
Songbook
for Beginners
Peter Upclaire
ONLINE MP3
100
Timeless
Folk and
Children
Songs
with Tabs
and
Chords

Peter Upclaire
3 Chord
Ukulele
Songbook
ONLINE MP3
50
Timeless
Children
Songs
with
Tabs and
Chords
C
G7
F

Peter Upclaire
Mandolin
Songbook
for Beginners
ONLINE MP3
45
Oldies and
Goldies
American
Songs with
Tabs and
Chords

Peter Upclaire
Mandolin
Songbook
for Beginners
ONLINE MP3
100
Timeless
Folk and
Children
Songs
with Tabs
and
Chords

Peter Upclaire
3 Chord
Mandolin
Songbook
ONLINE MP3
C
G7
F
50 Timeless
Children Songs with
Tabs and Chords

Peter Upclaire
Guitalele
Songbook
for Beginners
ONLINE MP3
45
Oldies and
Goldies American
Songs with Tabs
and Chords

Guitalele
Songbook
for Beginners
Peter Upclaire
ONLINE MP3
100
Timeless
Folk and
Children
Songs
with Tabs
and
Chords

Peter Upclaire
3 Chord
Guitalele
Songbook
ONLINE MP3
50
Timeless
Children
Songs
with
Tabs and
Chords
C
G7
F

Printed in Great Britain
by Amazon